STARTING UP SMARTER

Why Founders Over 50 Build Better Companies

MARY J. CRONIN
EDITOR

Printed in the United States of America
ISBN: 978-1-7379893-2-5 (hardback)
ISBN: 978-1-7379893-0-1 (paperback)
ISBN: 978-1-7379893-1-8 (ebook)

Produced with TEX. Typeset in Helvetica
Cover design by Graphic Details https://www.graphicdet.com/

First Edition
14 13 12 11 10 / 10 9 8 7 6 5 4 3 2 1

4Q CATALYST PUBLISHING
Chestnut Hill, MA 02467
www.4qcatalyst.com

MDV
Every minute
More than ever

Contents

Part I

Building Better Companies
Mary J. Cronin

Chapter 1

Entrepreneurial Imperatives for the 21st Century

by Mary J. Cronin

Meet eight entrepreneurs who have started twenty-first-century companies that aim to change the world:

- Bill Behrens heard the earth's environmental clock ticking in the 1970s, when his research highlighted the toll of natural resource depletion and pollution. As the decades passed, that ticking became ever louder, leading Behrens to co-found Revision Energy with the mission to save the planet with solar energy.

- Wendy Gutterson was at the peak of her healthcare management career when she decided to step off the corporate career ladder to found her own company, Physician Management Resources, with the goal of transforming healthcare at the medical practice level.

- Forty years in supply chain management and an unexpected layoff at the age of sixty-four combined to shape Paul Tasner's mission for PulpWorks: replacing one of the world's most toxic forms of plastic with planet-friendly molded cardboard packaging of his own invention.

- Doug Peck learned firsthand from caring for his mother how essential peer companionship and at-home support are for aging in place, inspiring him to launch a Seniors Helping Seniors business as a better model for providing home services.

3

- A decades-long dream of redirecting consumer appetite from industrially raised meat to a vegan alternative took hold of Jeffrey Harris and wouldn't let go until he teamed up with like-minded co-founders to start Plant Power Fast Food.

- Bryan Eagle switched career paths to co-found Glanris when he realized that solving a double-sided pollution and water scarcity problem by transforming agricultural waste into an innovative water filtration media was the impact opportunity of a lifetime.

- Caroline and Garry Myers achieved national recognition as child development and family life experts based on decades of writing and lecturing. Then they risked it all to launch *Highlights*, a magazine totally devoted to children.

These founders come from all around the United States and work in very different industry sectors ranging from fast food, to solar energy and water filtration, to healthcare consulting, publishing, and home care for seniors. While they don't know each other, as startup entrepreneurs they have a number of very important characteristics in common.

The brief profiles above highlight some of their fundamental common ground. Each founder started with a strong commitment to making a positive impact through their company. Like most entrepreneurs, they are risk takers, solution builders, and charismatic visionaries of a better world. One other factor they have in common also predicts that their startups are significantly more likely to succeed over time and become profitable, well-established businesses. That common factor is their age. All of these founders were over 50 when they launched their companies.

Perhaps being over 50 sounds like an improbable predictor of startup success. It is certainly counterintuitive in a world where fast-growing firms are closely associated with entrepreneurs who started their companies while in their twenties or thirties.

The US venture capitalists (VCs) who pour over $130 billion into newly formed businesses each year certainly don't seem to believe in the potential of older founders. Venture firm portfolios show that VCs rarely fund startups with management teams over forty, though only a few venture investors are willing to go on the record regarding their attitudes about age and entrepreneurial potential. Some revealing quotes include Paul Graham of YCombinator saying in a *New York Times* interview that the "The cutoff age in investors' heads is thirty-two," and venture capitalist Vinod Khosla saying at a conference that "People under thirty-five are the people who make change happen . . . people over forty-five basically die in terms of new ideas." Even more telling than these remarks is the stark reality that in the past twenty years, the dollars invested by VCs in firms with founders over 50 is a tiny fraction of their total venture investment amount.

It may be that an aversion to investing in age and experience is one reason why venture capital portfolio companies seem to underperform the average survival rate for all startups. The Small Business Administration tracks the status of newly formed businesses in the US, and it consistently reports that over half of all new companies fail and are out of business within five years from their start date. One would expect that venture-backed firms would have a significant survival and success advantage due to the funding they attract. However, a study of over 2,000 startups that received a million dollars or more in venture funding between 2004 and 2010 showed that about 75% of the companies did not provide any cash return to their investors (Hoque 2012). The data from "Age and High Growth Entrepreneurship," in the *American Economic Review* in 2020 provides a particularly strong antidote to negative preconceptions about the relationship between a founder's age and the likelihood of startup success. In this study, researchers from the University of Pennsylvania, Northwestern University, MIT, and the US Census Bureau analyzed the trajectory of 2.7 million US founders who launched companies between 2007 and 2014. One factor in the analysis was the age of the founder; another was whether the company had at least one employee and was still in business after five years. A third factor was whether the company overcame the one in a thousand odds of being ranked among the top performers of all high-growth startups.

One widely published finding from this research article was that founders in their forties are, on average, the most likely to be successful. As the article states, "Across the 2.7 million founders in the United States between 2007 and 2014 who started companies that go on to hire at least one employee, the mean age for the entrepreneurs at founding is 41.9. The mean founder age for the 1 in 1,000 highest growth new ventures is 45.0" (p. 67) Far less attention has been given to unpacking the phrase "or beyond" in the researchers' summary of their findings, where they note, "We find no evidence to suggest that founders in their twenties are especially likely to succeed. Rather, all evidence points to founders being especially successful when starting businesses in middle age or beyond" (Azoulay P et al. 2020).

A closer look at the research data analyzed by Azoulay et al. reveals exactly how much advantage founders over the age of fifty have in comparison to the entrepreneurs in their twenties and early thirties who garner so much investment from venture capital firms. An ingenious interactive calculator designed by data visualization specialist Frank Elavsky draws on the data analyzed in "Age and High Growth Entrepreneurship" to compare the likelihood of success of founders at different ages between twenty-two and sixty-five (Meier 2018).

Using this calculator provides details about just how consistently and impressively founders who start their companies between the ages of fifty and sixty outperform younger entrepreneurs. A fifty-year-old founder is 2.8 times as likely to launch a successful startup as a founder who is twenty-five. Compared to founders in their early twenties, the advantage of being decades older is almost mind-boggling. A fifty-three-year-old is thirteen times as likely to found a successful startup as a twenty-three-year-old, and a sixty-year-old founder is ten times as likely to succeed as a twenty-two-year-old. To dispel any notions that older founders gravitate to low-risk, low-growth lifestyle businesses, the data also show that founders between fifty-three and sixty are 4.1 times more likely than twenty-two and twenty-year-olds to launch a highly successful, high-growth technology company. Even when looking beyond twenty-year-olds to compare the success of founders at the age of thirty, older entrepreneurs do significantly better. A person who is sixty is three times more likely to found a successful startup than a person who is thirty, where success is defined by high growth in sales revenue and the number of employees.

Of course, this data shouldn't come as a complete surprise to anyone who is reading a book with the subtitle "Why founders over 50 build better companies." But I hope that it serves to sharpen the reader's interest in the disproportionate level of success that older founders demonstrate, as well as the opportunities inherent in this success for society as a whole. The "Age and High Growth Entrepreneurship" article ends with a judiciously academic understatement:

> We can say now however that venture capital, a major source of early-stage financing that can help drive creative destruction and economy-wide-growth, does not currently appear allocated to the firms with the highest growth potential.

Beyond this bland conclusion loom a number of pointed questions. What is it about older founders that drives their achievement, even in the face of VC investments being allocated on the mistaken premise that younger is better when it comes to entrepreneurship? Even more vital, what are the opportunity costs to society in failing to provide resources to firms with the highest growth potential, especially when their older founders have demonstrated a commitment to positive social impact? Most importantly, what more can be done to enable older founders and entrepreneurs of all ages to collaborate on building companies that will change the world for the better? These questions are at the heart of each chapter in *Starting up Smarter*.

Among the common sense reasons advanced to explain the success rates of older entrepreneurs are that they have accumulated a wealth of experience in one or more career tracks; that they have had time to grow deep and extensive professional networks that bolster their pipelines for acquiring customers and ecosystem partners; and that they are likely to have both personal funds and supportive friends and family members to help them to bootstrap a new venture.

These are all credible insights about the advantages older founders can leverage for the benefit of their startups. But the reasons behind the massive difference in success rates enjoyed by entrepreneurs over 50 compared to their younger counterparts surely deserve much deeper analysis. Defining the key components that shape the success of older founders, especially their widely shared commitment to addressing social issues and making a positive change in the world, will benefit society as a whole, not just older entrepreneurs. The next section begins by analyzing the shift in social expectations for business in the 21st century and the resulting imperatives for entrepreneurs of all ages. It posits that entrepreneurs over 50 have an intrinsic advantage as founders in today's business landscape, due to their commitment to social mission and the values they embed in their companies.

A Transformation in Society's Expectations for Business

A long-term shift in social expectations for business that had been building over several decades reached an inflection point during the pandemic years of 2020 and 2021 to become a sweeping transformation. There has been a noteworthy uptick in demands from employees, customers, investors, and other stakeholders for corporations to step up and address a variety of social issues. Stakeholders are no longer satisfied by promises about corporate social responsibility or by pledges to mitigate negative consequences at some future date. They are scrutinizing actual outcomes and demanding quantitative impact data for accurate, objective measurement of current performance.

To understand the long-term implications of this seismic shift, and its effects on startup success, one must first step back from the current context to a broader view of business and society in the last two decades. Since 2000, we have witnessed a dramatic escalation in expectations about all manner of corporate behavior. There has been a rising tide of discontent with the outcomes of business as usual, the winner-takes-all mentality of the global corporate landscape, and the outsized rewards for executives, often seen as coming at the expense of the workforce. Stakeholders are increasingly unwilling to pay the costs in personal, community, and civic well-being levied by some of the world's largest corporations in their pursuit of growth and profitability.

The increased intensity of social demands on the private sector shows no sign of abating. In fact, it's clear that 2020 and 2021 marked the end of an era for shareholder primacy as a publicly acceptable business goal. Amidst an upsurge of management declarations, investor commitments to sustainable business models, and social innovation, a new era of twenty-first-century business is taking shape. Social impact, shared value, and regenerative sustainability are now key features of the external competitive landscape that all companies will have to navigate in the coming decade.

The three entrepreneurial requirements that most directly address society's expectations for corporate priorities and behavior are:

- Focus on positive social impact
- Demonstration of shared stakeholder value
- Commitment to regenerative sustainability

In addition to addressing these external imperatives through their companies, founders must also embody important internal characteristics to meet and overcome the inevitable challenges of building a new enterprise. Three key internal imperatives for twenty-first-century entrepreneurs are:

- Urgency, agility, and resilience
- Cross-generational cohesion and inclusive diversity
- Organizational and technical innovation

Asserting that older entrepreneurs often start their companies with an intrinsic advantage because of their alignment with these six imperatives is by no means a claim that they have any monopoly on them. Given that the external imperatives reflect a widely held belief that business should be a positive force for social change, we would expect that founders of all ages will begin to embrace these imperatives. Indeed, there are vocal advocates of shared value and regenerative sustainability among all generations of entrepreneurs. Many younger founders launch companies that prioritize changing the world for the better. Similarly, younger stakeholders often lead in raising their voices to hold corporations accountable for their impacts and pushing for a transformation in the role of business in society. As stakeholders, they are influencing companies with their career decisions as well as their buying choices.

Nonetheless, additional decades of life experience give older founders an entrepreneurial profile that differs significantly from that of their younger counterparts. As the following chapters will illustrate, older entrepreneurs are especially attuned to each of these imperatives. This alignment with today's business and social environment contributes significantly to their startup success.

In the next section, we will take a closer look at the major turning points in the evolution from a twentieth-century tradition of voluntary, philanthropic corporate social responsibility to today's sharpened public scrutiny of corporate social impact. This sets the stage for understanding how the three external imperatives are shaping social expectations for business today, and why these imperatives will play an outsized role in startup success in the next decade.

From Prioritizing Profits to the Public Good

In fall 2021, a former Facebook employee turned whistleblower testified before Congress that Facebook executives were aware of internal research findings reporting that the regular use of Instagram had a significant negative effect on the mental and physical health of many adolescent women. The whistleblower shared internal company reports that Facebook decision makers were unwilling to alter Instagram to make it less detrimental to teen users because such changes could decrease its popularity with this major market segment. In summarizing her motivation to go public with this issue, the whistleblower said she couldn't stay silent when her former employer put its profitability ahead of the welfare of its users and the public good.

In the not-so-distant past, companies prioritizing their profitability would not be headline news; it was generally accepted as normal business and chief executive behavior. Twentieth-century companies, especially public companies, were expected to put their profitability first, fulfilling their responsibilities to their investors. Corporate CEOs were evaluated on their ability to deliver increased shareholder value, and fired when they didn't meet the expectations of their Board of Directors. The overarching priority of shareholder value was memorably framed by Milton Friedman in his 1970 *New York Times* article, "The Social Responsibility of Business Is to Increase Its Profits" (Friedman 1970). Friedman explicitly contrasted fuzzy statements about corporate responsibility and good citizenship with the clear-cut, objective metrics of revenues, profits, and return on investment for shareholders. He asserted that corporate executives and boards were directly responsible to their shareholders, and thus obligated to prioritize increasing shareholder value. Indirectly, higher corporate revenue and profitability would create stable employment and generate tax revenues for local communities. Corporations were not in business to solve social problems, Friedman concluded. That was best left to philanthropists, nonprofit organizations, and the public sector.

Throughout the twentieth century, smaller local firms and family-owned businesses seemed to counter the philosophy of shareholder primacy. These firms had a strong inclination and practice of giving back to their local communities and looking out for the welfare of their employees, even though they often lacked formal employee benefits programs. Business owners were often individual philanthropists, and their firms also sponsored local sports teams and civic activities. However, this behavior fits within the overall pattern of voluntary decisions to support local stakeholders, rather than a long-term commitment to sharing value with all stakeholders.

During the 1990s, environmental and consumer activist groups coalesced around demands for global corporations to more formally disclose their impacts on stakeholders and on the environment. This concept of a

Triple Bottom Line became a rallying point as a more responsible model for corporations to consider impacts on society and the environment, and to report on these impacts alongside of their financial results and profitability (Elkington J 1994). In this period, however, the practice of Corporate Social Responsibility (CSR) remained voluntary and largely secondary to profitability. Many CSR reports highlighted employee volunteerism and educational programs that put the company in a favorable light without mentioning negative impacts.

With the rise of Environmental, Social, and Governance (ESG) reporting in the 2000s, public corporations were expected to disclose all of the material factors that might present significant risks to investors, including regulatory investigations. Risk factors could include supply chain issues, fines for pollution, lawsuits and labor disputes, and other issues that could impact financial performance and future growth prospects. Specific metrics and reporting templates for ESG were proposed by the United Nations Principles for Responsible Investing (PRI) in 2006, accompanied by impact reporting guidelines developed by organizations such as the Global Reporting Initiative (GRI).

Focus on Social Impact, Shared Value, and Regenerative Sustainability

The practice of firms selectively addressing social and environmental issues within a continuing focus on profitability has been supplanted in recent years by a more data-driven approach to reporting on ESG impacts. One marker of this shift is the sharp increase in the corporations that regularly report on their environmental and social impacts. KPMG, which publishes an annual survey of Corporate Sustainability Reporting, reported that in 2011 about 20% of companies in the S&P 500 Index produced a formal sustainability report. By 2020, over 90% of the S&P 500 companies and 96% of the top 250 global companies produced a formal report covering ESG related data (Threlfall R et al. 2020).

Reporting on social impact is no longer limited to the world's largest corporations or publicly traded companies that must comply with federal financial reporting requirements to disclose material risks related to ESG factors. A 2021 survey from Thompson Hine detailing the levels of ESG engagement among companies with annual revenues ranging from over $1 billion to less than $50,000 shows that a commitment to ESG tracking and reporting is now widely shared among companies of all sizes. According to the survey, even the smallest companies in the US plan to adopt formal ESG strategies and performance measurement. While only 14% of companies with annual revenues under $50,000 currently have ESG strategies and measurement in place, an impressive 57% of these small companies reported that they will implement formal ESG strategies in the next one to two years (Thomson Hine 2021).

With more detailed and objective reporting of social impacts being produced by so many US firms, and ESG reporting of sustainability, climate and other material risk factors required for US public companies, social impact transparency is the expectation rather than the exception. The social impact data included in these corporate reports is scrutinized by the media, by government, environmental, and consumer activist groups and nonprofits, and increasingly by internal stakeholders, including corporate employees and ecosystem partners. The insights revealed by this close scrutiny, and conclusions about whether corporations are meeting social expectations, are widely shared with investors, consumers, and policy makers. Media articles publicizing corporate and executive behavior that is harmful to society and the environment, and accounts of employee whistleblowers, have become the norm over the past several years.

A 2019 survey of US consumers reported that 70% of respondents believe that it's either "somewhat important" or "very important" for companies to make the world a better place. In contrast, only 37% responded that it's most important for a company to make money for shareholders, a notable change in attitude from prior decades (Aflac 2019).

In the same survey, 77% of consumers stated that they are motivated to purchase from companies committed to making the world a better place, and 73% of investors said that whether or not corporations are prioritizing programs to improve the environment and contribute to society was an important factor in their investment decisions.

Even more striking is the consensus among employees that corporations must make positive social impact a priority in their business strategy. In a 2020 workforce survey by Porter Novelli, 93% of employee respondents stated that companies must lead with a social purpose. In an echo of the testimony by the Facebook whistleblower in fall 2021, 88% of these employees believe that it is no longer acceptable for their companies to make money at the expense of stakeholders, or society at large. Almost 70% of survey respondents say they do not want to work for a company that lacks a strong and positive social purpose.

As more and more stakeholders express strengthening preferences for companies that demonstrate positive impact, the negative repercussions for corporations that are found to have violated social impact expectations and/or misrepresented their impact are multiplying (Porter Novelli 2020).

Employees and investors are equally insistent that corporations should share the value they create with all stakeholders. In the Porter Novelli survey, 95% of respondents believe that businesses should benefit all stake- holders, including employees, customers, suppliers, and the communities they operate within. The majority of investor respondents say that they ex- pect companies to put shareholder value on a par with, and not above, the interests of other stakeholders, and that positive social impact and shared value is a primary driver of their investment decisions.

Employees, investors, and customers are also demanding a change to business as usual by holding corporations accountable for environmental damage and sustainability solutions. In Deloitte Global's 2020 Millennial Survey, for example, a third of respondents said they stopped or lessened business relationships because they perceived companies were doing harm to the environment. A Deloitte article on the company's 2020 Global Climate survey, "How Stakeholders Can Make or Break Companies' Sustainability Efforts," identifies two primary reasons for corporations to take sustainability more seriously: shareholder pressure and a notable increase since the start of the global pandemic in what the Deloitte report calls societal and employee activism:

> The survey shows that environmental sustainability initiatives are primarily being driven by stakeholder pressure. Investor demands became the top motivating factor for these efforts, up five percentage points from last year's survey. Additionally, activism—by people who are calling for change—and ongoing media coverage of this issue are vital to ensuring that climate threats stay top of mind for business leaders and policymakers (Deloitte 2021).

While the escalating stakeholder scrutiny of social impact, shared value, and sustainability practices put additional pressure on corporations, there is growing evidence that committing to these imperatives benefits companies and their owners. In its September 2021 report on "Shaping the Sustainable Organization," Accenture, in collaboration with the World Economic Forum, reported that the companies with the most deeply embedded sustainability practices outperformed their peer corporations by 21% on both profitability and positive environmental and societal outcomes (Accenture 2021).

Expectations for companies to demonstrate positive social impact, shared value, and regenerative sustainability will escalate in the decade ahead. These imperatives define the common business context for all sizes and types of companies from multinational publicly traded corporations to privately held, venture-backed firms, to small and medium-size companies. By building companies that embody their social impact and sustainability goals, founders over 50 are well-positioned to thrive in today's ever more demanding business landscape.

Prioritizing positive social impact, shared value, and regenerative sustainability does not, of course, ensure that a startup will succeed. Companies must still provide valuable products and services, differentiate their offerings to attract paying customers, operate efficiently, and generate revenues that exceed their expenses. In the next section, we will consider how the six entrepreneurial imperatives serve as catalysts for success at four critical startup stages: company launch, accelerating growth, withstanding external shocks, and charting a sustainable flight path to the future.

The Six Imperatives as Catalysts for Startup Success

Like all entrepreneurs, older founders must overcome a number of challenges at every stage of launching and growing their companies. They must also deal with inevitable external disruptors such as economic downturns and even unexpected shocks such as the global pandemic. How do the six entrepreneurial imperatives serve older founders as they face these inevitable business challenges to grow and expand their startups into businesses built to last?

In this section we'll share some of the ways that the founders featured in Part I have boosted their ability to overcome the challenges of four critical stages of business formation, growth, and longevity. The entrepreneurial imperatives have combined to provide these founders and their companies with:

- Launch Propellants
- Growth Accelerators
- Shock Absorbers
- Flight Paths to the Future

Launch Propellants

In transitioning from vision and pre-launch planning to an operational business, startup founders need financial resources. Finding capital for their launch is a challenge that stops many aspiring entrepreneurs at the starting gate. There are typically three available sources of funding. A common approach by older entrepreneurs is to use their own savings or obtain a loan to self-fund their company in advance of generating any revenue.

A second popular strategy is to bootstrap company growth with a plan to attract early revenues, often supplemented by a small investment from a group of co-founders, or from the founder's friends and family members, or possibly through a crowdfunding campaign. A third, much-desired source of startup funding, is attracting a significant investment from venture capitalists or angel investors. However, as discussed earlier, these investors very rarely agree to put funds into startups with older founders.

Another essential launch propellant is attracting a highly motivated and talented startup team, and possibly a co-founder. Unless they have investor funding, many founders find it difficult to pay for top talent. One alternative is to convince team members to join based on the startup's mission. Potential founders over 50 can leverage resilience, cross-generational cohesion, and organizational innovation in tandem with social impact goals to attract mission-oriented team members and sometimes even social impact investors. Three examples from the companies featured in the following chapters will illustrate the power of this combination:

- Bill Behrens joined forces with Phil Coupe and Fortunat Mueller, two younger co-founders who knew Behrens' reputation as a solar energy guru, and shared his urgency about saving the planet with solar power, to bootstrap the launch of ReVision Energy. Each co-founder invested $30,000 as operating capital along with a commitment to work without a salary until the ReVision could generate sufficient operating cash from revenues.

- Paul Tasner and his younger co-founder Elena Olivari spent a frustrating year trying to attract angel investors for their original PulpWorks vision of designing and manufacturing planet-friendly packaging from recycled cardboard to replace polluting plastic. After repeated rejections, they pivoted away from a manufacturing model and established a global ecosystem of manufacturing partners who shared their sustainability goals. Their lead partner agreed to produce and deliver the orders from early customers on credit, allowing PulpWorks to launch more quickly, and manage its cash flow to achieve profitability and accelerate growth.

- Jeffrey Harris and his Plant Power Fast Food co-founders needed outside funding to build their first restaurant and pay their front-line team members. With a deep-seated belief that vegan fast food would be transformational, Harris repeatedly pitched the Plant Power vision of shared value and sustainability until he convinced early investors to fund the company's first location. When early investor backing wasn't quite enough to build the second restaurant, he quickly organized a crowdfunding campaign to bridge the gap.

Growth Accelerators

Once a startup is successfully launched, the next challenge is to accelerate growth and generate revenues. This stage requires cost-effective strategies for building brand recognition and attracting customers, expanding the workforce and ecosystem, and providing differentiated products and services—all within the context of stakeholder value and environmental sustainability. Both external and internal imperatives come together during this stage to create the conditions for strong, predictable, and profitable growth, as the following thumbnails illustrate:

- Thanks to an extensive network built during a decades-long career in healthcare organizations, Wendy Gutterson attracted her first consulting clients by word of mouth almost immediately after launching Physician Management Resources (PMR). As a solo consultant with very low overhead, she quickly became profitable serving a small group of clients. It was a comfortable lifestyle, but that had not been her founding vision. To make an impact on improving healthcare practices, she needed to accelerate growth. Her solution was a shared value strategy for client acquisition and for recruiting PMR employees. Gutterson spends significant time talking with prospective clients, learning about their challenges, and recommending solutions even before they commit to engaging PMR. She feels this is time well spent, since those free consultations result in a prospect conversion rate of over 80%. As the PMR team grows, Gutterson strives to be a model employer, as well as a healthcare changemaker. She recruits new staff based on their commitment to the company's mission and willingness to learn new skills, rather than just for prior expertise. As a result, the PMR team's skillset and capacity has grown in parallel with the company's expanding client base.

- Doug Peck's commitment to shared value at his Seniors Helping Seniors home care agency attracted many loyal clients. He was meeting revenue goals, but management tasks kept him away from the seniors he had set out to serve. Rather than investing in administrative infrastructure, Peck approached an equally mission-focused entrepreneur who was much younger, and proposed a cross-generational merger of their firms. The merged Seniors Helping Seniors business has exceeded its revenue and growth goals, and Peck can now focus on his passion for serving seniors.

- At Glanris, Bryan Eagle highlighted the company's transformational impact to attract customers, grow revenues, and locate outside investors. Unable to convince traditional venture firms to take a risk on the Glanris filtration solution, Eagle didn't give up. Instead, he focused on the shared value that he and his co-founders could create for their community to attract local social impact and strategic investors. Family offices and community funders invested in the Glanris mission to reduce global pollution and address urgent water scarcity issues while bringing new jobs and innovative technology to Memphis. Riceland Foods, a billion-dollar leader in rice production and processing, became a strategic investor recognizing the shared value of transforming tons of its discarded rice hulls into a valuable filtration medium. This combination of regenerative sustainability, global impact, and shared value made it possible for Eagle to raise $2.5 million to accelerate growth, enabling Glanris to open its own processing plant in 2020.

- ReVision Energy developed an innovative option for individual social impact investors to help accelerate the installation of solar power at local schools, nonprofits, and municipal buildings through Power Purchase Agreements (PPAs). These community organizations get the benefit of lower electricity costs without having to pay directly for the installations. Investors receive tax credits as well as an annual return on their investment. ReVision can count on the revenues from these projects to hire and train more employees.

Shock Absorbers

The six entrepreneurial imperatives also come to the fore to reduce the negative consequences of business setbacks and external disruptions. In 2021, analysts reported an unexpected trend; employees quitting their jobs in record numbers. According to the US Bureau of Labor Statistics, four million Americans voluntarily terminated their employment in July 2021, continuing a trend that started early in the year. The trend has been dubbed the "great resignation" and the "turnover tsunami" by the media. Clever names aside, the difficulty of filling open positions and the continued pace of employee resignations has led to severe disruption for many firms. The result has been cutbacks in production, supply chain and fulfillment challenges, and a variety of shortages that threaten the growth, and in some cases the survival, of companies in multiple industries.

Older entrepreneurs' decisions to share value with their employees, suppliers, and customers are now serving as shock absorbers for their companies. Even in industry sectors that have suffered the most from employee turnover and supply chain issues, the companies built on shared value are retaining their workforce and customer base, and even managing to expand.

- At PMR, Gutterson's practice of hiring team members who shared her vision, including them in designing high-value services for medical practice clients, providing flexibility to work from home, and investing in a strong benefits program combined with the loyalty of her clients has enabled faster than ever growth during the pandemic. PMR retained its talented workforce, got more referrals, and earned more revenues in the past year than it had before the pandemic started.

- At Seniors Helping Seniors, the commitment to caring for their employees as well as for their clients allowed Doug Peck and Josh Obeiter to maintain their level of services and continue to their business during an especially challenging period for all senior care providers.

- The ReVision Energy founding team made a series of major commitments to sharing the value of their company with all stakeholders. In 2015, ReVision Energy became a certified B Corporation, explicitly pledging to a long-term future as a purpose-driven business that creates benefit for all stakeholders by making the welfare of employees, customers, suppliers, the community, and the environment a consistent priority. In 2017, ReVision adopted a 100% employee-owned organization structure, ensuring that all employees would benefit from the company's future financial success. In 2018, it established an internal Energy Training Center to provide employees with no-cost in-house training to advance their technical expertise and potentially become licensed electricians. And in 2020, the ReVision Energy co-owners formed the company's Justice, Equity, Diversity, and Inclusion (JEDI) initiative to recognize the intersectional relationship between environmentalism and social justice and to support a more diverse workforce, and a more equitable society.

- Plant Power's co-founders invested in increasing the compensation and advancement opportunities for their front-line restaurant team members, committing to higher wages at a point when that was a big financial risk for their startup. As Jeffrey Harris recalls in Chapter 6:

  > We realized that we had to look at our team in a new way. What if we started people above whatever that local minimum wage was, and won employee loyalty and trust with a more inclusive, participatory culture? If the net result was that we had lower turnover, that would reduce our costs in the long run. Staff turnover is expensive, especially when you include the costs of recruiting and training. High turnover also takes a toll on customer service and satisfaction. Even though the upfront cost was daunting, we decided to try a more equitable, less spreadsheet-oriented

strategy. On the surface raising salaries would blow our labor costs off the spreadsheet, and it wouldn't work. But we decided to take the risk.

Plant Power also implemented an employee-led Diversity, Equity and Inclusion (DEI) Council to provide input to corporate decision making. It broadened the recruitment of diverse talent, and committed to DEI training at all levels of the company.

The commitment these founders made from the start to share the value with their employees in turn motivated their employees to stay the course and allowed the companies to continue recruiting top talent, even in the midst of the turnover tsunami.

Future Flight Paths

Companies dedicated to solving urgent social and environmental problems are more needed than ever. Startups grounded in purpose, resilience, cross-generational cohesion, and supportive stakeholders are well-positioned to withstand external shocks that will often derail businesses that prioritize profit to the detriment of their stakeholders. Founders who successfully lead their social impact-focused startups through the challenges of launch and growth by embodying the entrepreneurial imperatives discussed in this chapter are the most likely to thrive well into the 21st century. Equally importantly, the companies they have created will contribute to changing society for the good of all, helping to make the world more sustainable and equitable, kinder, and more caring.

For founders over 50, making the world a better place is not a cliché. It is the urgent call that motivates them to implement transformational, world-changing solutions through their companies. For Bill Behrens at Re-Vision Energy, that call was expressed in his mission to save the planet with solar; for Paul Tasner at PulpWorks, it led to his determination to help stem the tide of toxic plastic packaging, for Doug Peck at Seniors Helping Seniors it took the form of providing peer companionship and social support for the legions of older adults who live alone. Whatever the founding purpose, accomplishing (and in fact even attempting) it is grounded in changing the world for the better. Bryan Eagle's reflection on his mission at Glanris encapsulates the vision of so many older founders to make a transformational impact through their companies:

> There aren't many technology innovations out there that can make a massive impact on essential resources like water and clean air, something that 100% of every living thing on the planet needs daily, right? And there aren't many opportunities to tackle such urgent global issues with solutions that are so powerful and so affordable. If Glanris is adopted worldwide, it will help to transform water availability, water security, and remove massive amounts of carbon from the environment. That's a transformation to be proud of.

The strong inclination of older entrepreneurs to partner with younger cofounders, and their willingness to recruit employees from every age cohort between eighteen and eighty, are the result of their own life experiences. The desire to create a cross-generational workforce is linked to their urgency to make a lasting difference. It's also an important advantage in putting their company on a flight path to the future.

As Bill Behrens notes, founders over 50 will inevitably become the elders in their companies over time. Their drive to build for the future is expressed in an openness to intergenerational teams, and a willingness to nurture new generations of leaders knowing that those new leaders will expand the founding vision in new directions:

> It has been fantastic to have younger partners who bring different interests and perspectives to the leadership table. For an older co-founder, it provides a sense of durability for the organization, because now you can see the company isn't limited to one founder's lifetime. ReVision Energy is going to persist

over time, and it's going to grow and improve. Of course, that means that over time this company will become something different than what it was when I started it. But that's okay, because I know that the next generation of leaders are smart, they are capable, and they are dedicated. I'm already working with that next generation, and that's actually a very good thing.

Jeffrey Harris believes that enabling a new generation to carry on with the Plant Power Fast Food vision is part of the wisdom of age. He is ready to share leadership, and let go of ego, to create a more diverse, future-oriented company:

As long as Plant Power continues on the path of being kind and respectful, as long as it's vegan and sustainable, as long as all our basic founding principles are safeguarded, I don't need to be in charge of it forever. I wanted to bring something like this to the world and watch it grow...I'd like to think my willingness to eventually transition to a different role in the company is a combination of the wisdom of age and the insight from my meditation and reflection. Keep to the intention, live your principles, and let go of your ego. It's a work in progress.

Conclusion

Older founders exemplify the characteristics that all twenty-first-century entrepreneurs and companies must embody to sustain growth, to innovate, to attract world-class partners and employees, and to win customer loyalty to become the leaders of tomorrow. They bring urgency, resilience, innovation, and cross-generational partnerships to their startup strategies, along with a deep-seated commitment to business as a force for good in society and for the planet.

Since research data and analysis are no substitute for hearing the lived experience of founders, the next six chapters in Part I feature in-depth startup stories, told from the perspective of older entrepreneurs at all stages of their company's trajectory.

I wrote the following chapters based on industry and company research as well as my interviews with one or more of the company founders. The founders candidly shared their pre-launch vision and motivations, experiences at every stage of company growth, lessons learned, and reflections that could benefit other entrepreneurs. I have included extensive quotes from these interviews, to incorporate the voice of the founders as much as possible in telling their stories.

These chapters illustrate how each founder has overcome the challenges encountered in launching their companies and forging a path to growth, social purpose, and profitability. Their entrepreneurial journeys are different in many ways, as are the career experiences and skillsets that they brought to their startups. Nevertheless, their common purpose and vision shine through. Their stories represent the motivations and mission of the millions of founders over 50 who are working to make our world a better place.

The company chapters are ordered based on the founding date of each company; ReVision Energy dates back to 2003 and its story is presented in Chapter 2. PulpWorks and Seniors Helping Seniors both started in 2011 and they are presented in Chapter 3 and Chapter 4 respectively. Physician Management Resources, which started in 2013, is featured in Chapter 5; Plant Power Fast Food which launched in 2016 is Chapter 6. Glanris, which started in 2018, is presented in Chapter 7.

Part II of *Starting Up Smarter* looks ahead to the urgent challenge of Changing the Future and the premise that our society as a whole has much to gain from the success of older entrepreneurs and their social impact-focused companies.

In Chapter 8, I present a model for Co-Generating a Better World with a framework for action to encourage decision makers and stakeholders in the public sector, educational institutions, nonprofit and community organizations, and social impact investors to prioritize steps to support older founders and empower them to be co-generators of world-changing solutions.

The remaining chapters in Part II analyze in more detail why older founders so frequently express these internal imperatives in their startup decisions and long-term path to growth—not exclusively, but as prominent motivations and characteristics that align closely with the external factors of impact, shared value, and regenerative sustainability.

In Chapter 9, Highlights for Children: Across the Generations, Kent Johnson, the fourth-generation CEO of Highlights, discusses how his great grandparents, Caroline and Garry Myer acted on their devotion to serving children to launch a risky new venture in 1946 when Caroline was fifty-eight and Garry was sixty-one. That founding purpose has guided the company during its seventy-five years, with an abiding focus on making a positive impact on the children they serve through a cross-generational vision of sharing value.

In Chapter 10, Leading with Purpose, Doug Dickson analyzes decades of research on the relationship between aging, resilience, and a strong desire to make a positive impact in the world that typically emerges after the age of fifty. He concludes that the deeply felt values and motivations of older adults, including their innate sense of urgency, passion to make a difference for others, and strong desire to deploy life skills and business expertise to help address the problems facing society, have created a convergence of individual and business factors that contribute to the success of older entrepreneurs.

In Chapter 11, Inventing Over 50, Scott Guthery analyzes the age of inventors of over seven million US patents granted between 1976 and 2021. His findings refute the widespread idea that inventiveness decreases with age, demonstrating that patents are regularly granted to inventors over 50, and that many older inventors continue to receive patents in their sixties and seventies. Guthery also notes a pattern of intergenerational collaboration in the data on patents with multiple inventors, reflecting his own experience of collaborating with younger colleagues to develop innovative ideas that go on to be granted patents.

In Chapter 12, Models for Regenerative Sustainability, Rick Terrien discusses the many synergies between older founders and a regenerative approach to sustainability, including developing innovative circular economy solutions. Having experienced a lifetime of environmental degradation, Terrien notes, older entrepreneurs are looking for solutions that can regenerate our planet. They will not be satisfied with just putting their finger in the dike to hold back the next wave of environmental damage and extinction triggered by centuries of unsustainable practices. In building sustainable companies, Terrien shows that older entrepreneurs are open and eager to share their experience and collaborate with younger generations and to share the value of new models for sustainability with their partners, employees, customers and community.

To sum up, entrepreneurs over 50 are not only ready, willing, and exceptionally able to adapt their businesses to meet the demanding social and stakeholder expectations for corporations in the years ahead—they are often leading this movement. Their founding mission is to address an urgent social problem, and make a positive change in the world. They are ready to share the value they create with their employees, their customers, and communities as well as their co-founders and investors. They are building their companies to become leaders in addressing these external imperatives, and models for sustainable twenty-first-century business.

References

Accenture (2021) *Shaping the Sustainable Organization.*

Aflac (2019) *2019 CSR Survey Results and Analysis.* Aflac.

Azoulay, Pierre, Benjamin F. Jones, J. Daniel Kim, and Javier Miranda (2020) Age and High-Growth Entrepreneurship. *American Economic Review: Insights*, 2(1), 65–82. DOI: 10.1257/aeri.20180582.

Deloitte (2021) How Stakeholders Can Make or Break Companies' Sustainability Efforts. *Forbes.* May 13, 2021.

Elkington, J. (1994) Towards the Sustainable Corporation: Win-Win-Win Business Strategies for Sustainable Development. *California Management Review*, 36, 90–100. http://dx.doi.org/10.2307/41165746.

Friedman, M (1970) The Social Responsibility of Business Is to Increase Its Profits. *New York Times* https://www.nytimes.com/1970/09/13/archives/a-friedman-doctrine-the-social-responsibility-of-business-is-to.html. Accessed October 19, 2021.

Hoque F (2012) Why Most Venture-Backed Companies Fail. *Fast Company* 12-10-12.

Meier, M (2018) How Old Are Successful Tech Entrepreneurs? *Kellogg Insight* May 15, 2018 https://insight.kellogg.northwestern.edu/article/younger-older-tech-entrepreneurs. Accessed October 1, 2021.

Porter Novelli (2020) *Employee Perspectives on Responsible Leadership During Crisis*, Porter Novelli, August 2020.

Threlfall R et al. (2020) The KPMG Survey of Sustainability Reporting 2020. KPMG Impact https://home.kpmg/xx/en/home/insights/2020/11/the-time-has-come-survey-of-sustainability-reporting.html. Accessed October 1, 2021.

About the Author

Mary J. Cronin, Ph.D. is a Research Professor at the Carroll School of Management, Boston College and the President of 4Q Catalyst. Her research and teaching focuses on corporate social impact, entrepreneurship, the future of work, and business transformation. She designed an interdisciplinary minor in Managing for Social Impact and the Public Good for undergraduates at Boston College.

Mary offers consulting services to social entrepreneurs and purpose-oriented companies. She is a nonprofit director for the Center for Ageless Entrepreneurship and the Encore Boston Network, and a co-founder of the Founders Over 55 Collective at the Cambridge Innovation Center AGENCY hub. Her research, consulting, and nonprofit work combined with her entrepreneurial advising to inspire *Starting Up Smarter: Why Founders Over 50 Build Better Companies*.

Mary has authored or edited ten prior books including Managing for Social Impact: Innovations in Responsible Enterprise with Tiziana Dearing (Springer, 2017); *Top Down Innovation* (Springer 2014); *Smart Products, Smarter Services* (Cambridge University Press 2010). Earlier books include the international best sellers *Doing Business on the Internet* and *The Internet Strategy Handbook*, as well as *Unchained Value: The New Logic of Digital Business*; *Banking and Finance on the Internet*; *Mobile Application Development* with Scott Guthery, and numerous entrepreneurship, management, social impact, and digital strategy articles.

Chapter 2

ReVision Energy

The founding story of ReVision Energy can be traced back to the 1970s, when Bill Behrens was earning his PhD in environmental economics at MIT. In addition to his graduate course work, Behrens was chosen as one of the principal researchers for an expansive research project that had been commissioned by The Club of Rome's Project on the Predicament of Mankind. His significant contribution resulted in his designation as one of four co-authors of the 1972 book that emerged from this project, *The Limits to Growth*. The *Limits to Growth* was a systematic and sobering examination of the emerging challenge of global resource constraints. A controversial bestseller around the globe, it was translated into over twenty languages and its conclusions were hotly debated. As noted in a 2012 retrospective review in *The Nation*, forty years after its publication, "The *Limits to Growth* remains the top-selling environmental title ever published. In many ways, it helped launch modern environmental computer modeling and began our current globally focused environmental debate. After *Limits*, environmentalists, scientists, and policy-makers increasingly thought of ecological problems in planetary terms and as dynamically interconnected" (Parenti 2012).

As Behrens and his coauthors concluded in *Limits to Growth*, the world's population and its political and corporate leaders had a time-limited opportunity to reverse the global trends that would inexorably deplete natural resources and increase pollution if left unchecked. As summarized in the book:

Our conclusions are:

1. If the present growth trends in world population, industrialization, pollution, food production, and resource depletion continue unchanged, the limits to growth on this planet will be reached sometime within the next one hundred years. The most probable result will be a rather sudden and uncontrollable decline in both population and industrial capacity.

2. It is possible to alter these growth trends and to establish a condition of ecological and economic stability that is sustainable far into the future. The state of global equilibrium could be designed so that the basic material needs of each person on earth are satisfied and each person has an equal opportunity to realize his individual human potential.

3. If the world's people decide to strive for this second outcome rather than the first, the sooner they begin working to attain it, the greater will be their chances of success.

These conclusions are so far-reaching and raise so many questions for further study that we are quite frankly overwhelmed by the enormity of the job that must be done (Meadows et al. 1972).

That conclusion and the "enormity of the job that must be done" continued to resonate with Behrens as he moved from post-doctoral teaching at Dartmouth College to the residential construction industry building homes for Maine residents. Fast forwarding the origin story of ReVision Energy to the late 1980s, when Behrens was forty, he recalls a pivotal moment when career and mission combined, "I took a contract to build a client's home that was entirely off-grid, fully solar powered. And that was a real eye opener for me. From that time on, I would say that I was consciously trying to figure out how to save the planet with solar power."

The path that Behrens chose was entrepreneurship with a solar and sustainability focus. His construction company took on multiple solar-powered homes and became the only contractor in Maine specializing in off-grid construction. In 1993, at forty-four, he co-founded The Green Store, a retail company in Belfast, Maine that stocked all sorts of practical products for customers interested in reducing their environmental footprint through a more sustainable lifestyle. The Green Store continues to be a popular source of sustainability products. But Behrens was looking to make a larger and more direct impact on the adoption of solar power. To accomplish that, he formed a second company with The Green Store partners to enter the solar contracting space in 1999. The new company, EnergyWorks, took its first contract with the State of Maine for thirteen solar hot water installations. Energy Works subsequently absorbed an electrical contractor (a former employee of The Green Store) and fully separated from The Green Store. As Behrens recalls, he could always hear the planetary clock ticking, and that ticking motivated all of his startups, culminating in ReVision Energy:

By the time the 2000s came along I had the same mission, which was how do you save the planet, and make an impact as fast as possible. I wanted to be able to have a larger, faster impact, because the clock is ticking very loudly, for those who hear it. For me, the ticking of the clock is very, very loud.

With that ticking comes a need for speed. You can't save the planet by talking about it. You can't solve the climate crisis by talking about it, or by thinking about solutions that you might implement ten years from now. You can only solve it by actively implementing the solutions that are available right now. That's really all you can do. So you should figure out how to do that as fast as you possibly can. That active implementation, figuring out how to have an impact as fast as we possibly can, became the core of my entrepreneurial and company mission.

In that sense the mission has been consistent, and my co-founding of ReVision Energy on the foundation of Energy Works was the next in a series of three or four entrepreneurial efforts to make solar deployment happen more quickly. My earlier iterations were effective on some level. But I could still hear that clock ticking.

Behrens' reputation and commitment to solar energy attracted people who shared his solar mission to join him at EnergyWorks. A believer in the power of a multigenerational workforce, he enthusiastically welcomed younger team members with a variety of experience and skillsets. Phil Coupe and Fortunat Mueller were at much earlier stages in their careers, but both were motivated by the same vision for making an impact with solar. They met with Behrens, and joined the team in 2006 to launch a branch of EnergyWorks in Portland, Maine. When it came time to move faster with solar installations by launching ReVision Energy as the successor to EnergyWorks in 2008, Behrens shared the title of co-founder and the responsibilities of leadership with Coupe and Mueller.

A Multigenerational Founding Team

As Behrens recalls, the formation of a multigenerational founding team for ReVision Energy happened almost spontaneously:

> In my case, the launch of ReVision Energy came along in my 50s. We were a multigenerational group from the start. Phil Coupe, who became a ReVision co-founder and our marketing director after joining the EnergyWorks team, is a great example. Phil drove into the shop dooryard and introduced himself. I remember that within twenty minutes of meeting Phil, I realized he was a person with a skillset that I would never acquire, never even want to acquire. I also recognized his skills were fundamentally valuable to our business. And, you know, within an hour, I was in a position of saying to myself, hey, this person ought to be deeply involved in this business from here on out. Holy cow, this person brings to the table something that I don't have, but that this business really needs. Similarly, Fortunat Mueller, who joined EnergyWorks at the same time as Phil has

another, different skillset. Fortunat is a system thinker with an absolutely brilliant engineering brain. It was clearly important to have him with us in the business.

For me, working with a multigenerational group of co-founders and employees at ReVision Energy has been absolutely super. I believe that a multi-age group is always considerably more dynamic than any collection of people of the same age. It has been fantastic to have younger partners who bring different interests and perspectives to the leadership table. For an older co-founder, it provides a sense of durability for the organization, because now you can see the company isn't limited to one founder's lifetime. ReVision Energy is going to persist over time, and it's going to grow and improve. Of course, that means that over time this company will become something different than what it was when I started it. But that's okay, because I know that the next generation of leaders are smart, they are capable, and they are dedicated. I'm already working with that next generation, and that's actually a very good thing.

From Phil Coupe's perspective, being one of a team of co-founders at ReVision Energy has been the most rewarding work experience in his life. He notes that the different ages and perspectives of the founding team are an asset to the company, "we work extraordinarily well together, because we have our own distinct styles, backgrounds, and interests that overlap very little, but complement one another almost perfectly. Bill is our CFO and division leader of ReVision Solar Impact Partners. As company president, Fortunat is focused on strategic direction, company-wide leadership and engineering. I'm a journalism major with startup expertise, focused on sales, marketing, culture and leadership." Coupe describes his path to becoming a co-founder of ReVision Energy as follows:

It was 2005 and the drumbeat of concerning information about climate damage was increasing steadily. On the personal front, my wife and I had recently welcomed our twin infant boys into the world, joining our two-year-old daughter. I was in my thirties, and working at a new job that had dubious long-term prospects. So I began some soul searching to find the type of opportunity that would let me support my family, and also help to make the world a better place for them in the future.

At that time, there was a lack of solar energy installers in southern Maine where most of the population lives. But rather than go into the business of solar installation, I decided to start a nonprofit called Smart Energy now. My hypothesis was that lots of environmental grant making foundations were poised to support solar energy for school buildings. My grand strategy was to get grant funding to install the solar arrays, and also deliver a curriculum to the students describing the negative impacts of fossil fuels including environmental pollution and geopolitical conflict. Things were going swimmingly until I submitted the first grant application. The foundation turned it down. Their feedback was that the ideas were great, but I didn't have any credibility in renewable energy, so they were not prepared to fund me. I took that feedback pretty hard.

The silver lining was that it prompted me to consider what a startup in the solar installation sector would need to be successful. I made a major pivot, and started seeking pathways to get into the installation sector. That's what led me to Bill Behrens and Fortunat Mueller. Bill, of course, was a well-known solar expert and had been a leader in the field at that point. He had started thinking about anthropogenic impacts back in the early 1970s, when he received his PhD in environmental economics at MIT and coauthored *The Limits to Growth*, the seminal book exploring our planet's resource constraints in the face of population and extractive industry growth. I learned after meeting him that Bill has an incredibly generous heart, brilliant mind, and natural instincts around entrepreneurship, company growth, and leadership, making him an ideal co-founder. Fortunat was an experienced mechanical engineer looking for an opportunity to work in the solar sector in Maine. Once I got to know them both, it was a no-brainer for us to go into business together based on our shared solar mission and our divergent but highly complementary skillsets. Within a few years of meeting, we officially incorporated our venture together as ReVision Energy which encompassed Bill's earlier company, EnergyWorks.

While each of us brings a somewhat unique skillset to ReVision, Bill is the oracle of good judgment, who has helped us make some of our best decisions through rational deliberation, and patient leadership. For example, he is one of the main architects of our solar impact investing program that has helped more than 140 schools, nonprofits and municipalities acquire solar at zero upfront cost through mutually beneficial power purchase agreements. Our fourth co-founder, Dan Clapp, joined us later in the game, in 2010. He is our strongest operational leader, helping to launch the ReVision divisions in New Hampshire and Massachusetts and serving as the General Manager overseeing both states.

Bootstrapping Growth

Even though the demand for solar power was slowly growing in the mid-2000s, there was still a lot of skepticism about its reliability and cost effectiveness, especially in the northern reaches of New England. Then and now, the majority of solar installation companies were small, very local firms, with fewer than twenty full-time employees. The co-founders decided early on to make ReVision Energy a mission-driven, values-led organization, and it was one of their best decisions. Recognizing it was ridiculously ambitious, but also true to their long-term goals, the co-founders settled on a mission to transition northern New England from a fossil fuel-based economy to a sustainable, renewable energy-based economy. They took a collective leap of faith in believing that ReVision Energy would be able to significantly impact the adoption of solar power in Maine and beyond. That faith extended to each of them investing their own cash and sweat equity to launch the new company, and support it during the early years. In lieu of third-party startup capital, each co-founder invested $30,000 and pledged to work their first 500 hours on the business without compensation. As Coupe remembers that period:

> We put in a boatload of sweat equity. In those early days, all three of us had to be masters of all trades. We all had to be involved in sales, we all had to spend time managing our operations. We shared the responsibility for leadership across the board, including hiring, policy making, human resources, financials, and of course, the actual installation of solar panels for our customers. Whatever was necessary to make the company go, we all chipped in to do it.
>
> Even though it was a small and self-funded firm in those days, starting with day one, and every day that followed, we wanted to drive a mission-first culture of excellence on a shoestring. We disciplined ourselves to not spend money we didn't have. We had the leanest possible operation and kept overhead to a minimum, so that ReVision could become sustainably profitable as quickly as possible. Our goal was to self-fund growth without taking out a lot of bank loans, or needing to sell equity to venture capitalists and somehow we were able to pull it off. One of the words that we use to describe our approach is Kaizen, the Japanese term for continuous improvement. I think that Kaizen is probably one of the most important key factors that has enabled us to accomplish our goals and jumpstart our growth without having to rely on enormous sums of outside money like a lot of other companies seem to do.
>
> Gradually, over time we were able to attract enough customers to prime the pump and get the business growing organically. Once that happened, the co-founders were able to self-select into our natural areas of expertise. I had to do less of the hands-on wrench turning for the business and could focus more of my time on sales and marketing, and develop a strategic marketing plan. Similarly, Fortunat got to spend more of his time on the intensive engineering design work that's required to make a tech and energy systems business like ours successful.

Bill was able to drill down deeper into the financial planning, and evolve into the role of Chief Financial Officer based on his educational background, deep business experience, and acumen. So over time, we focused on our respective sweet spots and hired other competent people to come in and backfill those aspects of the business where we had spread ourselves too thin.

We bootstrapped the company to the point where we had very healthy annual profits. Basically, we clawed our way up to a financial inflection point where we could access relatively cheap money. Once we had grown to where ReVision was reliably profitable at a certain scale, we could access very advantageous bank terms on lines of credit and access to capital. That inflection point in our revenues was like an accelerant that we could pour on to the business to help it expand and keep on growing.

A co-founder who could hear the planetary clock ticking as loudly as Behrens would not, of course, refuse to consider the support of mission-friendly outside investors. In this early phase, social investors could potentially have added their own accelerant in the form of investment capital, to speed up ReVision's growth and the number of solar installations it could implement. Behrens, Coupe and Meuller did in fact approach a number of potential social impact investors in an effort to obtain additional capital for the new company. Despite the clear environmental benefits of ReVision Energy's mission however, even environmental investors were not prepared to provide venture funding for a small solar installation company in Maine. As Behrens puts it:

> Early in the company, we spent quite a bit of time looking at the mission-focused, social enterprise investor realm. We must have talked to more than 100 different organizations that provide mission motivated capital to companies that focus on alternative energy and sustainability. We also had a long period, a couple of years, where we considered merging with two similar companies in New England. But we came away from

that experience realizing that we didn't want to grow by way of mergers, or through outside investors. We wanted to invest in the people who were working at ReVision. Ultimately, those are the people we wanted to have owning our company, not venture investors from outside. So ReVision is somewhat unique in that way, it's been bootstrapped from the very start, with just a small amount of capital from each of the co-founders.

Finally, we reached the level where we had multiple geographic locations, multiple crews leaving from each geographic location to do major installation work every day, and we were putting up new solar arrays every day. At the same time, state and local solar incentive structures and market conditions came together to create a situation where solar installation demand was always greater than supply in our region. At that point, we were confident that we could count on having more projects pending in the installation list than we were capable of building in a given day, or month, or year. So we could allocate revenues to support hiring more people, and doing more installations, and everyone could see a pathway to expanding this activity, and accomplishing our ambitious mission at a sharply accelerating pace in more and more locations.

As many founders discover, the hardest time for a startup to raise outside capital is when it's most needed. Once a company is profitable and has demonstrated that it can scale and grow quickly in a high-demand market, investors tend to become more interested. That was the case with ReVision Energy. After they had demonstrated their potential and profitability, the company attracted many queries from private equity firms, and several overtures from larger companies about a possible acquisition or merger. By that time however, the founding team was no longer interested in venture funding. To focus on the mission, and to have the ability to share the value ReVision was creating with employees, customers, and local communities, the co-founders decided to continue using the company's own revenues to fund future growth. Over the next several years, Behrens would also lead ReVision Energy in opening a new door for social impact and environmental investors to directly support solar installation for nonprofits, schools, and municipalities, through Power Purchase Agreements (PPAs).

By 2014, ReVision Energy had expanded its services into New Hampshire, and it was ranked number twenty-five of the 100 Top Solar Rooftop Installers in the US by *Solar Power World* magazine. With consistent profitability, and a fast-growing workforce and customer base, the company had moved beyond its bootstrapping mode. ReVision had become a stable, well-established business with a relatively predictable pipeline of new residential and commercial customers, amidst a rising demand for solar installations. The co-founders were able to broaden their original mission of saving the planet through solar, to develop a more integrated vision of social change, equity, and shared value for all of the company's stakeholders.

Committing to Broader Social Change

Behrens recalls one catalyst that prompted the co-founders to prioritize this broader mission was a talk by climate activist Bill McKibben who was invited to give a guest presentation to the ReVision team around the celebration of the tenth anniversary of the founding of EnergyWorks. Given the celebratory occasion, it was natural to expect that McKibben would focus on ReVision's impressive track record of growth and solar installations in Maine and New Hampshire. However, their activist guest took a different tack, exhorting the assembled workforce to take on broader sustainability and social challenges. As Behrens remembers the talk:

> Instead of just congratulating everyone about the progress we had made, Bill McKibben said, well, you probably all think that you are rock stars, that you're saving the planet by putting up solar every day. But I'm here to tell you that you have to do more. You have to organize, you have to become active in your communities, you have to be part of the social movement that is behind a broader adoption of sustainable practices. To change society, it's not enough to just be a very active solar

worker.

That message was kind of a jolt for all of us. I think at that point, because we were growing so fast, it did feel like we were doing everything we could. We really believed that the solar work we were doing at ReVision was all about saving the planet. That was what got us up in the morning, and made everyone excited to see more and more solar panels installed.

McKibben's message was, there's more that has to be done to enable change at the level that actually makes a difference to the future of our planet and our society. Yes, that includes creating broader support for solar, and reaching a critical mass of people who understand the reasons for solar adoption. That means spending time on changing attitudes and increasing understanding of solar as a viable alternative. So we started putting more effort into influencing public policy and into paying attention to what was going on in the state capitals and getting people organized to show up at energy hearings at the Public Utilities Commission and legislature.

Beyond these public policy and educational activities, the co-founders were ready to push ahead with meaningful changes in the company itself. How could the success of ReVision Energy deliver a more positive impact for all of its employees and for the community? Taking on this challenge required a fundamental rethinking of the role of the corporation in today's society. As Behrens notes, by 2015 the company had reached a critical inflection point in defining its strategic priorities and long-term goals:

That inflection point allowed us to start thinking more about our role in the community and our overall impact as a corporation and a commercial entity. That was the point where we started looking at participating in the B Corp certification process, we started thinking about employee ownership structures, and we committed to addressing social equity issues.

Our goal in all these efforts was, over time, to make ReVision Energy more than just a successful company that puts up solar panels. To accomplish our original mission, we wanted to become the type of company that looks like the future, a company based on what we believe is the most sustainable sort of social structure for the future of the planet. To achieve that, you can't just focus on solving the energy crisis, you also have to think about how to solve the social crisis. That means, you have to create opportunities for people to have access to wealth creation. You have to enable equality of access to different ethnic groups, different cultural groups. In a more sustainable structure, the corporate entity can be the leader, a beacon of a sustainable future that includes not just renewable energy, but also renewable social structures, sustainable and renewable structures that are equitable for all.

One concrete expression of this expanded vision of the leadership role that corporations should play in enabling a sustainable society is ReVision's certification as a B Corp.

Becoming a Certified B Corporation

Certification as a B Corporation (or B Corp for short) has been a signal of corporate intention to balance the interests of all stakeholders since the certification process was developed by the nonprofit B Labs in 2007. Aspiring B Corporations must demonstrate in their application that they consistently prioritize the welfare of employees, customers, suppliers, the community, and the environment, as well as providing a return on investment to shareholders and company owners. Applicants are scored on their performance under four categories: Governance, Workers, Community, and Environment. They must achieve a minimum score in order to be certified, and must support core B Corp principles, including the following "Declaration of Interdependence" from the B Corporation website https://bcorporation.net/

THE B CORP DECLARATION OF INTERDEPENDENCE

We envision a global economy that uses business as a force for good. This economy is comprised of a new type of corporation—the B Corporation—which is purpose-driven and creates benefit for all stakeholders, not just shareholders. As B Corporations and leaders of this emerging economy, we believe:

- That we must be the change we seek in the world.
- That all business ought to be conducted as if people and place mattered.
- That, through their products, practices, and profits, businesses should aspire to do no harm and benefit all.
- To do so requires that we act with the understanding that we are each dependent upon another and thus responsible for each other and future generations.

Phil Coupe recalls that from day one, he and his ReVision Energy cofounders were working to create a business that would benefit the environment, employees, and the community as a whole; in essence, they were aiming to build their company as a force for good. Becoming a certified B Corporation was seen as a reflection of that mission and a reinforcement of their commitment. As part of their strategic planning in 2014, the management team decided to pursue certification to join the ranks of B Corp companies like Patagonia and Ben & Jerry's that are widely known for their social responsibility priorities.

In 2015, ReVision Energy became a certified B Corporation, joining over 4,000 companies worldwide that have committed to using profits and growth as a means to a greater end: positive impact for their employees, communities, and the environment. The commitment to social impact and balancing benefits for all company stakeholders doesn't end with initial certification. B Corporations must continue to share detailed data on their performance with the B Labs nonprofit behind the certification process, and must be recertified every five years. To create transparency, company certification scores are published on the B Corporation website as B Impact Reports. Figure 1 shows the total score that ReVision received in its 2020 recertification, along with its score in each of the four categories.

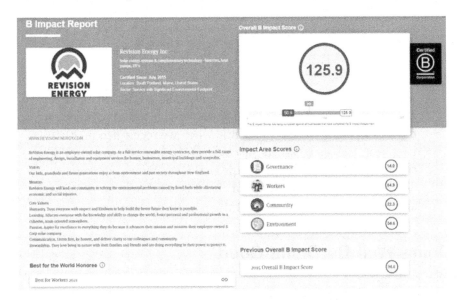

Figure 1: ReVision Energy B Impact Report for 2020

Becoming a B Corp was a clear statement to ReVision Energy's current and prospective workforce that the company valued and empowered its employees, and a signal to the clients and organizations with whom ReVision wished to partner that the partnerships would be mutually beneficial. According to Coupe, while the brand value was important, the fundamental driver for him and his co-founders was the social mission:

> We saw many compelling reasons to become a B Corp. We also thought it was just the right thing to do, purely from the standpoint of wanting to disrupt the traditional winner-take-all capitalist business model that we think has led to many of the economic, social, and environmental problems that bedevil us

today. So we followed our instinct and mustered the courage to go for it. And it did take some courage and a lot of persistence, because the certification process turned out to be really time consuming and challenging. It involved many hours of collecting data, carefully analyzing our business practices and our policies, and then making as many changes as possible to align with the B Corp guidelines and achieve our initial certification in 2015. Over the next five years, we did even more to benefit employees, and the community, and to make company governance more transparent. We were really proud to improve our certification score significantly when we recertified in 2020. Last year, ReVision earned the coveted "Best for the world" status as one of the leading B Corps worldwide. It was definitely a worthwhile effort, and overall it helped us to more consciously and consistently align our operations with our mission.

Doing Well By Doing Good

The centuries-old aphorism "doing well by doing good" originated as pithy advice for living a life that encompassed good deeds as well as personal well-being. More recently, this popular catchphrase has come to represent the more complex connection between business success, profitability, and the social good. The implicit premise is that adopting policies that serve the public good, having a good impact in social and environmental spheres, will create business value that contributes to a company's long-term success. In other words, companies that commit to a positive social and environmental impact for all their stakeholders will come out ahead in business terms. Their commitment to shared value may even generate a competitive advantage in the marketplace, accelerating the company's growth and profitability.

This link between doing well as a business and doing good in society means that the corporate motivation to pursue positive social impact is multifaceted. Even companies that prioritize saving the planet with solar must generate enough profits and resources to do well by employees, community members, and other stakeholders beyond investors and owners. In this context, it's helpful to consider ReVision Energy's commitment to doing good in the context of the broader competitive landscape of solar energy solutions and installation services in the United States.

A 2020 report on Solar Panel Installation in the US from IBISWorld characterizes this sector as having high and increasing levels of competition, decreasing barriers to entry, high volatility, and very low market concentration. Total revenues for all solar installation firms were about $14.8 billion in 2020, but this amount was spread across 19,000 very small firms, most of which had fewer than ten employees, and only a handful of medium-to-large providers. These industry characteristics betoken a very challenging landscape for market differentiation, and for sustaining long-term growth and expansion (Roth 2020).

The report also identifies the following Key Success Factors for solar businesses: a strong reputation for quality and high performance, close contacts within key markets, ability to attract and retain a skilled workforce, and ability to submit competitive proposals for large-scale institutional, municipal, and commercial projects. It notes that one of the biggest challenges for solar installation operators is attracting and retaining skilled workers who are qualified to complete the labor-intensive process of wiring solar panel systems, as well as the roofing components. Depending on local regulations, solar system installers may be required to have a certified electrician at the installation site as part of the team. Even when a company has attracted customers, training and retention of employees may create a bottleneck that limits the number of installations that can be completed.

The industry's competitive challenges have combined to limit the average revenue growth rate for solar companies to just over 5% per year, with an average profit margin of 5.9%. In contrast, ReVision Energy has achieved a growth rate of between 20% and 26% since its launch in 2006 (with the exception of the Great Recession in 2009). In 2020, the company reached $85 million in annual revenues, with a profit margin of about 11%, in the midst of a global pandemic. At a time when ReVision had to deal with daily obstacles to carrying out its mission, the company's workforce and customers came through. This sustained growth has enabled ReVision to make significant progress on its environmental mission and, importantly, to demonstrate its commitment to broader social impact and sharing value with its stakeholders. To the extent that shared value commitments create an advantage for ReVision in its industry sector, the company is demonstrating how a business can do well commercially by focusing on what is good for society instead of just its own profitability.

ReVision Energy's certification as a B Corporation in 2015 was just one step in the company's trajectory of doing well by doing good. In October 2017, ReVision Energy announced that it had converted to a 100% employee ownership structure by establishing an Employee Stock Ownership Plan (ESOP). Among the many benefits of this approach for ReVision's employees and all its stakeholders, there is a clear value for future business growth in attracting in-demand talent, as well as increasing employee loyalty and retention over time. As ReVision stated in its ESOP announcement press release:

> According to the ESOP Association, 84% of companies that convert to ESOP report higher levels of employee motivation and productivity. This overwhelmingly positive effect on the company creates broad-based ownership among all employees and fosters an environment in which everyone understands his or her role in helping the company achieve its triple bottom line. Research has proven that employee ownership builds successful, competitive companies, and creates equitable wealth for employees. It has been shown that ESOP companies pay better benefits, have twice the retirement income for employees, and pay higher wages than non-ESOP companies.

Shared Value Through Employee Ownership

Phil Coupe described the decision to pursue an ESOP structure as being similar to the co-founders' discussions about becoming a B Corp. There was a strong desire to increase ReVision Energy's social impact in a strategic way that would make the company resilient and mission-focused for the long term. ESOP was a path to directly sharing the present and future success of the business with all employees, recognizing their hard work that contributed to the company's success. An employee ownership stock plan would also benefit the co-founders, giving them some return for their upfront investment and the sweat equity that they had provided at the launch of ReVision. By pursuing the model of shared value for all stakeholders, employee-owners would all have a common stake in the future growth and success of ReVision. As Phil notes, the value of ESOP also extended to customers, communities, and potential partners:

> The ESOP transaction occurred in 2017, so now we are in the fourth year of that ownership model. It has really been transformational for the company. On the one hand, we strengthened our connection to our 300 co-owners in our workforce in a way that I think would be impossible to do other than through an ESOP. That's just been fantastic.
>
> Now we have this mantra that our workforce should think like a customer and act like an owner. And that really resonates with everyone. Our customers seem to really like the fact that when our crew shows up on their property to do a bunch of pretty intensive clean energy work, they know that each ReVision employee on the site is a co-owner. We have also had a great response from the general public about what we're doing, along with a lot of positive feedback from clients and potential partners in the public, private, and nonprofit sector.
>
> That said, it was not an easy step to take. Unless a company is well established and has reached an annual revenue rate of at least $10 million a year or more, it's probably not going to be cost effective to set up an ESOP, because the transaction itself is fairly expensive. There are a lot of legal filings, paperwork, and costs involved. Even with leadership from Bill and the company's general counsel, we had to bring in consultants to help with all the requirements. We were a little surprised by

how time consuming and complicated the process turned out to be.

However, we believed that the cost of setting up the ESOP was itself a kind of investment in ReVision employees and in all our stakeholders. That investment has delivered an awesome return so far. The ESOP has an expected life of forty years, that's how far the paperwork documenting all the ownership the agreements go out. This is just year four, but I can say without a moment's hesitation, that it's just been an absolutely tremendous advantage for all of us at ReVision Energy and one of the co-founders' best decisions in the history of the company.

Strategic Workforce Training

In addition to adopting a 100% employee-ownership structure, ReVision has been proactive in advancing the careers of employees who are interested in additional technical training and becoming licensed electricians. The company's internal ReVision Energy Training Center (RETC) was launched in 2018, as the first dedicated and state-certified electrical training program in the country operated by a solar company. The company covers the cost of the training courses and offers them onsite. It also provides employees with convenient access to the required registered apprenticeship training. By 2019, RETC had a cohort of sixty-six electrical apprentices in its program. As the company notes on its website, the Training Center is enabling ReVision to overcome the potential barrier of a scarcity of qualified electricians by building its own internal expertise and electrician workforce:

> State and federal regulations concerning the installation of solar electric systems and complementary technologies are becoming increasingly stringent, requiring the majority of our clean tech installation work to be done almost exclusively by licensed electricians with the help of registered apprentices, in very specific license-to-apprentice ratios. The ReVision Energy Training Center was developed as a way to resolve the acute

shortage of licensed electricians in New England, and to inspire our employee-owners to further their electrical skills.

ReVision Impact Investments

When ReVision had just launched, Behrens and his co-founders made a concerted attempt to attract social impact and alternative energy investors, only to come up empty. They bootstrapped the company by contributing hundreds of hours of sweat equity, until ReVision had enough of a revenue stream to be a going concern. Years later, when their company had an impressive record of growth and profitability, they turned down private equity and acquisition offers to ensure that the company's mission was not derailed by outside investors. At the same time, the ReVision co-founders were well aware that access to social impact investors would enable the company to expand its services to schools, nonprofits and municipalities that were eager for the benefits of solar power but lacked the capital to pay upfront for a solar installation and as 501c3's could not take advantage of federal tax incentives for solar. The solution was to leverage an innovative form of impact investing for solar power through what are called "Power Purchase Agreements" (PPAs).

Through an initiative led by Bill Behrens, ReVision Energy became the first company to implement PPAs in Maine and New Hampshire, using the Solar PPA investment structure to complete over 100 solar installations for nonprofits and municipalities between 2010 and 2017. Operating as ReVision Solar Impact Partners, this solar investment program is another example of combining social good with business benefits, including benefits for the schools, nonprofits, and municipal buildings that save money on the cost of electricity, for the investors who receive IRS approved tax credits as well as a favorable annual rate of return, and to ReVision which has access to additional funding to bring solar power to an expanding group of community organizations.

The details of the PPA agreements are described on the ReVision Impact website as follows:

Solar PPAs are an innovative, IRS-approved structure whereby a host agrees to purchase the electricity generated by a solar array (not the actual solar array itself) financed and built by an investor. The investor takes tax credits and other incentives available for the solar equipment, and sells the power generated by the solar equipment to the host, generally for a rate lower than the local utility.

After an agreed upon term, the host will have the option to purchase the system at a discount, often 30% to 40% below the original cost—or they can continue to purchase the power from the investor. Meanwhile, the investor earns a return on their impact investment in the form of federal and state incentives, and electricity payments from the solar host.

ReVision Impact aggregates our highly qualified, mission-aligned solar hosts and packages solar construction projects as impact investments. The unique win-win is that investors get a competitive return-on-investment, while making a positive impact on the planet, and the hosts receive the benefits of clean energy without upfront cost.

Even as ReVision partners with impact investors to accelerate the pace of solar installations and expand solar power access to a broader community, the company's owner-employees have launched a program to focus on the company's mission for social change.

The JEDI Initiative

In 2020, ReVision Energy co-owners formed the company's Justice, Equity, Diversity, and Inclusion (JEDI) initiative to recognize the intersectional relationship between environmentalism and social justice, and to highlight the work that needs to be done in the clean energy industry and beyond. The JEDI initiative aims to amplify the voices of under-represented groups to educate and lead, both within ReVision Energy and with our customers and communities. Under the values of ReVision Energy, JEDI members will actively promote and participate in an inclusive mindset to ensure a more equitable future.

A Clean Environment and a Just Society for Future Generations

As Phil Coupe looks back on his younger self, he realizes that his post-college aspirations to change the world were often just vague concepts, not practical plans. After spending fifteen years working to help achieve ReVision Energy's vision and mission, and turning fifty in the process, Coupe's understanding of social change is more grounded in reality. He believes that committed individuals and mission-driven companies together are a powerful force:

> One of my biggest takeaways from our meteoric ride here at ReVision Energy is that individuals, and groups of individuals, have immense power to create positive change. But you have to live it to really grasp that power. People have to dive into the work of making big, vague statements about changing the world come true in a way that dovetails with what needs to happen with your business. If you commit to the work and engage with everyone in the organization, then I think that opportunities to change the world exist for every business on the face of the planet. But that change will happen only if the leaders stay focused on their social mission and weave it into their business planning.
>
> At ReVision, we're all working together to transition northern New England from a fossil fuel-based economy, to a sustainable, renewable energy-based economy, and at the same time spreading social and environmental justice and equity. Pursuing that mission has been our North Star from day one. Our company's extraordinary growth, our success, and awards and accolades, and forward progress have all been the byproduct of our staying focused on our mission. We have confidence that

with a focus on mission, we will continue to grow and succeed as a business. So we are not interested in being caught up in stand-alone strategies for geographic expansion, or even an overriding annual revenue or profit goal.

At this point, we know that if we continue to drive the mission forward, we're going to attract the people to make it happen, and we're going to attract the clients who want to see that mission get accomplished.

Bill Behrens, after hearing the planetary clock tick faster and louder for many decades, has expanded his personal quest to save the planet through solar power. With his co-founders at ReVision Energy, he is committed to redefining the role of the corporation in society, and to making ReVision a model for what can be accomplished when owner-employees and all company stakeholders work together to solve both environmental and social problems. As Behrens concludes:

The traditional corporate model is destined for failure. It's just not sustainable. That model was a wonderful stimulus for economic development over a long time period, starting as far back as the 1850s and stretching all the way up to the 1970s. But in the past fifty years, the corporate structure and mission that focuses only on creating value for shareholders has become obsolete.

Companies like ReVision Energy are set up to show that commerce and worker interactions can actually be done in a different way—a way that is respectful of all participants and responsive to everyone's need to create a sustainable future for themselves and their families and communities. That sustainable future depends on a new economic and corporate structure. At ReVision, our B Corp status, the ESOP employee ownership structure, our JEDI initiatives, these steps reflect our expanded mission beyond saving the planet and solving the climate crisis to joining forces to also try to solve the social crisis.

The company's mission reflects this commitment to long-term environmental and social change. It states, "We will lead our community in solving the environmental problems caused by fossil fuels while alleviating economic and social injustice."

Reflections for Entrepreneurs Over 50

Behrens' experience in working with a multigenerational founding team, and co-founding several startups, never led him to define himself as being a certain age, or to act like someone in a later stage of life. His first reflection for entrepreneurs over 50 is to ignore your age and believe in the mission that inspires you to take action:

Number one, ignore the fact that you're over 50 and focus on the mission and the business idea that's moving you. If surrounding yourself with twenty-five-year-olds helps you do that, which I believe it does, be sure to create a multigenerational founding team and workforce. Imagine yourself as a person who has unbounded energy and time, because you actually are such a person.

Entrepreneurs don't think necessarily of themselves as being older, or in a later stage of life. At least, I certainly didn't, and others I've met don't define themselves in terms of their age. When I think about what motivates anyone to become a founder, at whatever age, I realize that entrepreneurs have certain traits that generally come into play. Entrepreneurs tend to have a lot more energy than others of the same age cohort. They tend to be able to express a strong vision, and get other people excited about a new idea. Entrepreneurs are usually able to make things happen in a way that a lot of other people just don't want to do, or don't know how to do. Overall, I think entrepreneurs have some uncommon personality characteristics that make it almost inevitable that they found startups and create new ventures.

You don't get to choose whether you have an entrepreneurial urge or not. You actually won't spend a lot of time reflecting on whether to become an entrepreneur and start a business, you simply find that that's how your life evolves. An idea takes hold, you convince other people to join in, and you realize that the business is starting.

When that urge strikes you at age fifty, instead of at age twenty or thirty, then you will find that you're working with many more who are younger and just a few who are older than you are. After a while you realize, everybody else I'm working with is twenty or thirty years younger than I am. But at the start of a new venture, moment to moment, you are focused on launching and growing your company, not thinking about your age.

Take advice from those younger than you. Listen to younger voices very carefully, because the future of any enterprise that you create is going to be in their hands anyway. Realistically, the future is not going to be in the hands of those who are older than you.

A good example from my own ReVision Energy experience is Fred Greenhalgh. Fred was in his twenties when he showed up at ReVision around 2010 and started working as a part-time contract web designer. He urged us to be much more active online. Even my co-founders Phil and Fortunat, who are fifteen or twenty years younger than I am, were not thinking about digital and social media as a company priority. Fortunately, we were smart enough to listen to a much younger voice, and we decided to hire Fred full-time to put ReVision onto the digital map. As a result, we became one of the first small solar companies to commit to making our website world class and having a strong presence on social media. That early commitment helped us to become much better known in our communities, among students and younger adults, and now all age groups.

It's essential for any company to be active on the platforms that will be going into the future. I would strongly advise anybody in their fifties who is starting a company to make sure to stay tuned to people in their twenties, and even younger. Their instincts and social context will tell you where the future is. Having younger people be part of your business planning and strategy is crucial. Have a multigenerational group help write the company vision statement, to conceptualize the mission, and figure out how to put it out there. You can't just teach yourself about the future. You have to learn from people who will actually live and breathe it.

Finally, there is one major asset that older entrepreneurs have, and that I think younger founders might lack. That is an awareness of the passage of decades. Along with that awareness comes an understanding that if the organization you have founded is of any value at all, it's going to last for decades, it's not going to disappear after a couple of years. And in order to last for decades, it has to have a sort of internal regeneration, and that structure has to be purposeful, and it has to be planned and implemented over time.

I think that's the one advantage that the older entrepreneur brings to the table that the younger ones might not fully understand. By the time you're in your fifties, you've actually seen a lot happen, decades have passed and you've seen how society and culture evolve. You understand as time passes, the future is actually large, but not unknown; it follows patterns that are visible in the present. And as you intentionally move into the future, your organization can and will have the long-term impact you envisioned from the start, so long as you build in the internal capacity to regenerate and evolve.

References

Meadows H D, Meadows L D, Randers J, Behrens III W (1972) *The Limits to Growth: A Report for The Club of Rome's Project On the Predicament of Mankind.* Universe, New York, p. 23–24.

Parenti C (2012) The Limits to Growth: A Book That Launched a Movement. *The Nation.* https://www.thenation.com/article/archive/limits-growth-book-launched-movement/. Accessed 21 Oct 2021.

Roth R (2020) Solar Panel Installation: US Industry Report OD4494. *IBIS World.* https://my.ibisworld.com/us/en/industry-specialized/od4494/about. Accessed 21 Oct 2021.

About Bill Behrens and Phil Coupe

Bill Behrens

Bill Behrens has been a leading force in renewable energy and global sustainability since the early 1970s when he earned a PhD in environmental economics from the Massachusetts Institute of Technology and co-authored *The Limits to Growth*, a seminal text of the environmental movement.

After teaching at Dartmouth College and working in the construction industry in Maine, Behrens co-founded The Green Store in Belfast, Maine to provide a variety of products for an environmentally sustainable lifestyle. From that foundation, he launched EnergyWorks in 2003 to design, sell, and install solar components.

Phil Coupe and Fortunat Mueller joined Behrens at EnergyWorks in 2006, and the three became co-founders of ReVision Energy in 2008. In addition to leading the company's financial management and planning, Behrens has spearheaded ReVision's initiatives in providing solar power to more than 100 municipalities and other tax-exempt institutions throughout New England via Power Purchase Agreements.

Phil Coupe

As a co-founder and managing partner of ReVision Energy, Phil focuses on community involvement, culture and strategic direction for the company's sales and marketing teams. After graduating from Boston College and prior to co-founding ReVision, he served as Vice President and Director of Corporate Philanthropy at a startup company in Washington, D.C. that twice made the Inc 500 List of fastest-growing companies  in America and won numerous awards for its social justice initiatives.

Coupe is an active member of his local and regional community. He serves as Chair of Maine Audubon's corporate partner program and he is on the boards of the Environmental & Energy Technology Council of Maine (E2Tech), the Conservation Law Foundation (www.clf.org), and Envision Maine. He is also a long-time mentor in the Big Brother/Big Sister program.

About the Company

Company	ReVision Energy
Website	revisionenergy.com
Founding Year	2003 as EnergyWorks; renamed ReVision Energy in 2008
Co-Founders	Bill Behrens Phil Coupe Fortunat Meuller Dan Clapp
Industry Sector	Solar Power Installation and Services
Address	91 West Main Street Liberty, ME 04949

Chapter 3

PulpWorks: Molding a Better World

Paul Tasner has packed a life-time worth of entrepreneurial experience into the past decade. After deciding in 2011 to start PulpWorks, Inc. with a mission to replace toxic plastic packaging with sustainable alternatives, Tasner pitched dozens of potential investors, recruited a co-founder, entered over twenty startup competitions, rose above repeated rejections by investors, and reinvented his business plan. Along the way, he encountered age barriers, discovered unexpected sources of support, built a scalable, global supply chain ecosystem, and enjoyed the satisfactions of creating a profitable company that lives up to its tagline of "Molding a Better World."

It's an impressive track record, not least because Tasner founded Pulp-Works as a first-time entrepreneur at the age of sixty-six. His story illustrates the power of older founders to stay the course while bootstrapping, partnering, and innovating their way to startup success even in a highly competitive market sector such as sustainable packaging.

To appreciate the challenges that Paul Tasner and his co-founder, Elena Olivari, have overcome in building a profitable company, it's helpful to start with an overview of PulpWorks today. The company's website, pulp-worksinc.com, provides a succinct statement of the founders' long-term mission and its current business model. It reads in part:

> Our mission is to "mold a better world". We will work tire-lessly to replace toxic plastic packaging—such as PVC (polyvinyl chloride) blister packs and Styrofoam® (expanded polystyrene)—with our compostable/biodegradable, 100% waste-based, molded

fiber products. Removing PVC and EPS from the waste stream is the foundation upon which the PulpWorks business is built.

Our flagship product, the patented Karta-Pack™, is Pulp-Works' environmentally friendly alternative to the toxic, dangerous and ubiquitous plastic blister pack. The Karta-Pack is comprised of two pieces of compostable and biodegradable material—molded pulp and cardboard—that are connected to create a single package with the saleable article nestled safely in a cavity in the molded pulp component. This product has enabled PulpWorks to spearhead efforts to reduce the amount of plastic—particularly, PVC—deposited in landfills everywhere. Short-lived products account for more than 70% of the PVC disposed in America's solid waste with two billion pounds discarded every year, including blister packs and other packaging, plastic bottles and plastic wrap. PVC production poses serious environmental health threats due to the manufacture of raw chemicals, including chlorine and cancer-causing vinyl chloride monomer. Similarly, expanded polystyrene foam (EPS, often referred to as Styrofoam is pervasive in the environment. It is extremely damaging throughout its lifecycle and is rarely recycled.

The advantages of the Karta-Pack, compliant with ISO 14000 and European Green Dot standards, versus a blister pack comprised of PVC, the most environmentally harmful plastic on our planet, are myriad.

A Career Twist and A Founding Vision for PulpWorks Version 1.0

In retrospect, Tasner's path to entrepreneurship started in 2009 with a sudden twist in his forty-year career in managing supply chains and contracted manufacturing services for global brands. That forty years had included an impressive list of high-level management positions that Tasner had held since earning his Ph.D. and M.S. in mathematics in the 1970s to complement his undergraduate degree in industrial engineering. During a 15-year stint at the Clorox Company, he rose to become National Manager of Contract Manufacturing with responsibility for over $300 million in business activity with the company's twenty-five contract manufacturers. He then spent five years at California Closets as Vice President of Distribution and Strategic Alliances, with complete P&L responsibility for the company's distribution business and the management of a complex, decentralized supply chain. In 2007, Tasner joined Method Products, Inc. He was attracted to the company's social purpose and its founders' stated mission of making healthy, non-toxic, and biodegradable household cleaners and consumer personal care products.

As Senior Director of Operations at Method Products, Tasner was responsible for managing the full spectrum of procurement, manufacturing, warehousing, freight, and customer service, along with a network of twenty contract manufacturers across North America. Reflecting his growing personal commitment to supporting the adoption of planet-friendly products, Tasner founded the San Francisco Bay Area Green Supply Chain Forum at the start of 2009. The Forum attracted dozens of companies to support its mission of promoting environmentally sustainable processes and sharing best practices across the supply chain ecosystem.

Then, in December 2009, Tasner's management career hit a drastic and unexpected road bump. At the age of sixty-four he was laid off from Method Products. His new year's agenda suddenly featured the search for a new position, or the unappealing alternative of an early retirement.

With his extensive network of contacts in supply chain management, Tasner decided to join a supply chain consultancy group, putting his skills to work helping clients to address a variety of supply chain challenges. It was a straightforward next step. For some managers nearing traditional retirement age, it might even have seemed to offer graceful options for winding down a long and successful career.

Traditional retirement, however graceful, was not in the least appealing. Tasner had set his sights on far more challenging goal; he wanted to tackle the seemingly inexorable rise of global pollution caused by the ubiquitous plastic packaging of consumer products. Like many consumers, he and his wife routinely struggled to open the rigid plastic encasing so many household products, from electric toothbrushes to cleaning fluids and kitchen utensils. His frustration with this pervasive plastic packaging went much deeper than the average consumer. As a supply chain professional, and founder of the Green Supply Chain Forum, he knew the severe environmental toll that hard molded plastic and other forms of packaging such as Styrofoam were taking on the planet every year.

Concluding that recycling and waste management efforts would never keep pace with the massive, fast-growing use of plastic packaging, Tasner was determined to take action by starting a company to design and manufacture a commercially viable green packaging alternative for consumer goods. He envisioned that his startup's green packaging would be made from fully compostable, biodegradable materials. What's more, a truly sustainable solution would exemplify the circular economy model, using previously recycled materials to create the new packaging. Ideally, he wanted this green packaging solution to be manufactured in a facility that was itself environmentally friendly, retrofitted or designed, and built from scratch to reduce emissions and conserve energy at every step of the manufacturing process.

The fact that non-toxic, recycled pulp could be molded into protective cardboard packaging inspired the name of his company-to-be. He called it PulpWorks.

Balancing Optimism and Startup Reality

Tasner was optimistic about his ability to manage a manufacturing facility for the production of PulpWorks packaging and to attract consumer brand companies to purchase its green packaging solutions. In addition to his career-spanning experience in supply chain management and contracted manufacturing for consumer products, his recent work with peers in the San Francisco Bay Area Green Supply Chain Forum had convinced him that the goal of reducing plastic package pollution was widely shared by consumer goods companies and contract manufacturers.

Tasner's original business plan was to launch his company as a small, environmentally advanced manufacturing plant in the Bay Area. By operating a green, model manufacturing company, he hoped that PulpWorks would attract positive attention from clients as the demand for non-toxic packaging inevitably accelerated over time. Even though adoption of alternative green packaging was still an emerging trend in 2011, it was already clear that the global damage caused by plastic-wrapped consumer goods would eventually trigger a backlash among environmentally conscious consumers and the public sector. At the same time, Tasner knew that in the short run, an investment in PulpWorks would require a leap of faith and a strong commitment to social impact investing. To strengthen the founding team, and add sustainable facility design experience, he recruited Elena Olivari as his co-founder. Olivari brought decades of global experience as an architect and recent training in solar energy and green building, together with a passion for sustainable, environmentally sound solutions.

Despite his optimism, Tasner was well aware that he would face challenges as a first-time entrepreneur trying to find investors for a company that didn't fit the typical venture capital profile of fast-growing, digital startups. As a manufacturing-based business, PulpWorks would require significant capital investment to set up the production facility. There would be a multi-year horizon for attracting customers, generating revenue, and becoming profitable.

In hopes of building public sector support, Tasner and Olivari approached municipal government and regional funding agencies to convince them that PulpWorks was an appealing candidate for economic development support. It would provide environmentally sound and well-paying jobs, along with apprenticeship opportunities for a diverse population of Bay Area residents. In addition, the plant would be designed, and become known, as a model manufacturing facility, enhancing the sustainability reputation of the Bay Area. As Tasner recalls, the co-founders did get initial meetings with local officials. It was 2010, just after the recession. Good career-track jobs were scarce outside of skilled high-tech opportunities, and well-paying manufacturing jobs were even more scarce in northern California. Environmental awareness was increasing, but model implementations of green manufacturing were still almost nonexistent. Building a green manufacturing facility would produce a much-needed non-toxic, recyclable packaging alternative, and create a model that could be replicated for the benefit of the community and the environment.

It seemed like a compelling plan, but it soon became clear that the municipal support and economic development path was a dead end in terms of funding for a PulpWorks manufacturing facility. Undaunted, Tasner turned his attention to pitching PulpWorks to private investors. He knew that Venture Capitalist (VC) firms were not a good match. However, he was hoping that deep-pocketed Angel investors would be excited about the positive environmental impact of green packaging. He came up against yet another brick wall. In Tasner's own words:

> We tried for about a year to raise money for our PulpWorks green manufacturing plan. We did get a hearing for our original plan. I was able to set up meetings with many investors to make a pitch for PulpWorks version one, and I'm well aware that even getting to the meeting stage is flattering in some way. I was savvy enough to know that our pitch would not appeal to traditional VCs. As first time founders with no startup track record, it was clear that we didn't fit the typical VC portfolio profile. So I put my energy into meetings with Angel investors, especially those with an interest in sustainability and the environment. At the start, I had a very romantic notion of Angel investors being more open to outside the box thinking and non-typical founder profiles. I started out optimistic, but boy, I was so wrong. It was quite naive to think that these Angel groups would be attracted to our green packaging innovations and excited about the high growth potential of the sustainable packaging sector. They had no interest in taking a risk.
>
> What I had not expected, and what really kind of shocked

me, was how negatively some potential investors reacted to me as an older founder. To say the least, the reality of pitching to investors at my age was very disheartening. I was prepared for concerns about my being a first-time entrepreneur but I had hoped that my experience in the sector and the strength of our idea would help to counterbalance that at least a little. Being a senior founder raised some pretty obviously ageist responses. At one event, I was part of a panel with myself and two other startup founders who each happened to be in their twenties. After we each gave our presentation to the whole audience, the organizer asked each founder to sit behind a table and invited the investors to line up in front of the table with the founder they wanted to talk with to learn more about the company. Everyone lined up in front of those two young men. Nobody came near my table. Even the young founders were embarrassed; they tried to make me feel better about it. There was no way to make me feel better. I had to admit that this was a dead end. The next day, I said to Elena, looking for investors is just pointless. That's the last pitch I'm doing for PulpWorks. It's just not worth it. We didn't give up. We knew we just had to find a different path to enter the market, a strategy that didn't require up front capital investment.

The Pivot: PulpWorks Version 2.0

PulpWorks couldn't set up its own manufacturing plant without a significant amount of capital and investor support for building a facility. The lack of investor interest was discouraging, but it didn't erode Tasner's conviction that becoming a source for green packaging was a viable and much-needed business idea. The next step was to develop another launch strategy, one that would build on his expertise in managing contract manufacturers. The plan for PulpWorks version 2.0 was to build a strong, distributed network of outsourcing partners, rather than take on the role of green manufacturer. Once Tasner decided on this strategy, he could see it was a natural fit with his prior experience. In some ways, it felt like an extension of what he had been doing for decades. The difference was that previously he had contracted with manufacturers as a representative of large, well-known corporations. The key negotiating points were price and delivery terms. Now he was working for himself, with a vision of reducing global plastics pollution. He turned to manufacturing firms that he already was familiar with, introducing PulpWorks as a startup with a mission to create biodegradable packaging using recycled materials.

PulpWorks pivoted its business model accordingly. Tasner reached out to his contacts among small manufacturers around the world, many of whom were already in the same business that he wanted to enter, producing packaging for consumer products. He received a positive response from many well-qualified firms. After the skepticism and rejection from investors, he was moved by the enthusiasm his supply chain partnering proposals received. Overseas manufacturing firms welcomed him with open arms, and were ready to start working with him even though he was an older entrepreneur and first-time founder of a new and as yet unproven firm. These partners offered more than best wishes and enthusiasm. One of the manufacturers that Tasner had worked with on behalf of a prior employer was willing to wait until after PulpWorks had been paid by its early customers before collecting their own payment. As Tasner remembers, "That's an amazing amount of trust to put into a startup, especially a startup operating in a different country with no revenues in the bank. It was such a boost for PulpWorks, and it really helped us to manage our cash flow during the launch period. That company certainly earned our loyalty, and not surprisingly they soon became our premier manufacturing partner and supplier."

Although Olivari's background and professional network was not in contract manufacturing, she could leverage her formal architectural training, environmental building experience, and outstanding design skills to help jumpstart the creation of packaging prototypes. With a strong commitment to sustainability at all levels, she was willing to dig into the details of the green packaging market and to work closely with a contracted design team to develop customized package designs to meet the demands of global consumer brands.

The advantage for PulpWorks of establishing a globally distributed, contractor-based supply chain ecosystem went beyond bypassing the need for a high capital investment in local production capabilities. Over time, Tasner established an expansive network of core production partners, with locations around the world. This networked ecosystem made up of multiple trusted partners provided PulpWorks with the scalability it needed to fulfill high-volume orders for its green packaging. It made the company a capable contender in a highly competitive global market. Importantly, adopting an outsourced manufacturing and production model eliminated most of the overhead costs of production, allowing the company to be flexible on pricing and fulfillment terms in their proposals. As Tasner notes, "Our current model means we are so lean that basically there's no overhead. That may sound like an exaggeration, but we literally have no overhead on the production side of the company. We just have to manage the cost of goods and fulfillment through our suppliers. That's been tremendously liberating when we are competing for a new customer with more traditional, overhead-heavy packaging manufacturers. We have the option to quote a price that gives us margins that are pretty small in order to win a piece of business, but even with those smaller margins we can be profitable overall."

Initially, Tasner was concerned about the optics of PulpWorks relying on overseas manufacturing, in case this would be detrimental to the company's ability to attract large consumer brands as customers. In reality, while many prospective clients raise concerns about manufacturing locations, their concerns are centered on time to fulfillment, supply chain complexity, and potential cost of delivery from overseas. In the past ten years, PulpWorks has only heard from one small US company that they wouldn't contract with them based on the lack of a local PulpWorks manufacturing facility.

PulpWorks currently has production partners in China, Taiwan, India, and Egypt, as well as in the UK and in North America. Each partner has their own talents and specialties. Many of them overlap with each other in some areas and PulpWorks doesn't use them all equally. These ecosystem relationships are very close, and have lasted now for almost a decade. Tasner has encouraged transparent relationships and communication among the partners. They talk candidly about margins and capacity and inventory. The ecosystem participants often work together collaboratively to win new business and new customers.

In retrospect, Tasner believes that the failure of PulpWorks version 1.0 to attract investors has been a proverbial blessing in disguise. He realizes that he may have been consumed by the details of setting up and running a local facility and never achieved the scalability and agility that the distributed supply ecosystem provides to his company. In addition, it's hard to see how he would have had the time to devote to building the PulpWorks brand and attracting customers on top of the manufacturing responsibilities. He would never have taken the time to enter multiple business competitions and talk to the media about PulpWorks' vision and strategy. As it turned out, those competition entries and published interviews created a global awareness and brand recognition for his startup that became an essential ingredient in attracting interested prospects for its green packaging products and converting those prospects into customers.

Patent-Protecting a Breakthrough in Sustainable Packaging

One potential downside of sharing the details of molded pulp production processes and packaging design with global supply chain partners was the risk of copy-cat products. To reduce this risk, PulpWorks needed to take action to protect the innovative thinking that had inspired its solution. Being granted a patent for their ideas would provide impressive legal confirmation that Tasner and Olivari had come up with a truly novel and useful alternative to plastic packaging. A patent would also provide notice to any potential copy-cat competitors that the new company was prepared to safeguard its intellectual property. There is, however, no guarantee that a patent application will lead to approval and a patent from the United States Patent and Trademark Office. Obtaining a patent is a time-consuming and expensive undertaking. It's a big investment for a cash-strapped startup, and aspiring inventors are well-advised to assess the chances of a patent being granted before embarking on the process. In a sign of their commitment to the PulpWorks mission and revised business strategy, Tasner and Olivari decided to file a provisional US patent application in April 2012 with the broadly encompassing title of "Package for Holding Articles."

Strikingly, and unlike the majority of patent applications that are dominated by arcane technical details and the complex legal language of patent claims, the PulpWorks patent narrative spends considerable time describing the environmental damage caused by plastic PVC packaging and the urgent need for a sustainable alternative.

The background section of the PulpWorks patent granted by the United States Patent and Trademark Office and issued in November 2016 as patent US 9,481,500 reads in part:

BACKGROUND OF THE INVENTION

1. Field of the Invention
Blister packaging is commonly used to display small consumer goods sold at retail. A clear PVC (polyvinyl chloride) blister, with a saleable article inside, is typically sealed to a sheet of cardboard.

2. Background Art
PVC is a commonly-used plastic found in baby shampoo bottles, packaging, saran wrap, shower curtains and thousands of other products—yet there is relatively little public awareness of its serious health and environmental impacts. . .
As much as seven billion pounds of PVC are discarded every year in the U.S. PVC disposal is the largest source of dioxin-forming chlorine and phthalates in solid waste, as well as a major source of lead, cadmium and organotins—which pose serious health threats to humans and the environment.
Short-lived products account for more than 70% of PVC disposed of in America's solid waste with two billion pounds

discarded every year, including "blister packs" and other packaging, plastic bottles and plastic wrap...

Contrary to popular belief, recycling of PVC is negligible,
with estimates ranging from 0.1% to 3% of post-consumer PVC
waste being recycled.

PVC is very difficult to recycle because many additives used
in PVC products make it impossible to retain the unique prop-
erties of the original formulation from a batch of mixed PVC
products collected for recycling...

Safer alternatives to PVC are widely available and effective for almost all major uses in building materials, medical
products, packaging, office supplies, toys and consumer goods.
Phasing out PVC in favor of safer alternatives is economically
achievable...

Therefore, the invention responds to an urgent and compelling need for improved packages that embody the intent of
a blister pack but have a significantly reduced negative impact
on the environment while providing consumers with enhanced
functionality and design features.

The patent goes on to summarize the invention of Tasner and Olivari
as follows, emphasizing the use of various types of recycled materials:

BRIEF SUMMARY OF THE INVENTION

Two pieces of recyclable/compostable/biodegradable material,
such as melded pulp, paperboard or cardboard, are connected
to create a single package that can be used in a retail environment in a manner similar to a blister pack.

The backing piece, which can be comprised of molded pulp,
holds an article in a cavity or depression designed for that specific article. The backing piece can be of any length, width or
thickness. The cavity or depression can be of any size, shape
or depth.

The front or face card, which can be comprised of recyclable paperboard or cardboard, covers the article and can be printed on one or both sides and/or die cut to highlight the features of the article within. The paper face card can contain the UPC bar code. The face card can be of any length, width or thickness. The locking tabs are proportional to the size of the card.

The molded pulp backing piece and face card can be of recycled content: post-industrial or post-consumer waste...

The decision to claim a breakthrough packaging invention on behalf of PulpWorks paid off for Tasner and Olivari when their patent application was granted in 2016.

Building the Brand and Attracting Customers

The PulpWorks business pivot was well underway, with a scalable global ecosystem of production and fulfillment partners and a patent to protect its green packaging inventions. But what about the customer acquisition challenge? As a small company without brand recognition or a budget for extensive marketing, how was PulpWorks going to get the attention of the consumer brand companies it wanted to land as clients? Tasner was already reaching out to his professional network to pitch the advantages of environmentally friendly packaging, but that wasn't enough to fill the company's pipeline for new orders over the long term. A fortuitous piece of free digital marketing advice provided Tasner with a low-cost brand-building strategy. Fueled by his willingness to commit to innovative promotional efforts, this strategy helped to put PulpWorks at the top of Google search engine rankings and attract global attention for its products. As a bonus, Tasner was able to transform his position as an older first-time founder from a funding liability into a digital marketing asset. In Tasner's own words:

In the early years after founding PulpWorks, I was searching for a strategy to build our brand and attract new customers without spending a bundle on marketing. I went to a local seminar on startup marketing strategies that covered search engine optimization (SEO) techniques. One of the main speakers was a marketing consultant, who was clearly there hoping to promote his own SEO consulting business. After the program ended, I went up to this consultant and said, "You seem like a great consultant, but I simply can't afford to hire you. If you had one pearl of wisdom to give me, what would it be?" In response, he recommended focusing on getting respected online media and other heavily visited, credible websites to link directly to the PulpWorks website. This type of exposure would over time boost our ranking in Google and other search engines, and our company would become known as a leader in our field. It would take consistent effort for the links to accumulate, but it wouldn't require a big marketing budget. I took that advice to heart, learned more about the power of backlinks, and made it a company priority to give interviews and generate as many online media mentions and articles as possible about PulpWorks as a company. Since that day, it has been our main marketing strategy.

Of course, we needed to find a way to get regular media coverage. Being based in San Francisco, I realized that we were surrounded by opportunities to enter startup business competitions. Fortunately for us, as an environmentally friendly, green packaging manufacturer, PulpWorks was a perfect fit for any competition that featured sustainability. In the past decade, there have been countless business competitions open to sustainability motivated startups in San Francisco and beyond. PulpWorks spent years entering every competition we could find, whether it was local, regional, or even international.

Our primary goal was to highlight the company name and our green packaging solutions in the competition entry materials, and in every pitch we made. By doing that, we increased our digital visibility, rising in the search rankings as more and more articles mentioned PulpWorks and our competition entry, and linked to our website. Over time, I also learned how to make a compelling pitch at these competitions, to stand out among the other entrants. It helped that we had a genuinely interesting product and green solution that was worth writing about. As a bonus, we also ended up becoming competition finalists and prize winners. In fact, PulpWorks has won quite a bit of prize money from the many business competitions we entered. Since we were not able to attract any outside investors in our early years, that prize money was very helpful in funding our business operations in the early stages of attracting customers and ramping up our revenues.

Just as we had hoped, being a finalist and winning competitions created a positive cycle of even more publicity and interview requests. It helped to attract media attention that I didn't fit the profile of a typical Silicon Valley founder. In standing out from the competition, my age was an advantage. Soon I was being interviewed for feature articles not just in the industry specific and local trade papers or magazines, but in publications such as the *New York Times* and the *Wall Street Journal*. Turns out, people like a good story about an older founder with an innovative solution for environmentally friendly packaging. Just as that digital marketing consultant had told me, there's a terrific marketing impact in having featured online articles with a direct link to your company website.

This type of coverage was especially powerful in our consumer goods packaging industry category where there are just a few global packaging giants, thousands of medium and small companies with low brand recognition, and relatively few innovative, green packaging solutions. The industry giants focus on volume and scale. They make cardboard cartons by the billions; they make drink trays like what you get when you take coffee out from Starbucks, and they make other disposable food service items, like the takeaway clamshells and plastic containers that you get from most restaurants. All those items are manufactured literally in the billions by the behemoth companies.

The thousands of small and medium size companies that make more specialized packaging for everything else are scattered all over the globe. PulpWorks is one of the smallest companies in that crowded landscape, there's no question about that. But there are no giants competing directly for the specialized packaging business. Most are single plant manufacturers and frankly, they're not very sophisticated about their digital marketing and internet exposure. So PulpWorks ended up appearing way above these competitors in the online search rankings.

A friend of mine told me that at a convention he met one of these small competitor companies that has been in this business for decades. They asked him if he had ever heard of this Pulp-Works outfit? Who are they and why are they listed so high in search rankings? That was a great compliment from the competition. It turns out that when global companies search for a supplier who creates the kind of packaging that we do, there's only a handful of terms that they search on. Molded fiber, molded pulp, biodegradable packaging, green packaging.

And when you plug those into a Google search, we are right up there at the top. I mean, literally at the top, next to Wikipedia. Once we landed in that top position, we started getting inquiries every day from potential customers all over the world. Honestly, it's been years since I've had to pick up the phone and make a cold call to a prospect. That's an amazing impact from that one piece of digital marketing advice that I took to heart almost ten years ago.

According to Tasner's estimate, PulpWorks has served over 250 companies in the past decade, from the very largest global brands to many small niche firms. In parallel to the demand for consumer packaging by different industry sectors, PulpWorks has drawn most of its customers from industry categories such as cosmetics, personal care and household items, and electronics. They have also developed specialty food packaging, veterinary and healthcare packaging.

One of their newest customers, and one that Tasner is very proud to have attracted, is the pharmaceutical company and insulin maker Novo

Nordisk, a well-known global brand with a commitment to sustainability. Tasner notes that there is a lot of exciting growth potential for this client, and he looks forward to having a long and fruitful relationship with them. Additional recent customers including Electrolux, the appliance manufacturer, Titleist, the golf equipment leader, and Estée Lauder, the cosmetics giant. These new customers are global, respected brands that are putting their trust in PulpWorks, in recognition of their established track record in designing and delivering a quality green packaging solution. Tasner is sure that these large companies first learned about PulpWorks because of its widespread media coverage and consistently high search rankings.

Planning for PulpWorks Future

Tasner continues to give interviews, answering questions about being an older founder as well as providing updates on PulpWorks business growth. He notes that recently he is fielding more and more questions about his long-term plans and where he sees himself and his company five or ten years into the future. In response, he notes:

> The reality of starting a new company in my mid-sixties is that by now I've learned to take one year at a time. Way back in 2011, being the CEO of my own company for ten years seemed like an ambitious goal, and building up PulpWorks to be a profitable company providing green packaging products that were a sustainable alternative to polluting plastics seemed like satisfying career capstone. Of course, as of 2021, I just blew right past that ten-year marker. I'm still CEO and I'm still not attracted to a traditional retirement way of life. I love getting up every day and hearing from customers and new prospects, and taking care of business. Some days I only have to spend a few hours on PulpWorks priorities, but sometimes I have to spend ten hours at a stretch. As with any business, it really depends on what's going on. I can do this work from anywhere. In managing the day-to-day operations, and in terms of revenue

and growth, there's nothing I really want to change about it.

On the other hand, I'm not planning on being the Pulp-Works CEO in another ten years. Elena and I are aligned on this question. Even though there's a twenty-year gap in our ages, both of us have similar needs around the business. In defining success, our goal has been to create a lean and consistently profitable operation. And we have achieved that goal. PulpWorks keeps growing from year to year. Sometimes the growth has been quite modest. Occasionally, we take a giant leap, and we've even gone backwards in our revenues some years. But the way our business operates and the way we are introduced to new customers, it seems to be a never-ending pipeline that shows up in our inbox every morning. We definitely want to continue this consistent performance as we think about transition to a different management structure.

Every year, the company is better known for green packaging solutions, and increasingly the business, regulatory, and consumer worlds are moving in our direction. In Europe, regulatory issues have pushed companies in that direction. Manufacturers like Electrolux are hearing from their business and consumer customers that they need to replace their plastic packaging with a sustainable alternative. That's what brought them to Pulp-Works. This is a story we expect to hear even more frequently in the next few years as anti-pollution regulations combine with a commitment in recycling and the circular economy around the world.

Thanks to the diverse manufacturer and design network that PulpWorks has in place, we have the capacity to meet pretty much any size packaging project that we might be asked to fulfill. We have responded successfully to really enormous opportunities in terms of volume. Prospects sometimes ask me questions about whether or not we can deliver on high volume orders. They can see that we are still a small business. In response, we've been able to successfully demonstrate how our ecosystem and supply chain partnerships support efficient timely fulfillment. Most of the time, we land the contract.

It's been a great ten years, and I won't be surprised if next week or next month, we get an inquiry from yet another block-buster company asking us to bid on a giant new contract. At this point, I'm well aware that we may or may not win that piece of business and the outcome will have an impact on our earnings. I used to worry that our pipeline of new customers and new business would suddenly dry up. But after ten years, it doesn't show any signs of drying up. The world wants and needs more sustainable packaging and I know we can keep on supplying it.

I am so fortunate to run a company that generates a livelihood and provides a solution that is good for the planet, a solution that I'm really proud of.

Reflections on Being an Older Founder

In his 2017 TED talk, Tasner summed up the accomplishments of Pulp-Works at its five-year anniversary as follows:

> Five years after PulpWorks started, I'm thrilled and proud to share with you that our revenues have doubled every year, we have no debt, we have several marquee clients, our patent was issued, I have a wonderful partner who's been with me right from the beginning, and we've won more than twenty awards for the work that we've done. But best of all, we've made a small dent—a very small dent—in the worldwide plastic pollution crisis.

Reflecting on over ten years as CEO, Tasner estimates that PulpWorks has provided sustainable, green packaging products for over 250 customers around the world, has demonstrated its ability to attract new clients, and has grown to about $3 million in annual revenues. In addition to accomplishing its mission to reduce pollution from plastic packaging, PulpWorks has become a model for sustainable product development.

During this decade, Tasner has given a lot of thought to his experiences as an older founder, and he is happy to share some of the lessons he has learned and challenges that he encountered since starting PulpWorks:

Becoming a TED Resident and giving a presentation to the TED audience in 2017 was a real stimulus for reflecting about all the things I've experienced and learned since 2011. When I started working on the TED Talk, I felt like the odd man out in the group of TED Residents and Fellows, mainly because nobody else had a manufacturing-related business there. I was also the oldest and I had certainly taken an unusual path to starting my own company. I started out talking about entrepreneurism, and about the environment, and then the ageism question kind of popped up. That kind of highlighted the ageism issues for me, and since then I've been invited to speak at many places about the realities of ageism.

Honestly, addressing the challenges of ageism that older founders need to think about really wasn't my intent at the start, but I am pretty passionate about it now.

The good news for older entrepreneurs, based on my own experience, is that I really only encountered that blatant ageism when I was trying to raise money, to get the business started. Even better news is that as soon as we launched PulpWorks with our new business model, and became a going concern, I didn't experience any evidence of ageism as a CEO. It never reared its ugly head with respect to anything else. It was only when I wanted to tap into an investor's deep pockets that all of a sudden, my age became an issue. It's never been an issue again. Most of my customers, unless we've met, have no idea how old I am. It doesn't matter. They're looking for quality, service, fast fulfillment, and reasonable prices. As long as I meet all those demands, they're happy. It doesn't matter on a day-to-day basis that most everyone I talk to in the business is younger than I am. From my perspective, it's a bonus.

Another lesson I have learned is that if you're unhappy at

your job, consider that it may not be your role that's causing that problem. Whether you are working as an accountant or an engineer, or in some other career where you feel burned out, it may very well be the organizational environment, or perhaps your boss, or the bureaucracy that is causing this unhappiness. So don't decide to abandon your expertise to find a more satisfying job without getting to the root of what you want to change. It strikes me that many days, I'm doing exactly what I was doing in many of my previous jobs in terms of managing supply chains and contract manufacturing projects. I love that work as the CEO of PulpWorks, but I was so unhappy doing similar work at some of those prior jobs. Believe me, starting your own accounting firm will feel a lot different than working in the accounts payable department of a corporation.

Find a co-founder who complements your own background and can be a true startup partner. Elena joined PulpWorks when we expected to leverage her architect's experience to set up a green manufacturing plant. Her green building background turned out to be a little off target for the business model we decided to adopt. But she was flexible enough to pivot along with me, and to step into helping manage the package design work that needed to be done through contractors. Most importantly, it's been fabulous having someone to celebrate with and someone to cry with. I mean, if you're hesitant to share the upside and ownership of a new company with a co-founder because you want to keep all the money for yourself, you probably shouldn't decide to become a founder when you are over 50.

Focus on building your company through partnerships and attracting early customers who can provide revenue. Don't waste your time trying to attract investors. I was pretty disgruntled by that experience. The more you can bootstrap your startup, the better. This is the time to think about putting your own funds into the company, if you've got some savings, or reaching out to friends and family who might help you to bootstrap. Hold off on more formal investor pitches at least until you have fully launched and demonstrated that you can attract customers, and have a clear goal in mind before you approach investors. Obviously, that comes from my own personal experience, which wasn't very good. With a different business model, or a track record of successful entrepreneurship, some older founders might be able to find investors.

Finally, being a founder is challenging, probably the biggest career challenge you will ever have. Don't give up when you run into roadblocks. Acknowledge your frustrations, but don't conclude that you will never succeed. Anticipate that like almost all founders, you will probably have to rethink or even completely change your start up plan. Just hold on to your long-term vision, whatever that is, and find a more flexible path to move toward that, one step at a time. From my personal perspective, think about the need and opportunity for innovative companies in the environmental sphere, providing solutions that support sustainability. This is where the world is heading. It's where I hope that we'll all be heading, companies and consumers together, from now on. So if your talents can be applied to solving the challenges of waste and pollution, I can confirm that it's a really wonderful direction for innovative and determined older founders to explore.

About Paul Tasner and Elena Olivari

Paul Tasner

Paul Tasner is the CEO and co-founder of PulpWorks. Prior to co-founding the company in 2011, Paul held leadership positions in procurement, manufacturing, and logistics in ventures ranging from start-up to Fortune 100. Included among them are: The Clorox Company (consumer packaged goods), California Closet Company (home furnish-

ings), Method Products (consumer packaged goods), Hepagen (vaccines), OM2 (supply chain consultancy), and the Reclipse Group (supply chain consultancy). His clients have included Clif Bar, Dreyer's Grand Ice Cream, GlaxoSmithKline, Novartis Consumer Health, Borden Chemical, Dial Corporation, Unilever, and Industrial Light+Magic.

In 2008, Paul founded and continues to lead the San Francisco Bay Area Green Supply Chain Forum—the first such assembly of supply chain executives anywhere. He has authored many papers and presentations on supply chain sustainability and currently lectures on this timely topic in the MBA Programs at San Francisco State University and Golden Gate University, as well as the Packaging Engineering Department at San Jose State University.

Paul is an Industrial Engineering graduate of the New Jersey Institute of Technology and holds a Ph.D. in Mathematics from Boston University.

Elena Olivari

Elena Olivari is the Chief Sustainability Officer and co-founder of PulpWorks. In 2010, she earned professional certificates in Solar Energy and Green Building as well as Social Corporate Responsibility Reporting at the University of California, Berkeley. Born in Vicenza, Italy, Elena has practiced as an architect and designer for twenty years in the US and internationally, managing projects of diverse complexity and scale and cultivating strong relationships with clients, consultants, and general contractors. Her prior employers and projects include Smithgroup, Chong Partners Architecture, Minami Tamaki, and  Hornberger+Worstel, with responsibility for projects involving historical restoration, and the construction and renovation of environmentally certified resorts, academic buildings, and urban mixed-use facilities.

Elena earned her M.A. in architecture from the Istituto Universitario diArchitettura di Venezia, Italy.

About the Company

Company	PulpWorks, Inc
Website	pulpworksinc.com
Founding Years	2011
Co-Founders	Elena Olivari and Paul Tasner
Industry Sector	Sustainable Consumer Goods Packaging
Address	50 Almenar Drive Suite B Greenbrae, CA 94904

Chapter 4

Seniors Helping Seniors

In 2020, there were more than 770,000 franchise businesses operating in the United States, representing about ten percent of all US companies. Spread across 200 plus industry sectors, franchises provide employment for an estimated 8 million people (Statista 2021).

Entrepreneurs of all ages are attracted to the franchise model for many reasons, including buying into a recognized brand and business model, reducing startup risk, the promise of centralized support and training, and access to a network of peer owners (Bevis 2020).

Like all founders, new franchise owners encounter their share of startup growth and operational challenges. In this chapter, Doug Peck and Josh Obeiter discuss the mission that inspired their entrepreneurship, what they have learned since opening their franchises, and how an intergenerational merger of their Seniors Helping Seniors companies has helped them to achieve both their business and social impact goals.

Entrepreneur at 64: Doug Peck

In 2011, at the age of sixty-four, Doug Peck was facing a major career decision. Far from thinking about retirement, he was weighing the risks and potential rewards of launching his own company. After a successful career in corporate human resources and temp agency management, followed by several years of solo consulting gigs, Peck was looking for an opportunity to make a difference in the world as an entrepreneur while doing work that he loved. Based on his experience caring for an aging family member, he was poised to enter the home care sector to achieve his entrepreneurial goals. As Peck recalls:

I had three main objectives in looking for an entrepreneur-ship opportunity. First, I didn't want to be a solo consultant any longer. I wanted to own a small business that involved working with other people.

Second, I wanted to have a hands-on role delivering services that were meaningful, instead of just sitting in an office and managing the business itself.

Finally, I wanted to start a company with a clear social purpose, knowing that the business was accomplishing something that was beneficial and useful for the community. Of course, I also wanted to bring in revenue and continue to make a living, but the financial goals were not my main motivator.

The inspiration for entering the home care sector stemmed from my own experience caring for my mother. My father had passed away and my mother was living alone. She didn't want to move into any type of senior housing. In fact, she was adamant about staying in her own home. As the eldest son, and closest family member geographically, I took responsibility for helping her to live at home for almost four years. During that period, I learned firsthand just how much work and time is involved in being the primary caregiver for an older family member. It seemed that there was an endless amount of work to do, taking care of my mother's house and yard and all sorts of chores, along with her appointments.

Fortunately, I was running my own consulting business at the time which gave me flexibility. But seeing me shuttling back and forth between houses trying to take care of all the chores, my wife gave me a great insight. She pointed out that what my mother wanted most was my time and attention, so she could socialize. I realized that was true. Despite my best efforts, my mother was alone for long hours every day, and she didn't have a lot of social interactions to look forward to. Even though she said she didn't mind being alone, it really became apparent that she needed more companionship. I just didn't have enough time available to fill her days, no matter how hard I tried.

This opened my eyes to the importance of providing services for families who were responsible for their older relatives living at home. When I began to explore caregiving services as a business opportunity, it struck a chord with me. I knew from personal experience that these services were much needed. Once I made the decision to start a business in services for at-home seniors, I had to figure out how to proceed. I didn't have the background to set up and operate a home care agency on my own. That's what attracted me to a franchise. As I researched the various franchise options, I particularly liked the Seniors Helping Seniors model. The idea of literally hiring older workers to be the ones providing the support and companionship for other seniors was so attractive. I just felt that it was a win-win for everybody. I didn't want to run a traditional home care agency. And Seniors Helping Seniors had a special affinity for me at the age of sixty-four. I could envision working with other seniors to support families and older adults to stay safely and comfortably at home. It seemed that this area of business was a good match for all of my objectives, and that the franchise structure would provide the support I needed to get started. I was ready to make the leap into entrepreneurship.

Making It Work: The Franchise Decision

The Seniors Helping Seniors corporate franchise headquarters is in Pennsylvania, which was also the location of the very first Seniors Helping Seniors business.

Doug Peck made it a priority to visit the franchise headquarters as part of researching this business opportunity. He was interested in the support services and training materials that were available for new owners like himself. He wanted to learn as much as possible about the financial and legal aspects of buying into this franchise license and the territory that he would be allocated for customer acquisition in the suburbs west of Boston, Massachusetts.

It was equally important to Peck to get a feel for the Seniors Helping Seniors corporate culture, including the goals and values of the other franchise owners he would be joining. His wife came along for this visit since launching a new business was a joint family decision for them. In 2011, Seniors Helping Seniors also provided access to regional representatives who were available to meet with prospective franchise owners and to help support new owners with their start-up questions. Peck met with the regional representative from Connecticut several times in the course of making his decision.

A fundamental question Peck had about the financial framework of franchising was how much upfront investment he would need to make, including the cost of the franchise license. The answer in 2011 was that a ten-year franchise license from Seniors Helping Seniors would cost him a one-time fee of $35,000. This was good news since it meant that he could afford to pay this startup cost out of his own pocket without needing to borrow any money. He was also pleased to learn that the ongoing fees would amount to about 6% of the monthly revenues he earned by operating the business. There was also a requirement to pay a minimum monthly franchise fee of around $275. He felt that he could cover that amount, even if it took him a while to become profitable as he worked to attract clients. Offsetting the payment of the monthly minimum fee was the advantage that Peck could start by operating his new company out of his home office, with no need to incur the cost of an outside office rental until the business was growing.

Like many older founders, Peck was ready to self-fund the startup costs of his new venture with prior income and savings. He had another advantage, in that his wife was working full-time with a predictable annual income and family health insurance benefits.

All in all, buying into the franchise model was a significant financial commitment, but not out of reach. Peck wanted the new company to generate enough income for him to contribute to overall family finances but he wasn't counting on Seniors Helping Seniors to provide any kind of financial windfall. As long as he wasn't losing money, and could eventually bring in enough revenue to sustain and grow the business, that would satisfy his financial objectives. He had done enough research to know that home care services were not a high margin business. Peck had experienced firsthand the value of home services for seniors like his mother who wanted to age in place and needed extra support. His primary entrepreneurship motivation was to own a company that helped to support older adults to age safely and happily at home. He was ready to commit.

Even with all this preparation and planning, Peck encountered some unexpected expenses and a few organizational surprises in his early years of operation. As he recalls:

> Seniors Helping Seniors did generate a positive revenue flow for me, but in my first few years there certainly were some surprises, especially in managing the operations and expenses. I had run my own consulting business as a solo entrepreneur, but it turned out I had a lot to learn about owning a company with twenty to twenty-five employees. I quickly found out that the employment laws in Massachusetts are strict, with piles of paperwork and frequent reports that had to be filed. There was a steep learning curve involved, and it wasn't the area where I wanted to spend most of my time. The solution was to hire vendors, such as a payroll services vendor, to handle that aspect of operations and reporting. But paying these vendors involved expenses that I hadn't anticipated.
>
> Another surprise was the communications and cultural differences in the home care sector. Based on my career in managing human resources for companies in the technology sector, including global corporations, I had a lot of valuable experience in hiring the best talent. But even in this area, I needed to learn

more about hiring and customer acquisition specifically in home care services. I quickly realized that the process for attracting both clients and employees in the senior care sector was entirely different. I couldn't rely on email and digital communications as I had in large companies. It took a lot of phone calls, and face to face meetings, and traditional networking to develop trust and credibility as a new home care provider in the region. I wanted to be completely transparent about being new to the field, and having a lot to learn. That presented challenges in ramping up as a new entrant.

To help gain both knowledge and credibility, I became certified as a CSA®—Certified Senior Advisor. The Society of Certified Senior Advisors educates and certifies professionals who work with seniors through its Working with Older Adults education program and the Certified Senior Advisor credential. The CSA is the leading certification for professionals serving seniors. I also started volunteering with the Alzheimer's Association and became a presenter of one of their most popular programs: Know The 10 Signs, Why Early Detection Matters.

I had to convince seniors and their families that my company offered the highest standards of care with reliable and supportive caregivers. At the same time, I needed to recruit a strong team of caregivers who could meet the demand for different types of client needs. It was a constant balancing act to attract enough clients to justify hiring a sizable group of caregivers, and then matching up the client service demand with available skills and hours of mature caregivers who typically worked part-time. Getting that balance right was a real struggle in my first few years of managing Seniors Helping Seniors. During those early days I was still doing 90% of the office and back-end operations work, like preparing and sending out all the invoices to clients. In addition, I was recruiting and hiring all the employees, and leading the training and supervising a growing group of caregivers. Even though the company grew steadily, and we became profitable, I was still stuck in the office most days, rather than providing the hands-on services I had envisioned.

Despite these early operational challenges, Peck was determined not to fail. Even though it turned out to require a lot more time and effort than he had expected, his new company was able to attract a core group of satisfied clients and dedicated caregivers. Revenues grew steadily, and the company was cash flow positive. Doug Peck wasn't making a lot of money, but that hadn't been his top priority. On balance, he was achieving his entrepreneurial goals.

A Twenty-Something Founder: Josh Obeiter

As a high school volunteer, and then as an undergrad majoring in business, Josh Obeiter always made time to work with older adults. At the University of Connecticut, he organized an extracurricular program that brought students from campus to visit a local nursing home on a weekly basis. Starting his professional career in Boston after graduation, Obeiter continued volunteering, visiting seniors in independent living communities. Like many new grads, he tried out a variety of management positions, with jobs in project management and account management, and a brief stint in college admissions work.

There were positives in all of these positions, but Obeiter never had the sense of fulfillment that came from his volunteer work with older adults. In 2014, at the age of twenty-seven, he was looking for a way to turn his commitment to supporting seniors into a full-time career. But where to start? He was attracted to entrepreneurship and well aware of the urgent need for home care services, but even with his undergrad business education and work experience, founding a company on his own seemed like a huge step. As Obeiter recalls:

> Ever since childhood, I had a special connection with my grandparents, especially both of my grandmothers. I just really

enjoyed their company and connected well with them and their friends.

In middle school, I started volunteering at a local nursing home and ended up spending every Sunday there from middle school until graduating from high school. My grandparents had passed away during those years, making me even more committed to continuing a connection with older people. My volunteer work was an eye-opening experience because I could see that many of the people in the nursing home were very isolated, even though they lived in a community setting. Some families didn't visit often, and staff mostly didn't have the bandwidth to provide the companionship that people crave.

Fast forward to college, where I continued to find myself drawn to working with seniors even while I studied marketing. After graduation I tried out a variety of management positions in a range of different industries, but I never really felt that strong sense of purpose and fulfillment that I got from volunteering. I was looking for a full-time opportunity to work with older adults that could become the foundation of a rewarding long-term business.

When I first heard about the Seniors Helping Seniors model in June 2014, I said to myself "I think I'm entrepreneurial enough to do this." I liked the idea of franchising instead of starting a company and building a brand from scratch. It seemed that a franchise would provide the backbone of how to build an organization, with some built-in business support. I could leverage the brand and structure of Seniors Helping Seniors because it was a known entity.

At that early point in my career, however, I didn't have enough capital to pay the startup franchise fees. Fortunately, I was able to convince my father to fund and advise my startup. He had been working in consulting and in business his entire career, and he agreed that the Seniors Helping Seniors model was a good joint business opportunity, as well as a really good match for my professional skills and passion. My father was involved that first year as an investor and business advisor, helping me to ramp up the business with practical advice along with marketing and strategic planning support.

Once I made the commitment to turn my life around, things happened really fast. I went from considering entrepreneurship, to researching the Seniors Helping Seniors franchise opportunity, to opening my own business in partnership with my dad by the end of 2014.

Just as Obeiter was opening his Boston-area Seniors Helping Seniors franchise, however, his parents' lives in New Jersey changed dramatically. His mother was diagnosed with young onset Lewy body dementia, which quickly took a toll on her health. Obeiter's father was now focused on caring for his wife's needs, and as her health declined, he had little time to devote to the new business venture in Boston. His father still provided some business support and advice from a distance, but in 2015, Obeiter was unexpectedly on his own to manage his first business venture without a lot of entrepreneurship training or experience.

At that point, Obeiter faced a steep learning curve, and he was glad he had decided to take the franchise route to entrepreneurship. There were multiple priorities that needed his attention and so much he didn't know about all the licensing and operating requirements for senior caregiving in Massachusetts. Being part of a national franchise provided him with some startup basics like the company's website design, general marketing collateral, and employee training materials. Even though a lot of the content provided from the corporate office was generic, it gave Obeiter a faster start than creating everything himself and at least he had checklists and samples of all the different forms, systems, recruiting and training materials he needed to operate the business.

But Obeiter quickly learned that in most areas, the generic materials didn't deliver what he needed to succeed in providing services to the Greater Boston area market. The demographics for seniors in Boston were very different from what Seniors Helping Seniors corporate headquarters had developed for its home base in Pennsylvania which was located in the heart of Amish country. So were the characteristics and expectations of the caregiver employees whom Obeiter needed to attract. Those differences impacted everything from the types of work that were most in demand, to the scheduling and invoicing systems that were most productive, to his company's cash flow projections. He started with the generic materials, then worked to modify and adapt them to suit the daily reality of operating in the Boston area. Eventually he figured out how to morph most of the templates into something that would work better for his market.

A Network of Franchise Owners

Ultimately, Obeiter found that his most reliable sources of advice and expertise were the other New England-based owners in the Seniors Helping Seniors franchise group. Meeting with these colleagues, he learned what back-end systems they were using for scheduling and payroll and other operations. This network of local owners helped to make up for the somewhat limited support available from franchise headquarters. It was an invaluable resource for Obeiter in his startup years, when he had so much to learn about everything including vital questions about how much to pay his employees and what were realistic margins to project in revenue planning. As the company grew, he turned to this network for insights into longer term business strategies and regional trends in the senior care industry. The other franchise owners were facing similar questions and challenges, and they were the group where Obeiter could lean in and lean on. Having that built-in network of people he could consult as needed was especially important to him as a first-time entrepreneur.

Doug Peck was one of the franchise owners who Obeiter reached out to early and often. Peck's market territory west of Boston was adjacent to the area where Obeiter operated. There were business advantages to collaborating rather than competing over client referrals and promoting each other's businesses to prospective clients when appropriate. Beyond the business advantages, Obeiter and Peck shared a deeply felt mission as entrepreneurs serving seniors, and they developed a strong personal synergy.

Even as he worked to master the business, operations, and marketing demands of his new company, Obeiter was determined to become more expert in the broader sector where Seniors Helping Seniors provided services, namely, nonmedical home care and healthy aging. He set out to learn as much as he could about the needs of seniors aging at home, including the most common physical and medical challenges they faced. He also made it a priority to get to know the other organizations and service providers in the senior services and healthy aging sector.

He believed that in order to be a good business owner, and to be able to do a very comprehensive job, he needed to know about the range of services that were available to potential clients. One of his goals as a business owner was never to turn people away without giving them another recommendation. That meant understanding the end-to-end experience his clients and their families faced when they went into a hospital for treatment, got discharged, were assigned to rehabilitation facilities, and so on. If clients couldn't return to their homes in the short term, he wanted to know about the range of offerings available to seniors, such as community living. Obeiter participated in as many external training programs as he possibly could, to immerse himself in the overall aging field, and to learn more about dementia care. He studied about living with Alzheimer's and other dementias and became a certified dementia care practitioner.

Planning for Growth

As is typical of a first-time entrepreneur entering a new industry, Obeiter started out making many business decisions on the fly. In the early years, he was personally managing multiple business processes, including the onboarding of caregivers and of clients, as well as overseeing all the required paperwork, documentation, legal, and human resources tasks that needed daily attention. He realized that an on-the-fly approach to handling those various tasks as they arose wasn't efficient. What's more, it prevented him from growing the business in a strategic way. Obeiter decided it was essential to formalize operations and hire administrative support staff. He wanted to stop being a one-man shop and start building a team and delegating. That would allow him to start putting all the things that he had learned in his first few years of operation to good use in scaling up his business.

While Obeiter negotiated this steep startup learning curve and arrived at the point where he was ready to expand his business, Peck passed his five-year milestone as a Seniors Helping Seniors owner and found himself approaching another major decision point.

An Intergenerational Path Forward

Five years after launching his Seniors Helping Seniors franchise, Peck was meeting his initial financial goals, as well as providing the high value services he had wanted to deliver to older adults. His company was generating a little over $400,000 in annual revenues, with about twenty-five part-time employees and a profit margin of around 10%. As Peck entered his sixth year, the business was reliably profitable. However, some of his early operational issues remained stubbornly unresolved. He was still doing a lot of the routine office work such as preparing invoices for clients. He was hiring and directly supervising all the caregivers. Some days, he still felt like a one-man show, tied down to the office routine much more than he had hoped. He realized it was time to make a decision about next steps:

> One of the important lessons I learned as an entrepreneur and founder, and my advice for anyone thinking about owning a consumer-facing franchise, is that you have to be ready to make a total commitment of time and energy. That's especially true for the early years. Be prepared to think about your company, its employees, and customers, and your operations seven days a week, and as many hours a day as you can. Franchising gives you a more predictable framework for some things, but like with any startup the pace of change is constant.
>
> Challenges and unpredictable issues keep coming up, no matter how much advance planning you might do. There's so

much involved in owning and running a small company that you have to address in real time. If you're a person who wants to take regular long vacations away from your job, founding a new company probably isn't a good match for you.

Personally, I don't regret a minute of the time and effort that I spent ramping up Seniors Helping Seniors. Over the years, I've done hospice with some people that have been clients, and even though it can be heartbreaking, it's so inspiring getting to know clients and their families and learning how important the work we do is to everyone involved, and how much they appreciate the support that we can provide. I have enjoyed meeting so many clients and families, and getting to know our employees as well as networking and becoming friends with other professionals in the home care sector. I've met some really, really interesting folks. Entrepreneurship opened a path with amazing people to be around, to work with and socialize with. Having these people in my life has been the best part of this journey for me, much more so than the financial rewards.

But I was always aware of the responsibility and the pressure of owning a business. And I never did manage to get free of all the office work involved. When I passed the five-year milestone and then the sixth year on my ten-year franchise license, I had some serious thinking to do. When a franchise contract is coming to an end, you need to make a decision to either sell your business, renew the license for another ten years, or leave the franchise. I already knew that I was not interested in signing up for another ten years of ownership. I would be eighty-four years old when that next ten-year term ended. No matter how much I valued the services we were providing, it wasn't what I wanted to do full-time when I was in my eighties. That decision wasn't just about my age—it was based on the changing dynamics of the home care industry. Beyond my own personal and work balance issues, I could see that the home care Industry sector had changed a lot since my entering it in 2011. And my company was at an inflection point.

Today, companies in this sector have to achieve a bigger

scale to be successful. It was clear that success, maybe even survival, required the ability to expand quickly and achieve scale. To stay in the business, I knew that I would need to grow, expanding the caregiver staff and hiring a management team, and spending even more of my time in administration instead of with clients and colleagues. That wasn't the direction I wanted to take. But I still loved the home care work, and I wasn't ready to retire. All of this confirmed my desire to find a good exit path, ideally through a merger or sale of the company to a compatible partner. And of all the colleagues I had met over the years, Josh Obeiter was high on my list of potential partners for a merger.

I got to know Josh soon after he bought his own franchise, in part because our territories were adjacent. Inevitably, there were some issues about clients who might be referred to us from each other's service areas. That could have been a bone of contention, but in fact we were able to talk things over and agree to collaborate right from the start.

As time went on, I realized that even though he was a lot younger than the average Seniors Helping Senior owner in our region, Josh was the most forward thinking, especially when it came to collaborating on marketing outreach and networking opportunities. Many of the owners were not interested in going to industry trade shows or senior health care conferences in other parts of our region. That took a longer-term strategic view about how to grow the business, and a willingness to keep up with new trends. Josh and I both felt it was important to gain a broader perspective by taking part in regional events and conferences. As we got to know each other by participating in a number of events together, it became clear that we shared a lot of ideas about the goals and values of our companies. I felt we could work together as a team, and eventually I talked with Josh about my franchise license and the potential for joining our companies.

After months of fairly casual conversation, in the spring of 2017, I decided to share with Josh that I was approaching a decision point. I was transparent about my company revenues and growth potential, and we talked about the pros and cons of a merger. Josh could see the advantages, and he wanted me to continue to have a role in the combined company. We agreed that I would focus on community relations, outreach, and networking. My title in the combined company is Director of Community Partnerships, which is a great match for me. Of course, there were a lot of legal and organizational discussions before the merger became official, including back and forth with the franchise corporate office. Josh took the lead on those aspects of our agreement, and he handled the negotiations with headquarters, since he was the acquiring company. Our direct discussions were less complicated. We had a lot of trust and good faith, and we both wanted to do the right thing by each other, and for our clients and employees.

Based on Josh's growth and revenue projections, I agreed to a buy out over time, rather than one lump sum payment. That involved some risk for me, if the combined business didn't continue to grow according to projections. But I was willing to take that risk, and continue to support the company in a new role. Honestly, I would have made the deal based on a handshake, but my lawyers wouldn't let me. There was a legal review and a fair amount of paperwork, and a lot of communication with all stakeholders, but for a merger of two franchises, we kept it as simple as possible. And when it was done, we both felt like winners.

An Expanded Company Becomes a Top-Rated Employer

Seniors Helping Seniors, Greater Boston & Metrowest is regularly voted one of the best places to work in Massachusetts in an annual poll by the *Boston Globe*. That award for their combined company is a particular point of pride for Peck and Obeiter, who were originally attracted to the model of hiring older adults to become companions and caregivers to seniors. As the company's website states:

> Our employees are themselves older adults, from age fifty to eighty. They are not medical assistants or health care aides. They are dedicated to providing companionship, helping with errands, appointments, and light household tasks.

In the entire franchise network, out of more than 100 locations, Seniors Helping Seniors of Greater Boston & Metrowest is currently one of the top two or three in terms of its financial and growth performance. While Obeiter is happy to achieve this milestone, he has still higher aspirations in terms of growing the business further. The challenge he sees is achieving future growth thoughtfully without diluting the brand or losing the personal touch that characterizes the company. It's a constant process of evaluating and resetting corporate and financial goals while nurturing the culture of caring that supports the employees and the clients.

Josh Obeiter acknowledges that he has poured blood, sweat and tears into his business since its launch in 2014 to achieve its current level of financial and market success. In fact, he has already exceeded his original revenue targets a few times over. When he first projected the potential for growth back in 2014, he was hoping to achieve a million dollars in revenue within five years. In part thanks to the merger, the company reached the million-dollar mark in annual revenues before its fourth-year anniversary. As of 2021, the expanded Seniors Helping Seniors of Greater Boston & Metrowest expects to achieve $2.5 million in annual revenue. Given all the disruptions and challenges of caregiving during the pandemic, Obeiter and Peck are justifiably proud of that achievement.

For Obeiter, working in caregiving for older adults is a labor of love and a long-term career. He doesn't envision himself moving to another industry. His goal is to continue to grow the business and eventually to step back from some of the day-to-day operations and details, to allow for a bit more work-life balance. There's a constant sense of responsibility with this work that can be weighing and stressful at times as well as challenging in a positive sense. In Obeiter's own words:

> I manage people who are older than me on a daily basis, whether they're part of our office staff, or Seniors Helping Seniors caregivers. For me, leadership and management is always about mutual respect. The skills and attributes that I bring to the table and the skills that older employees bring are mutually reinforcing. For so many reasons, an intergenerational workforce is a beautiful thing.
>
> Most of my office staff is also over fifty, somewhat by design, and partly because they are the best qualified among candidates who apply for positions. Of course there are also some younger people on the staff as well. I think a mixed age work staff is great, because everyone's coming at things from a different angle, different perspective, different life experience and work experience. From the start, working with Doug, I knew that there was a lot that I could learn from him. His skills and life experience provide me with insights that I wouldn't have had access to. I was happy that he could be a mentor and coach for me. It's a bonus that he's very open and receptive to my ideas. I'm always surprised to hear him say things like "I'll check with my boss," because even in my office I don't always see myself as the boss, even though I am.
>
> My approach as a manager is always to be very collaborative, bringing everyone to the table. I know that my best ideas may not be the whole answer, or even as good as someone else's, especially someone older with different experience. I certainly have a vision and a lot of ideas for improvement, but I always want to hear what other people have to say before making any decisions. After discussion, my role is to consolidate and condense and take what I think are the best recommendations and execute. In this particular business, there's a lot of trial and error in terms of seeing what things work and

what don't work. So it's essential to be flexible and adaptable. That's an approach that Doug, and I share, regardless of the difference in our ages, and the mutual respect we have for each other extends to everyone else in our company.

Our caregivers are part-time employees, with an average employee of ours working anywhere from ten to twenty hours per week. The last time I took a deep dive into our data it looked like people were averaging around twelve to thirteen hours per week, which is very part-time. And our employees come from all walks of life, which makes our caregivers so unique and diverse and interesting.

Some of our employees still have children at home, maybe high school students. Those employees are working what we call parents' hours. Other employees may have recently become empty nesters. Often they have not been in the workforce for years, but now they want to give back and do something meaningful as well as earning a regular income.

Our biggest employee demographic is people who have retired from a full-time position. Sometimes, they have been retired for several years, and at some point they realize that they need a more structured schedule along with a way to connect with other people through serving a purpose. That's really an ideal demographic for Seniors Helping Seniors employees, people who are passionate about giving back who have vast life experience and work experience that allows them to connect with the clients we're serving. Many of these caregivers are over sixty-five; currently the average age of our employees is sixty-seven. Sometimes they start out looking for purposeful volunteer work, and they're thrilled to combine that type of work with earning additional income. Many retired people count on the extra income, of course. Maybe they have experienced going through a divorce or family member illness that depleted their savings so they are working to supplement their income. In fact, our ideal employee is someone that does need to work, who is eager to work with older adults, and who is reliable in keeping a regular schedule.

Fortunately, the older adults we hire tend to be very reliable, more so than younger caregivers based on what I hear from other home care providers and agencies. Older employees are also very loyal and attached to their clients. Having that peer relationship between two older adults makes all the difference, not only for clients, but also for the caregivers. They often become incredibly invested in the clients that they're serving, perhaps because they remind them of their parents, or maybe of a sibling or spouse.

Often the caregivers and the clients are just a couple of years apart in age. Maybe it's a five or ten-year difference, and sometimes the caregiver is even older than a client but they are more robust in terms of their health. Caregivers often develop a sense of advocacy and this is just an added level of investment into their client. It's way more than a job for them. Their heart is in the work, and it shows.

So one thing I try to hire for is heart. We do not require people to have a specific background or education. Even among the company's office staff, employees have a wide variety of different professional backgrounds. I firmly believe that people who come in with a commitment to caregiving can learn the business skills for office work, and they can apply their prior experience to do a great job. But if you don't have the heart for the work that we do, you're going to be less successful. And I really feel like a caring heart and passion for doing good will spill over into the kind of client experience we strive to provide. That's certainly a point of pride for us. It's something that I take very seriously because a culture of excellence and a great client experience starts with happy employees.

If you look at our employees, many of them are themselves isolated to some degree. They're coming into this work, as I mentioned, because they care, they have a heart and a passion. But many of them are widowed. Some were never married. When they join our company, they're looking for some sense of community as well as purposeful, fulfilling work. But as it happens, the work that they do in the field can be somewhat isolating. We're not working in a team environment, we're not working in an office setting, we're working one on one. And working with a client who maybe is nonverbal or someone with Alzheimer's can be quite challenging for a caregiver.

To counteract that, we work to create a strong community, by treating employees and their clients as our biggest and most important asset. Without them, we are nothing. So it comes down to acknowledgement of their birthdays, milestones in their life, to doing lots of celebratory things throughout the year from a summer picnic to an annual holiday party, to celebrating small things like Valentine's Day and other holidays in the office, sending them cards and small gifts, as well as providing lots and lots of training for them and regular support group meetings.

We carve out time for our caregivers to reflect and talk about the experiences that they're mutually encountering, with lots of open forums for caregivers to connect with one another. It comes down to doing our best to make every staff member feel really important and valued. Now that we have about 125 employees, I still know every employee by name. When they walk in the office, they get a warm greeting, a smile, and always a thank you for the work they do.

Another point of pride for me is that our caregivers often become friends with one another. In addition to the employee events that we sponsor, they will socialize outside of work, and support each other.

In the long term, Obeiter can envision being attracted to a new venture that involves innovations in the next generation of communal living models and community-focused housing for seniors. Instead of today's assisted living models, he would like to be involved in something more future oriented, designing and managing intentionally communal spaces for older adults to share with peers and other generations. He loves the idea of co-housing for seniors.

Reflections for Founders of All Ages

One thing Obeiter has learned from owning a Seniors Helping Seniors company is that he is happy as an entrepreneur. He has come to terms with the accountability and responsibility of owning his company, and he enjoys being responsible for overall planning and the vision, as well as the operations. He also has some lessons from his own experience to share with aspiring entrepreneurs off all ages:

> When thinking about being an entrepreneur, no matter what age you are, don't only look at the bottom line. Be clear about your passion, be committed to your vision, and the big picture of what you want to accomplish, don't just chase money. Because no matter how much you plan ahead, and how smoothly your company takes off, you have to be prepared to put a massive amount of time and effort into your first few years as a founder. And if you're not happy with the work that you're doing, if you're just financially motivated, you're much more likely to burn out. Your motivation and commitment is going to be clear to your employees and to your clients and other stakeholders. My job is sometimes more of a cheerleader, helping other people in the organization to problem solve and be motivated to do the work because it can be challenging whatever industry you are in.
>
> In hindsight, I didn't do a lot of market research into other home care agencies when I was considering purchasing Seniors Helping Seniors. I had never really strongly considered owning a business before I came across the model, and I came across it in an airline magazine on my way to my brother's wedding. While I did my research on Seniors Helping Seniors and I did my due diligence in terms of speaking to other partners, and looking at the financials and the Franchise Disclosure Document and had it reviewed by attorneys, I didn't necessarily fully understand what the marketplace was for my particular industry.
>
> I didn't realize how saturated this market is, in particular,

in the Boston area region where I was going to run my business. So I think for a potential franchise owner, if you're really drawn to a particular brand, you also have to have to research the market, learn who the competitors are, and where they're located in your market, and make sure that whatever you're offering is different enough. For example, our unique differentiator that has allowed me to be successful quickly, is that we employ older adults exclusively. And we do it really well. So while there are over 100 senior care agencies within a five-mile radius of mine, we're one of the only ones delivering the types of services in the mode we deliver them. So I think it's important that you really understand that if you're entering a competitive landscape, that your brand is different enough to break through.

Being a passionate, fully committed founder and owner, being outgoing, and personable and hard-working is not necessarily enough to ensure success. When it comes to starting any business, and especially in the franchise world, do your due diligence and make sure that you're speaking to a wide range of constituents and stakeholders in the franchise network.

Remember that the people that are selling the franchise, their goal is to sell you the franchise, and you want to talk to people with different years of tenure with the organization, and see what their insights were. I certainly did that. And I will admit that I knew some of the deficits of this particular franchise before I bought into it. But I was so passionate about the model, because through my experience of volunteering with seniors for so long, that the concept of Seniors Helping Seniors was so needed and unique, that I was confident that I could successfully launch the business.

Moving Forward: What's Next?

Through their shared responsibilities at Seniors Helping Seniors both Peck and Obeiter have developed new insights into the ever-evolving senior care landscape. It almost seems that with each year new challenges, innovations and opportunities present themselves, as the rest of the country (and world) recognizes the significant impact that a rapidly growing aging population has on society as a whole.

Being part of their Seniors Helping Seniors business has given both Peck and Obeiter the opportunity to meet and collaborate with leaders in the senior care space, people who address different challenges around aging and senior care from different perspectives and areas of expertise. With the rest of the world now paying attention advancements in technology to keep older adults safe, for example, are accelerating at a rapid pace, a marked change from even the mid-2010s. While the Seniors Helping Seniors founders are encouraged to see that the senior care industry is slowly but surely getting the attention it needs from many different business sectors, their core reasons and shared founding mission of combating social isolation and building lasting interpersonal and helping relationships, remains more important than ever.

As Peck and Obeiter reflect on their entrepreneurial experience to date, they are proud of what they have accomplished, and looking forward to the challenges and opportunities ahead, "We strongly feel that certain businesses, like Seniors Helping Seniors, which at its core is a people business, will always be much needed. There's no replacement for the human touch that a service like ours provides. As we move forward, the sky's the limit."

References

Bevis, J (2020) Reasons a franchise business is even more important today. *Forbes* https://www.forbes.com/sites/jeffbevis/2020/11/11 /5-reasons-a-franchise-business-is-even-more-important-today/ ?sh=491f265a5ba4. Accessed 12 October 2021.

Statista Research Department (2021) Franchising in the U.S. *Statista* https://www.statista.com/topics/5048/franchising-in-the-us. Accessed 12 October 2021.

About Doug Peck and Josh Obeiter

Doug Peck

After a thirty-year career in Corporate Human Resources and Human Resource consulting, and at sixty-four years of age, Doug Peck had three important insights. One, he knew he had more to contribute and was not ready to retire. Two, ageism is real. Three, taking care of an elderly parent was more complicated and took much more time than he had imagined. A chance encounter with the Seniors Helping Seniors franchise model inspired him to become an entrepreneur. As a business owner, he could provide meaningful work for other seniors who wanted to remain active while supporting those who, like his mother, needed companionship and a little help to remain independent.

In 2011, Doug took the plunge and opened a Seniors Helping Seniors business serving Metrowest Boston. He became a Certified Senior Advisor as well as a Certified Dementia Practitioner. Most importantly, he became involved in the larger senior community. His volunteer activities include Chairperson of the Southborough Council on Aging, Vice President of the Board of Directors for BayPath Elder Services, board member of Better Day Social Day program, and volunteer trainer for the Alzheimer's Association. He is also an active member of the Elder Care Collaborative in Marlborough and the Metrowest Alzheimer's Partnership.

At the end of 2017, Doug merged his business with the Boston-area Seniors Helping Seniors owned by Josh Obeiter, and stepped into his present role as Director of Community Partnership. He continues to work with several long-term clients on a regular basis.

Josh Obeiter

Josh Obeiter is the Executive Director and Owner of the Seniors Helping Seniors of Greater Boston & Metrowest, a non-medical home care agency that provides companion and caregiver support to seniors, by seniors. Its unique model provides meaningful employment for older adults who have an intrinsic desire to help and make a difference in the lives of seniors in need. The Seniors Helping Seniors  relationship based model is focused on the social-emotional connection between caregiver and client, and is intentional with all of the matches that are made.

For the past twenty years, Josh has been intimately involved with volunteering with seniors, primarily providing intergenerational programming at local nursing homes and assisted living communities; he is well-versed in the challenges that seniors and their families face when it comes to providing care and combating social isolation. Josh is active in several other Boston organizations, including the MA/NH Chapter of the Alzheimer's Association and the Aging Life Care Association. He is a trained Dementia Ambassador through the Alzheimer's Association, a Certified Dementia Practitioner and sits on the Board of Directors for Little Brothers Friends of the Elderly as well as Better Day Adult Social Day Program.

About the Company

Company	Seniors Helping Seniors of Greater Boston & Metrowest
Website	shsboston.com
Founding Years	2011 Doug Peck 2014 Josh Obeiter 2017 Merged company
Co-Founders	Doug Peck and Josh Obeiter
Industry Sector	Non-medical Home Care
Address	330 Bear Hill Rd #305 Waltham, MA 02451

Chapter 5

Physician Management Resources: Consulting with a Mission

The healthcare consulting sector in the US is a $7 billion-dollar services industry (Spitzer 2021). Companies within this industry range from multi-billion global giants to thousands of small, niche consultants with fewer than ten employees. Barriers to entry for solo and small boutique consulting groups are low, but the obstacles to growth for small consultancies are enormous, and differentiation is a major challenge in the crowded consulting landscape.

Wendy Gutterson was well aware of these challenges. Nonetheless, at a pivotal moment in her decades-long career in healthcare management, she decided to step off the organizational career path to launch her own consultancy. Several factors combined to provide a strong impetus for entrepreneurship with a mission. Health care services had become critical inside her own family as her daughter and her mother simultaneously faced serious illness and hospitalization. In the midst of this stress, Wendy experienced firsthand the limitations of traditional health management, including physician visits hemmed in by time constraints and the imposition of computers for taking electronic medical notes. Her own annual physical was dominated by computer note-taking rather than face-to-face consultation and advice. That was her personal wakeup call that healthcare management systems were failing both physicians and patients. Could she leverage her experience at leading health provider organizations to help transform the management of healthcare practice groups and give physicians more time to spend with their patients?

Inspired by this goal, Gutterson founded Physician Management Resources in 2013 as a solo consultant in her early fifties. Her long-term vision was to empower physicians to offer the level of personalized care that she and her family, and all patients deserved, to receive. To achieve this vision, her new consultancy would have to develop innovative solutions for health practice groups. As a startup, she would face the challenge of attracting enough clients who would value and pay for those solutions. And to become a long-term success in a crowded competitive landscape, she would have to master a new set of entrepreneurial skills. Eight years after launching her startup, Wendy Gutterson is the proud owner of a thriving consulting practice with over twenty employees serving over 125 clients around the United States. In this chapter, she shares the lessons learned, milestones achieved, and the challenges she anticipates in the years ahead.

Making the Leap

Wendy Gutterson clearly recalls the moment that shaped her startup decision:

> In 2013, my career as a health care services manager was flourishing. I was working in my dream job at an organization that I loved. This was the place I honestly thought I would retire from. And my work was about to get even better. Thanks to a reorganization, I was offered a promotion. In a few months, I was slated to be reporting to the organization's president. This was a terrific opportunity, and I was excited about the prospect. But with more reflection, something started to gnaw at me. There was a nagging feeling that maybe I could accomplish more by getting off the track of working inside of a large health care provider for the rest of my career. Maybe it was time to try a totally different approach.
>
> Even though everything was going so well in my career, with a promotion just ahead, I was painfully aware of the limitations of the health system from a family, patient, and physician per-

spective. During this period, my daughter was quite ill, and spent time in the hospital. At the same time, my mom was diagnosed with metastatic melanoma. Then came the 2013 Boston Marathon bombing, with dozens of marathon runners and spectators seriously injured. This tragedy touched my family in a different way, since my husband, an M.D., is an amputee rehabilitation specialist. That spring, he took an intensive part in the round the clock care of seriously injured Marathon bombing survivors, while our daughter was in another hospital. As a family, we barely had time to breathe.

During this stressful, emotional period, I went to my primary care physician for my annual checkup. My physician was a dedicated doctor. I knew she cared about me and I had always enjoyed seeing her. But on this visit, it seemed that she spent the whole time I was in the examining room for my physical typing furiously on the computer, taking medical notes. Finally, at the end of my visit, she took just a minute to look me in the eye. But all she had time to say to me was "I know that you have a lot of really hard things going on in your life right now. Sorry. I'll see you in a year."

I left that visit thinking, there has to be a better way to provide health care. My talented, caring doctor was seeing me and her other patients as part of a treadmill, following a rote script that she had to get through to close. Maybe that treadmill was fine for routine visits, but for patients who needed special attention, or just a little extra time, it just wasn't working. I had spent decades learning a lot about health care management, and I understood how the system worked. But now I wanted to find a way to get rid of that treadmill and change the system for the better. My goal was to find a better way to support physicians so that they had the time and resources to become the healthcare providers they wanted to be, and that I wanted to take care of me and my family. Staying on the same career track was safer, but I would be missing the opportunity to make a more personal mark on the future of healthcare.

At that moment, I took a deep breath and resigned from my dream job to start my own health care consultancy. In retrospect, getting started as a consultant was the easy part. I made up new business cards, and announced my new career path. Almost overnight I had landed my first and for a while, my only client. As my own boss, I could work from home. That gave me the time I needed to take care of my family while I figured out what it would take to manage a startup. My consultancy that first year was literally me working out of our family room with my dog for company. But even at this stage, I was planning for bigger things. Instead of just Wendy Gutterson, Consultant, I named my new business Physician Management Resources (PMR). I wanted a name that would resonate with my broader potential market, and signal my vision for future growth.

From Solo Consulting to a Scalable Business Model

Looking back on her first few years as a solo consultant, Gutterson remembers being focused on helping physician groups improve their healthcare practices one client and one issue at a time. When her startup began serving clients, she hadn't done any significant long-term planning or developed a full-fledged business model. As founder and a solo entrepreneur, she took care of everything that needed to be done to operate the business. That included answering the phone, responding to email queries, developing proposals, and pricing her consulting work. When new prospects got in touch, she was responsible for convincing them to become regular clients. Once clients were on board, Wendy analyzed their issues, then walked them through her recommendations and the practice management solutions that they needed, providing her support for new process implementation. Then she put on an administrative hat, sending out invoices as well as tracking payments. She became familiar with the details of every single client, from the goals and priorities of their practice to the level of in-house support available to manage IT and operations.

PMR's basic strategy in those early years was leveraging Gutterson's understanding of healthcare management to provide each client with the most effective solutions. With her goal of improving healthcare delivery in mind, she allocated time for in-depth conversations with every single prospect, getting to know their practice management issues and then developing and implementing solutions that were customized for the needs and size of their specific practice, however small or large.

Marketing and customer acquisition were not an urgent priority. Thanks to Gutterson's extensive professional network and the enthusiastic endorsement of her early clients, new prospects learned about her consulting services through referrals. She was happy to grow mainly through word of mouth in those early years. In addition to reducing any pressure to develop a formal marketing and customer acquisition strategy, regular referrals demonstrated that PMR clients believed in the value of the services they were receiving, and benefited from following her recommendations. From a financial perspective, it also meant that the company quickly became profitable, even with a relatively small number of clients and billable hours. Working from home, handling both the consulting services and the administrative work without any employees, Gutterson's overhead costs were low.

That combination of low overhead and profitability is understandably appealing for entrepreneurs who launch solo consulting practices. The tradeoff, however, is that this model imposes a limit on how many clients a solo consultant can serve, and ultimately how much impact they can have in changing the healthcare sector. For Gutterson, it seemed like her company had reached a plateau in its growth after just a few years of operation. While she enjoyed developing and implementing practice management solutions for her small and steadily growing client group, she had founded PMR with broader goals and impact in mind.

Accomplishing these goals would mean expanding PMR beyond the solo consultant model. She would have to design more scalable services for a larger group of clients. And to deliver those services, she would need to recruit a talented, motivated consulting team.

A Path to Growth

While PMR only had a small number of clients, many of the practice groups it served were experiencing a broad spectrum of healthcare delivery and administrative challenges. In developing solutions for these challenges, it became clear to Gutterson that a key path to business growth for PMR would be moving away from the design of one-off, highly customized client implementation projects to develop a modular set of core practice management solutions.

By focusing on scalable solutions to the most frequently requested client projects, PMR would be prepared to serve a much larger group of clients, identifying high-priority issues facing thousands of small and medium size health practice groups in the US and developing solutions that could be implemented with far less customization per client. With a well-designed suite of practice management services, it would be feasible to acquire and serve a broader range of clients.

Analyzing the pattern of consulting requests that she was addressing on a regular basis allowed Gutterson to develop a list of core services for PMR. As she remembers, "my early clients were already asking for my help in developing and implementing a bundle of different practice management services, including scheduling, HR support, and insurance credentialing and billing." Frequently requested client projects included:

- Redesign of patient appointment and staff scheduling systems to reduce waiting times and motivate patients to keep their appointments.

- Human resources support, including setting up processes to recruit the best providers and support talent and establishing ways to retain and motivate the workforce with the right combination of salary and benefits

- Implementing an efficient coding and billing system, to facilitate reimbursement from the multiple insurance providers and regulations so that doctors can focus more on their patient's health and well-being and less on completing a crushing load of daily paperwork.

- Insurance credentialing

The decision to focus on a solution for insurance credentialing became a growth and client acquisition accelerator. Insurance credentialing expertise was a widely recognized need and improving the reimbursement claims processes in small practice groups had a visible return for clients. Inefficiency in submitting insurance claims means lost or delayed revenues for all health care providers. Improving the process creates measurable value. The insurance credentialing services that PMR provided soon became the company's most important gateway to more referrals, higher monthly billing per client, and faster expansion.

That was the start of a growth spurt for PMR as Gutterson's focus and time shifted from developing customized services for each client to creating the foundations for a model that could service dozens and eventually hundreds of clients, with a well-trained team. She realized that bundling various services into a high quality, robust package would enable PMR to offer a broad range of solutions to practice groups without reducing the quality of services. In fact, expanding the PMR offerings turned out to be a strategic boost to the long-term goal of improving the health care delivery experience for physicians and patients, by making clients more efficient at administrative tasks and freeing up more time for seeing patients.

Recruiting, Training, and Deploying a Professional Services Team

A critical element in the next stage of PMR's growth was Gutterson's willingness to transition from being the sole consultant and personally managing every aspect of the business. It was time to recruit and train a team of professionals to serve a much larger group of customers. These two elements—designing scalable core services and hiring a dedicated professional team—created a foundation for PMR to grow at a faster pace, while keeping its personal touch and continuing to serve the best interests of clients.

Gutterson had recognized the path to growth, but it still took some time to bring it into operational focus and to begin hiring the team that would allow PMR to deliver on it. When she hired her first employee, she had to come to grips with a whole new set of challenges around hiring and team building. There weren't any standard position descriptions to guide her selection. In fact, Gutterson was hard pressed to describe to candidates exactly what she most wanted her first employee to accomplish. Without a clearly laid out list of responsibilities and expectations, it was a challenge for new team members to understand Gutterson's expectations and priorities. This was an instance where her decades of management experience and the confidence it generated came to the fore. She didn't let a fear of ambiguity or making a mistake become a barrier to progress. Her early hiring premise was to hire the smartest, most motivated people she could find, and encourage them to ask questions and learn by doing. Her slogan as the leader of PMR became, "We're smart, and by working together, we can figure this out."

Of course, that same management experience meant that Gutterson didn't rely on instinct alone in building out her team. She proceeded to develop written position descriptions and implement standard HR best practices. But, she recalls:

> I also listened to my instincts. I think this was a benefit of my being an older founder. If I had started PMR earlier in my career, or when I had just completed my graduate degree, I would have been more inclined to seek out candidates who were the best match in terms of credentials and probably would have hired applicants based mainly on their having exactly the right experience in handling a specific aspect of medical practice management. I've learned over time that this approach to recruitment doesn't work out well in a fast-growing company

in a fast-changing industry with so many moving pieces and regulated processes. Now my strategy is to screen candidates for their commitment, their demonstrated willingness to work hard and smart, as well as their past experience. I still believe that learning on the job, listening to clients, and working smart are essential characteristics for success.

As a result of this strategy, the PMR team consists of talented, dedicated professionals from a variety of backgrounds. Gutterson trusts her own judgment in hiring, and in turn, she has come to trust the judgment of her team members in carrying out their roles at PMR.

As PMR expanded its insurance credentialing and other core services, customer acquisition growth continued and so did the pace of hiring. As of the middle of 2021, there were twenty team members, serving more than 100 clients each month. Those clients are now located all around the United States, in over forty different states. That rate of growth has in turn transformed how Gutterson manages the organization. In the early days, even after she had hired a support team, she was the only one who spoke directly to clients. The other PMR team members worked mostly behind the scenes. She has now built a cohort of team leaders who manage various company operations and interface with the clients. In taking responsibility for managing a growing team, she has expanded her founding mission to include a second purpose—a commitment for PMR to become a model employer; the kind of company where she herself would want to work. What does this mean in practice?

In Gutterson's own words:

> I'm really proud of the entire team, and what we've accomplished in the past few years, I'm especially proud to have followed through on my founding vision of helping front line health care providers be the caring and effective health professionals who have time to listen and think about each individual patient, in part because their practice is managed efficiently

behind the scenes. I still believe that our services are help-ing physicians and their practice groups to become the kind of providers that every patient wants and deserves to see.

As PMR has grown, I've shared that vision with every new hire. And now I've added a second guiding principle that has helped me transition from a solo founder to the head of a grow-ing company, a principle that shapes my day-to-day decisions internally and externally. I want PMR to exemplify the type of employer that I always wanted to work for.

These two goals have become my guiding principles for man-aging and expanding PMR. I've built this team and this com-pany to a level I honestly didn't know I could achieve back in 2013. I feel really good about what we've accomplished to-gether in improving healthcare practice management and mod-eling employer best practices to the extent possible for a small, still growing company.

When I first decided it was time to hire a team, PMR didn't have any formal benefit program. That's the norm for small consulting groups, and it's common among the healthcare prac-tice groups that we serve. PMR paid people well, and provided regular salary increases. But team members only got paid when they worked, and it was up to employees to take care of their own health insurance. For the past three years, I've started to address that situation. When the pandemic started, one thing that worried me was that some employees didn't have health insurance. I couldn't bear the thought that in this healthcare space, I had employees, some of whom have children, who had no health insurance. So we rolled out health insurance as our first company benefit, and then we rolled out paid time off. And we'll see what comes next. Every year, as long as we can do so, I want to roll out some additional employee benefits.

Today, I'm proud to be creating really good jobs. All the team members working at PMR have flexible schedules, good pay, good benefits, good mentoring, and opportunities to learn on the job. Whereas some of my clients don't let staff members take any time off during the day, to me that's not the right approach. I have high expectations. There's no doubt about it. Anybody who works for me will tell you that they are expected to produce the highest quality work. But I will never, ever throw anybody under the bus. If anyone on the team makes a mistake, I expect them to let me know. And either we fix it very quickly, and it gets resolved so that it's no longer a problem, or we make it right by the client. Everybody on my team will tell you that one of the great things about working at PMR is that they will continue to learn and grow and be rewarded for doing a great job. Even if someone needs a little boost to do a really good job, there will be support available. When you are part of the PMR team, we care about you, and you will have the resources you need to be successful.

At the start of the pandemic, Gutterson was concerned about what would happen to her clients, and to PMR's ability to survive. She was expecting the worst, knowing that many medical practice groups were struggling. It seemed that would inevitably reduce PMR's client base. But the opposite happened. The company was well positioned to continue working closely and productively as a team throughout the pandemic, because Gutterson had been open to hiring the best talent regardless of location. That meant PMR had hired employees in Oklahoma, Tennessee, South Carolina, and Pennsylvania so that a number of team members were already working virtually. The team came together to ensure that productivity didn't suffer once everyone started working from home. The first year of the pandemic brought continued expansion, and currently the company is growing faster than ever. During 2020, Gutterson would interview candidates and tell them that there was plenty of work to be done at present, but she wasn't sure what was going to happen in the year ahead. It felt like she was asking new hires to make a leap of faith, to join PMR in such uncertain times.

Having come through the trials of the pandemic, Gutterson has increased confidence that PMR is established enough to be a stable company, and a going concern. Now she has the track record and financial data to make decisions about team expansion based on calculating how the increased HR costs will be covered through new clients and expanded deliverables to the existing customer base.

Client Loyalty, Conversion, and Retention

In growing her business by word of mouth, Gutterson realized early that saying "yes" to clients whenever possible was a key strategy for customer retention. The loyalty of existing clients is a testimony to the quality and value of the services that PMR provides. As part of her mission to free physicians and clinical providers from the distraction of administrative overhead, she was highly motivated to design core services and processes in ways that would help clients to manage their practices more effectively, always aiming to lessen their administrative burden across as many areas as possible. To achieve this for PMR clients, the team is ready to spend the time necessary to drill down on a variety of individual client back-end processes and really get into the weeds of these practices' day-to-day operations. With this level of detail in hand, it was easier to advise clients on increasing their reimbursement from insurance payers by billing more accurately and consistently. As noted, providing streamlined reimbursement solutions turned out to be a major lever for PMR to generate revenue and attract new clients. Learning the details of client processes also means that PMR is ready to assist in the next steps in practice management improvement and to help clients adapt to new reimbursement and regulatory policies at the state and federal level. That in turn contributes to an impressively high level of client retention and loyalty.

PMR routinely converts between 80% to 90% of the prospects who set up exploratory conversations into clients. That's an amazing track record for any company. At this point in time, Gutterson is almost surprised when a prospect fails to convert after their introductory call. "I sometimes can't believe they didn't sign with us, because we really seemed to be a great match for their needs after an amazing conversation."

She also notes that some companies that don't follow up immediately to engage with PMR actually will come back four to six months later to sign up. These prospects may have engaged a less expensive, local consultant in the meantime, and then discovered that they were not getting the level of service they had anticipated. Sometimes those prospects become clients because the insights and advice that Gutterson shared on the exploratory call resonated so strongly that they decided the proposed PMR engagement price would be well worth it.

In terms of average client size, PMR's sweet spot is the small to medium size health care practice groups. Larger practices tend to have implemented their own in-house infrastructure. Even the larger groups may become clients, however, to receive the expert support that PMR can now provide in dealing with many different practice management, billing and insurance reimbursement systems.

PMR is committed to serving healthcare practices of all sizes, including groups with only a few providers. Unlike many consultancies, Gutterson won't tell a client that they are too small to be eligible for personalized services. "We don't say you're too small for us, because we were founded on the principle of helping small businesses, we are proud to be a small business, and we want to see other small businesses do well."

Analyzing the factors that have been most important in attracting and retaining clients, Gutterson sums it up as follows:

> We communicate well, we pride ourselves on meeting our clients where they are and improving their ability to operate their practice more productively and profitably. At the same time, PMR is still a very boutique consultancy, in the sense that we listen carefully and deliver a carefully crafted suite of services to each client rather than a one-size-fits all standard package.
>
> It's essential to take the time to learn about our clients. Before you even become my client, I have typically spent substantial time on the phone with you, learning the issues you are concerned about, and offering ideas about how to solve them.

The motto is, everything should be value added. So even when we are taking a prospective client's first, exploratory phone call, I want that prospect to come away feeling like it was time well spent. I'll do a better job if I know who you are. And I can do a better job if you know who I am, and you trust me, and you know that I'm on your team.

Looking back on the past eight years of running my own company, I have a clearer perspective on the growth trajectory that many solo founders have to prepare for. I would say in any solo consultancy's first year, be prepared to do a lot of ground-work to acquire relatively few clients. In my case, because of everything that was going on in my family in terms of personal health crises, I didn't expect to spend endless hours on client acquisition and service delivery. Compared to the management position I had left behind, it actually seemed that I worked very little on PMR on a daily basis. But I did work at a steady and increasing pace during those early years. I was happy with the progress my clients were making, and I believed in the value of the work that I was doing. When I did start to focus on growth and strategies for increasing revenue, I had already learned a lot about the high-value, high-demand services that would be key to attracting more clients and generating higher revenues.

The last three to four years have seen so much growth. I'm really proud to say that in the current year, my regular payroll every two weeks has a higher total than all the revenue PMR brought in during the company's entire first year of operation.

Building an Infrastructure for the Future

Even with this impressive track record, Gutterson is well aware that there is a lot more work ahead to enable continued success. One priority is developing a formal marketing and customer acquisition strategy to maintain that growth into the future. Gutterson readily acknowledges that PMR has been very slow to implement the types of marketing tools used by many companies its size. Aside from maintaining its website, there has been very little investment in digital marketing and brand building. Today, 100% of the company's new business continues to come from referrals. There are some important advantages to attracting prospective clients through referrals, including that the prospects who visit the PMR website and then decide to reach out to Gutterson via email or phone have already heard from a trusted source about the quality of PMR's services. That means she has confidence that those contacts are pre-vetted and well worth her spending significant time learning more about their issues because there is a very high likelihood that they will become paying clients.

Nonetheless, a stellar referral and conversion rate isn't enough to sustain growth over the long term. So adopting additional marketing and brand-building tools is on the priority list for the coming year.

Internally, best practices such as documenting every conversation with clients is a work in progress for PMR. When the number of clients was small, and Gutterson was the only person delivering consulting solutions, she was comfortable giving clients advice, answering their questions, and sharing information on demand. The priority was to quickly address the problem that the client was dealing with. Sometimes that solution is as small as confirming the policy change in reimbursement, or clarifying how to code an invoice to a particular payer. But even with simple support consultations, it is important to track and record all the interactions and information being shared.

Gutterson is ready to lead the change in team behavior and model full adoption of follow-up documentation, especially since she is still having so many regular conversations with clients. At the same time, she now has a well-qualified team to delegate this and other internal process changes that need implementation. And she welcomes their input about the priorities for PMR, from IT infrastructure and cybersecurity implementation to the design of additional client services. Her plans for the future are now grounded in being the leader of a fast-growing company, providing the encouragement and support that her team needs to continue their own growth as professionals. It's an exciting moment on her entrepreneurial path:

From the start of our hiring a team, I prioritized recruiting people who could be smart, independent thinkers, like-minded enough to take this journey with me, without having exactly the same mindset. Top managers and founders need to encourage team members to come up with their own new ideas and out-of-the box suggestions. A healthy team environment includes being supportive and also comfortable pushing back as appropriate, being able to have candid discussions and air out any disagreements on how to solve a challenging situation. That's healthy and necessary for serving a growing clientele. As PMR has grown, team member suggestions and experience have been key to expanding our service offerings. Planning for that far into the future means asking different questions than I had to think about in my solo consultant start-up years. Now I focus on building the scaffolding for more growth in all areas of the company. And I know that I can rely on my team to help solve any new challenges for our clients and for PMR as a company.

Reflections and a Family Entrepreneurial Legacy

After making a successful transition from solo consulting to a growth-oriented company, Gutterson is considering her personal and entrepreneurial goals for the decade ahead. She reflects:

Future goals and transition planning—those are always major questions for older founders, right? When I think about how much longer I want to be the CEO, responsible for the future of PMR, I can honestly say at least for the next five years. I'm also working with a CEO coach right now because I realized that there are so many possibilities and I needed an appropriate sounding board. With this coach, I have a place to talk about growth, about strategy, and about how to be the best CEO I can be now and in the future.

What happens beyond five years, in the ten or twenty-year timeframe, isn't something that keeps me up at night all that often. That said, I definitely have a commitment to building this company for the future and I'm thinking about options for keeping the mission of PMR alive. Given our success as a consultancy, the skills of the team, and the growth of our clientele, finding a larger buyer with a similar vision to transform healthcare practice may be a good strategy. I'm not in any hurry to explore that option, but perhaps it will be appealing in a few more years.

Now that my two daughters have graduated from college and started their own careers as teachers, I can't help wondering occasionally about whether one or both of them might be interested in joining the company someday. One daughter is already helping PMR in a part-time role, alongside her teaching work. My younger daughter is starting to look at going back to earn a business degree. Currently she's thinking about switching from teaching to a very different industry sector, not healthcare consulting. Knowing that they are both so talented, I enjoy thinking about becoming a family business down the road.

There is actually a long-standing family entrepreneurship legacy that I believe was part of my own decision to resign from organizational healthcare management and start my own company.

My father started his own company early in his career, managed it successfully, and then sold it when he was approaching seventy. Finding that retirement didn't suit him nearly as well as entrepreneurship, he then started a second company, and worked into his eighties in that business. In that entrepreneurial spirit, my brother started his own business as a tax attorney right out of law school. My nephew also graduated from law school and has now joined his father in that company.

An even deeper family legacy comes from knowing that my grandmother, who was born in 1921, owned her own business. It was a retail children's clothing store on Long Island, and was still open when I was a child. As a result, I remember always being the best-dressed girl in the neighborhood when I was six or seven years old. What made an even more lasting impression on me was watching her operate the cash register, and balance her accounts at the end of each business day. The ledger seemed to be such an exotic and exciting book, where my grandmother would write down important, mysterious numbers at the end of the day. I just loved watching that, thinking that my grandmother had a fascinating life.

Whether or not my daughters decide to join the business, I am happy that they get to drop into the PMR office and see their mother as an entrepreneur who was willing to take a risk to achieve her goals and live her dream.

References

Spitzer, D (2021) Healthcare Consultants: US Specialized Industry Report OD5496. *IBISWorld*, February 2021.

About Wendy Gutterson

Wendy Gutterson is an expert and innovator in healthcare management, and her career has spanned diverse leadership roles at organizations ranging from large nonprofit providers to independent physician practices to consultancies in the sector.

Recognizing both need and opportunity, in 2013 she founded Physician Management Resources, a consulting group that provides wraparound services to independent medical practices. Blending strategic planning with hands-on leadership, Wendy and the multi-specialty PMR team has partnered with several hundred client organizations of various sizes and helped them navigate the healthcare landscape, become more resilient, and achieve results.

For clients of PMR, she and her team have successfully conducted diverse projects, implementing thoughtfully to stabilize innovations. These include practice assessment to identify trends and opportunities; revenue analysis to capture provider cost, volume assessment, capacity and projections; transition strategies to manage partnership changes and new systems; and overall practice management to align perspectives and expectations across the care continuum.

Prior to founding PMR, Wendy worked in large and small physician practices, as well as academic departments at Lahey Clinic, Cambridge Health Alliance and Hebrew SeniorLife.

About the Company

Company	Physician Management Resources
Website	physicianmanagementresources.net
Founding Year	2013
Founder	Wendy Gutterson
Industry Sector	Healthcare Practice Management
Address	475 Hillside Avenue, Suite 4 Needham Heights, MA 02494

Chapter 6

Plant Power Fast Food

Changing the World with Kindness and Plant Power

Jeffrey Harris has grounded his professional life on a few simple principles, "I found that by being kind, being respectful, calling people back, and telling them the truth, I was able to build a career and make a decent living." In retrospect, his success over two decades in professional and sales management roles strikes Harris as a bit accidental. He grew up without much interest in pursuing a commercial career, much less in earning his living as a sales manager in the corporate world. He became a vegetarian at the age of fourteen, suddenly struck by the connection between his hamburger and the routine slaughter of livestock. That insight triggered deeper thoughts about how society's indifference to animal suffering is inexorably linked to a long chain of unjust and unethical human behavior within our larger human culture. Years later, motivated by the same ethical considerations, he went fully vegan. As a teenager Harris had no idea that his personal decision to stop eating meat might be magnified a million-fold by giving the average consumer a plant-based alternative to the billions of hamburgers and chicken nuggets consumed every year. It was a long time before his individual motivations for adopting a plant-based diet coalesced into the vision of Plant Power as a positive force to change the world.

In 1981 before graduating from California State University at Northridge Harris left college to spend time living in an ashram in India, intent on studying meditation and learning more about Vedanta and other eastern spiritual philosophies. After returning to southern California, he spent his early twenties as a self-described hippie, living in a semi-converted garage and working at a local vegetarian restaurant as a dishwasher, a busboy, a host, and then finally a waiter. His commitment to a mindful life, rooted in respect for all living things deepened, but he was struggling to support himself through restaurant work.

In 1986 Harris began working at a retail music store in Hollywood called Nadine's Music. It was there that his passion for the kind of equipment and technology used in professional sound recording and live sound systems was ignited. In addition to building out a home recording studio where he produced his own music and that of other artists, he fell in love with the process of helping artists, producers, and engineers create their own dream recording environments. He also enjoyed helping local bands put together their own performance sound systems. In other words, he fell in love with sales. But for him, the sales process was never just about closing the next deal. He was passionate about connecting with his customers and helping them realize their own goals and dreams. From this start in audio sales, he went on to work as an account executive with a well-known independent sales firm in Southern California where he represented professional audio brands to music stores and professional installation companies. After five years as a sales rep on the road in Southern California, he joined Alesis Studio Electronics, a manufacturer of audio and musical equipment. In 2001, he joined Harman Professional Products, a subsidiary of Harman International.

Harris remembers feeling that this work was a bit like getting into the music business, specializing in the equipment rather than the performance side. The experience of turning an extension of his personal interests into a viable long-term career path inspired him to think more seriously about his personal and social change goals. As he recalls:

> Eventually, I joined the Pro Division of Harman International and expanded my scope to become a regional sales manager for a number of top professional audio, video, and lighting brands. We sold everything from the kind of large sound and lighting systems you'd see at concerts and performing arts

venues to background music systems for restaurants and retail stores. The equipment included the type of large installations you'd find in arenas, stadiums, and airports. It was challenging and there was always something new to learn. I worked with some really talented and wonderful people and I had a lot of fun. That said, working in sales at a publicly held company was a pretty high-pressure environment. It turned out that I really enjoyed leading sales teams and after almost thirty years on this career track I found myself making a good salary, enough to buy a house and a nice car. That was more stability and success than I had ever imagined for myself.

But instead of being satisfied with the status quo, in my mid-forties I started asking myself some big questions: What else could I be doing? Was there something I could create that might really contribute towards making this world a better place? If I could live by my principles and be a success in the corporate world, what was keeping me from doing something much more meaningful for the larger world, something that could make a real difference outside of just my own limited sphere?

I started thinking, if these principles worked in one career track, what would happen if I applied them to a larger goal? Something more meaningful? So, I asked myself the question that so many people ask in their mid-forties: What would I like to do with the rest of my life?

Thinking through these questions ultimately brought Harris back to one thing that he had always been passionate about: bringing the benefits of a plant-based, cruelty-free, and sustainable diet to more people. Motivated by his concerns for the plight of animals and aware of the increasing body of evidence linking animal agriculture to environmental devastation, Harris wondered about how to inspire millions of people to ask themselves important questions about their food choices and in doing so, inspire wide-spread change. He found himself coming back to an idea that wouldn't go away: What if someone created a vegan version of a traditional fast-food brand?

He could envision a way to change America's eating habits on a massive scale through a vegan fast-food restaurant chain as popular and omnipresent as McDonald's. That was a bold, outlandish idea in itself. Even more outrageously, Harris felt a calling to turn this crazy vision into an actual company, by founding a business that he would help to make a household name and a force for social change. No matter how much he told himself that this was a foolish, totally unrealistic next step for his career, the vision of transforming the world through vegan fast food took hold and wouldn't leave him alone. Harris recalled that way back during his years working in vegetarian restaurants, he and a friend brainstormed about opening a small vegetarian restaurant that would feature live music performances, and maybe even a spiritual bookstore. They got as far as building out a detailed business plan and pitching the idea to potential investors. As Harris remembers it:

> We were young and inexperienced; we obviously didn't know what we were doing, but we were certainly inspired. Understandably, no one had much faith in us as potential business owners, and we weren't able to raise enough capital to get our idea off the ground. Even so, I did manage to find a few people who might have invested if our vision had been much larger. What they told me was something like, "We're not willing to give you a few hundred thousand dollars to open just one little restaurant but if you wanted to build something big, something that could scale, we could probably come up with a few million dollars of funding." That response shocked me, and I never forgot it. There was obviously money out there, but the people who had it were looking for big ideas, not something that felt like 'Jeffrey's Veggie Shack'. So, I realized that if I could come up with the right plan, the money might be there. Years later, when I started to think about the potential of what I liked to call the "vegan version of McDonald's", the idea just wouldn't leave me alone. Something about it was really exciting to me and I believed that it might be big and bold enough to attract investors.

In particular, Harris found himself thinking about the importance of intention and the impact that building a major vegan fast-food brand could have on changing the world for the better:

> What if a new brand could attract millions of people to a plant-based version of traditional fast food and in doing so, demonstrate a new model to the world, a way of eating that was cruelty free, sustainable, and healthier? A vegan fast-food brand could be a fun and engaging way to connect people to some very important ideas about animal welfare, the importance of preserving the planet's resources, and maybe even a path towards rethinking the whole food system, but doing so without preaching or hitting anyone over the head with a guilt trip. How powerful would it be if we could simply offer consumers a delicious plant-based version of traditional fast food and serve it with love?

It was a compelling vision, but Harris also realized that he could not turn it into reality on his own. Building a vegan fast-food brand that might one day be as popular as McDonald's and Burger King required more than intention and commitment. It would take business acumen and operating expertise in actual restaurant management, as well as significant investor funding to build out a new restaurant chain and attract customers. Harris had developed a strong core of business skills by this time. What's more, he enjoyed communicating new ideas, and knew that he had a gift for enrolling others in a vision if it was something he believed in. These were essential skills for any aspiring entrepreneur. His experience talking with potential investors many years earlier still resonated, and he was excited about pitching a bigger, bolder business venture. What could be bigger than a concept that could literally change the world for the better, while also making money for investors and founders? In his optimistic moments, he believed that he had a lot to offer as part of a founding team.

It was still a huge, scary, and unbelievably ambitious vision, but Harris decided to pursue it.

Searching For Partners

It took Harris several years to go from the dream to its implementation. To even get started, he had to find the right partners. Harris was very well aware that his own skillset did not include the nitty-gritty expertise of running a popular restaurant. His next step was to locate willing, talented partners whose strengths would complement his own:

> I realized right away that a vision this big was too much for me to create without a team. I'd have to find one or more partners who had the skillsets that I lacked. I had developed some solid business and sales skills in my career. But those skills didn't include much that directly applied to developing a menu and kitchen layout, hiring team members and then managing a busy restaurant. I had no experience in selecting locations or negotiating leases. Obviously, I needed help.
>
> I decided to think of the next step as a search, almost a quest, for the right partner or possibly partners. I needed to find the other piece or pieces of this puzzle. I wondered if there might be someone out there that shared the same crazy vision I had, and who also had the operational expertise that I lacked. And I hoped that, just maybe, I would have the skillset that they were looking for. It seemed to me that it would be like finding a needle in a haystack, but I thought, hey, if I don't make this effort, nothing will ever happen.
>
> So, I went on a deliberate search for a like-minded partner who could help me manifest this vision. It was literally an active search. I googled vegan entrepreneurs, and I hired consultants. Something in my heart told me that if I kept knocking on doors, eventually, one would open, but for a long time, it just didn't happen. I spoke to a lot of good people, but it was never quite a match. After a few years I was pretty discouraged and wondered if I should just let this go. I certainly didn't want to end up as a crazy old man chasing a dream. So, at one point, when I was close to giving up, I literally went out onto

my back porch and I said to the universe, 'Okay, if this is really supposed to happen, show me a sign. Give me some help. I can't do this by myself.' Looking back, this was a moment of trust, a moment of surrender.

A few days later, I got a phone call from my dear friend Susan. She was very aware of my fast-food vegan restaurant dream and my search for a partner. She excitedly told me that she had found my guy. A friend of hers named Joelle had a friend named Mitch Wallis who had founded a well-known vegan fast-food restaurant in San Diego called Evolution Fast Food. It opened in 2004 and as far as we knew, it was one of the very first vegan fast-food restaurants in the country. It was also a local icon, but being from Los Angeles, I had never heard of it. Susan said that Mitch had always hoped to create a national vegan fast-food brand, and had been looking for the other part of his own puzzle for years to help make his vision a reality. I called him up out of the blue to introduce myself. After about ten minutes on the phone with Mitch, I was elated. We hit it off immediately and I just really loved his heart and his intention to be part of creating change. It felt like I had finally found what I was looking for.

Of course, one phone call was not enough to create the foundation for a long-term business partnership, especially one that involved such an ambitious venture. Inevitably, there were some roadblocks ahead. When Harris visited Mitch Wallis at the Evolution Food restaurant in San Diego to continue their conversation in person, he also met with Mitch's partner at the time. The rapport with Wallis was still strong, but the partner was clearly skeptical. He expressed doubt about what value Harris would bring to a new business partnership, and questioned his lack of experience in starting anything near this big. Even with this rocky start, Harris was willing to spend time working with the pair on a startup planning effort. He even hired a consultant to help move the planning ahead and spent a considerable amount of his own money. But after months of discussions, Harris had to admit that the puzzle pieces were just not fitting together.

He wasn't about to give up on his vision, but at some point, he realized that he had to walk away from this very frustrating potential three-way partnership and go on searching for a better match.

Months later, Mitch Wallis reached back out to tell Harris that his former partner was now out of the picture and suggested getting their startup discussions back on track. Wallis invited him to return to San Diego to meet the restaurant manager at his restaurant, Evolution Food. That employee was Zach Vouga, a committed vegan in his mid-twenties, who also aspired to transform the vegan restaurant landscape. Harris headed back to San Diego, excited that he and Wallis were reviving their partnership idea, and now looking forward to seeing if Vouga might be a good fit. As Harris recalls:

> I thought that I was there to get to know Zach to see if I felt that he would be a good fit to join Mitch and I. I didn't know this until years later, but Zach thought that he was interviewing me to see if I would be a good fit to join him and Mitch. It's hilarious now, but looking back, I can see why that first meeting was a bit awkward. But I knew right away that Zach, like Mitch, shared the same vision that had possessed me. Even before the three of us knew each other, each of us had been thinking the same thing: 'Why isn't anyone creating a chain of plant-based fast-food restaurants?' We had all become vegan for ethical reasons. We all believed that the world was ready for something completely different and revolutionary in the form of vegan fast food. And I'm not sure why, but we really believed that together, we could make it happen.

Harris came away from that first meeting with both Mitch and Zach knowing that he had finally found his founding partners. He sensed that each of them would be able to make their own unique and powerful contribution to the effort and that they'd very likely coalesce into a powerful and dynamic founding team. The multigenerational aspect of the team would add an important positive component as well. He and Wallis were both in their mid-fifties at the time and Wallis was an experienced and successful restaurant owner. Vouga was almost thirty years younger with a lot less business and restaurant experience than Wallis. But Vouga seemed like a natural leader. He had a strong, palpable passion for vegan food, and he was on fire with innovative ideas for everything from menu development to the look and feel of what this brand could be. All three were committed to making their planned startup a transformational consumer brand.

Together with these two partners, Harris was ready to take the next step in launching a vegan fast-food brand. Importantly, despite their different backgrounds and ages, the three felt like a team of equals. In recognition of that, they agreed to move forward as co-founders of the venture they named Plant Power Fast Food. They even decided to share the title of co-CEO in their new company.

Building a Startup into a Sustainable Business

Being the newly minted co-founder and co-CEO of Plant Power Fast Food changed Jeffrey Harris's life in many ways, but some things stayed the same. The most profound change was that he had found his partners and the new venture was underway. What he had thought of for years as a personal and perhaps unattainable vision of changing the world finally had a strong collaborative foundation. He was working with two experienced restaurant operators who, like him, believed it would be possible for their new venture to expand over time to open hundreds of restaurants around the US and create a well-known fast-food brand.

One thing that didn't change for Harris was his day job. For the first several years after co-founding Plant Power, Harris stayed in his full-time career position and managed his co-CEO and founder responsibilities on top of that. He made the decision to forgo a CEO salary in order to help conserve Plant Power's cash flow so that the new company could hire additional experienced team members and devote resources to run the company. There wasn't any money in the Plant Power budget to pay Harris a salary he could survive on. So he stayed at his corporate job, and put in as many extra hours as it took every week to be a fully present leader and co-CEO of Plant Power.

An all-too familiar challenge that Harris also faced in the company's early years was self-doubt. Had he embarked on an impossible mission? Could he really convince enough investors to support the launch of Plant Power? His meditation practice provided a way to acknowledge those doubts without allowing them to sap his energy for the work ahead. He focused on the mission and intention that Plant Power embodied, and took one step at a time, treating every stage of the new venture as a learning process and opportunity to extend his skills:

> Some skills I had already developed and practiced over the years, in business and in my personal life. I had learned how to give a talk that might inspire listeners or tell a memorable story to illustrate an important point. I had experience officiating at wedding ceremonies and memorial services. I had taught meditation to some friends and family. I always enjoyed adapting the skills I learned and then using them in new situations. Now I was doing that adaptation on a daily basis, learning as fast as I could. As a new entrepreneur, I had to educate myself about things like finance, various types of deal structures, Limited Liability Companies, and in recent years, the advantages and disadvantages of private versus public financing. These are all things that I had no interest in learning while attending college all those years ago when I majored in psychology and minored in philosophy. I wouldn't have described myself as having a head for business. At the start a lot of the needed skills were pretty clear cut, like learning how to build a business plan or how to put together a spreadsheet of financial projections for ourselves and investors. I had a basic idea of how to create those materials. But the rest was all about figuring things out in real time, often learning from my mistakes and occasionally getting it right the first time.

Crafting a compelling story, pitching potential investors, and raising money are key capabilities for any founding team reliant on outside capital to grow their business. At Plant Power, Harris took on the essential roles of chief fund-raiser, storyteller, and investor relations manager. He leveraged his previous business and communications skills to find potential financial backers and convince them to support Plant Power and its vision. At every step, he overcame his own doubts to focus on the enormous impact that this venture could have on the world as well as the income that a successful vegan fast-food brand would deliver for its investors. Harris recalls experiencing a mix of high anxiety and exhilaration as the first Plant Power restaurant opened its doors:

> One of my first big tests as a co-founder was winning over investors. I had to convince enough people to believe in Plant Power in order to raise the money we needed for building out and opening up our very first restaurant location. My partner Mitch was known by some of our first investors as having launched successful restaurants so he brought some early-stage credibility to the project. But this particular team hadn't done anything together before and the vision for Plant Power was huge—much bigger than just one restaurant. So I had to sell that vision to new investors without any real evidence that Plant Power Fast Food was even going to survive, let alone become profitable. I was focused on raising capital, while Mitch and Zach were managing the operational and restaurant planning side of the startup. I did a lot of the early marketing, food photography, and social media as well. Fortunately, communicating a vision is something I'd been doing throughout my many years of leading sales teams at Alesis and then Harman and I really enjoyed it.
>
> I was persistent. I kept pitching our vision and our business plan and we managed to scrape together the money to fund our first Plant Power Fast Food location in Ocean Beach, California. We opened that first restaurant in January 2016, knowing full well that if this unit failed, the big dream was over. I was

very honest with our early investors. There was risk. I told them 'You'll either do really well on your investment or you'll never see that money again.' That was often my closing line and it often got a laugh. But I think that those early-stage investors were responding to our passion and our honesty by writing those first checks. It was an exciting time.

I actually remember sitting at the counter in Plant Power Ocean Beach on opening day waiting for the first customers to come in and buy our food. I was anxious, imagining what would happen if no one showed up, and we never made any money. I might end up selling my house and car and liquidating whatever I had in my 401(k) to somehow pay back those who had placed their trust in us. My partners think that I worry way too much and maybe that's true. Happily, my fears were misplaced. Customers did show up, and in large numbers. They bought our food; lots of it. Our first Plant Power location was a success. At the end of the first year of operation, we had exceeded our pro forma financials, which frankly had been an imaginary best guess at what we hoped would happen. We ended up that year at over a million dollars in revenues. Back then, that revenue number was amazing to us.

Looking at what Plant Power Fast Food restaurants are earning annually today, Harris realizes that the first location was actually a pretty small opening. Even so, it was an essential business validation of the founders' ambitious vision, the first step that allowed them to keep going on the journey. Raising funding from angel investors, leasing and opening the physical restaurant, hiring employees, preparing and serving the food, attracting enough customers to meet and then exceed their annual revenue goals— that was a big deal for all three partners. All those steps had worked as planned. Not only that, but Harris was proud and relieved that he and his partners were able to begin to make profit distributions to investors by the end of the second quarter of operation.

Success at the first location was an essential, but far from sufficient proof of Plant Power's long-term business potential. Much more was needed to become a profitable vegan fast-food chain, a high-growth franchise model, and ultimately a well-known consumer brand. The next step was to build on that first location's success in order to open a second restaurant. For the next opening, the co-founders selected a site in Encinitas, California about twenty-five miles north of San Diego. The site had been both a Burger King and also a gas station in its history and the team decided to transform it into a drive thru with a nicely landscaped outdoor dining area. The cost for construction and everything else needed to complete the project meant going back to raising the necessary funds. Once again, Harris developed a pitch, identified potential investors, and worked to scrape together enough cash to open their second location. Costs were higher than expected on the project and Plant Power ended up struggling to build out the restaurant while Harris was still working on raising money. He recalls the stress that was involved:

> Until then, I'd never considered taking medication for anxiety, but suddenly I understood why people do. We started building Plant Power Encinitas before we had all the money we'd need to complete it. I was raising as fast as I could, but it was just enough to keep the construction moving forward month to month. It seemed to me that the cost of failure would be catastrophic. I had no idea how we'd ever pay back all those investors if we didn't open. Even more critically, failure so early in our journey would probably kill the dream. Our second location had to open for our larger plan to have any chance of succeeding. Between equity investors and a hastily designed, but successful last minute crowdfunding campaign, we got it done. And when we finally opened Plant Power Encinitas for the first time, it felt like a real milestone. We weren't just one restaurant anymore. We were officially a restaurant 'chain' even if just barely. Two successful restaurants looked more like the proof of concept we'd need to convince investors that we might really be onto something. For the founders and our

new team, this second opening boosted our confidence that the Plant Power menu and brand would work in a community that was a little more mainstream than our first restaurant in Ocean Beach. Ocean Beach had a natural food co-op, a few local yoga studios and seemingly, on the surface at least, more plant-based types. Encinitas appeared to have a wider demographic, with doctors, nurses, and staff from the hospital across the street, a population from local businesses and homes, and the types of families who might otherwise be enjoying burgers and chicken nuggets at a traditional fast-food restaurant.

Attracting that mainstream demographic of fast-food diners would be the key to long-term revenue growth and geographic expansion for Plant Power.

Managing for Growth

After two successful restaurant openings near San Diego, the Plant Power co-founders were ready to think more expansively. Even as they searched for a third corporate location, they knew that in order to scale the business as rapidly as they would like, it would be necessary to franchise. In order to franchise, they would need to simplify their operation.

Up until now, Plant Power prepared all of its plant-based burger patties, sauces, dressings, and its popular "chicken" products from scratch at each individual restaurant location. To continue to expand, they'd need to transition to a centralized manufacturing facility, or as it's often known in the restaurant world, a commissary. That commissary would also distribute proprietary Plant Power products to corporate and franchise locations. So, in 2018 the team opened up Plant Power Wholesale, their new manufacturing arm in Escondido, California, which was a twenty-five-minute drive inland from their Encinitas location.

Centralized prep and the distribution logistics were both big expenses that would only pay off if the company was able to open enough new locations. Since the funds to build corporate locations at a rapid pace were not available, an essential next step for growth was to create a successful Plant Power franchise program. With his co-founders focused on operations, Harris was the logical choice to recruit potential franchise partners, negotiate the agreements, and integrate new franchise partners into the organization. He took on the role of de facto franchise development manager, in addition to his continuing responsibilities in identifying potential new investors and raising capital.

The first potential franchisees approached Plant Power to talk about opening a new location. Harris was happy to find that these two entrepreneurial brothers were experienced restaurant franchise owners who had been successful operating multiple Subway restaurants, as well as developing new units for a popular juice and smoothie franchise. As committed vegetarians however, they were a bit troubled by the karma of selling animal-based products and they were looking for a plant-based brand to franchise. No one at any of the other well-known plant-based brands would return their phone calls, but Harris established a quick rapport with them that soon turned into a formal franchise agreement. In his words, "Of course, I fell in love with these guys."

These first franchisees opened a Plant Power restaurant in Redlands, in the Inland Empire section of California. That location was a hit, and quickly became a moneymaker, leading to a second franchise location with this new team in Riverside. Plant Power's expansion was on a roll.

While the franchise segment of their business would allow Plant Power to expand its footprint and gain market share without a large expenditure of capital, the founders understood that additional corporate locations would be needed to generate the kind of revenues that the company required to build a larger team and scale up their infrastructure. Also, if Harris had to convince a small group of trusting investors to provide the cash needed to open new restaurants one at a time, the company might take years to achieve its goals. What's more, the sophisticated private equity and venture capital investors he was looking for weren't interested in investing directly into a single unit. They wanted to be part of the entire enterprise.

Up until this point, each Plant Power corporate restaurant was a separate business unit, technically disconnected from the other locations, except through the founders and a nascent management team. With the next stage of growth in mind, the founders began planning for a new umbrella parent company. Revenues from corporate and franchise restaurants would be used to build up the kind of infrastructure and team required to operate a growing enterprise. This new structure would also allow Harris to attract a larger amount of capital from a more sophisticated investor base including private equity, venture capital, and family offices. In 2019, the Plant Power Restaurant Group, LLC was born. By 2020 the new company began recruiting top level industry professionals from well-known brands like Chipotle, Hard Rock Café, and Yum brands. By 2021, it had grown to a robust team of fifteen people covering everything from operations, new store openings, graphics, marketing HR, finance, and guest relations.

In quick succession, the company opened new corporate-owned restaurant locations in San Diego and Long Beach and a new franchise location in Fountain Valley. In five short years, the company had demonstrated its ability to grow fast and to operate profitability. Enterprise-wide net sales grew from $1.1M in 2016 to $14.5M in 2020 and Plant Power is on track to hit $19M by the close of 2021. From its humble beginnings in 2016, the company had grown to nine restaurants and a Los Angeles-based Food Truck by September 2021. Five more restaurants are slated to open by June of 2022 including flagship locations in Hollywood and Las Vegas. To support this expansion, Plant Power signed with a national distributor in order to enable regional and eventually national development.

Another major milestone for Plant Power came in April 2021, when the company announced it had completed it's $7.5 million Series A capital raise. Harris had taken the lead in this challenging endeavor which began shortly after the formation of the Plant Power Restaurant Group in 2019. Although he had made tremendous progress by the end of 2020, he said that it took the addition of new CFO Ed Har to help him get it over the finish line. To

Harris, the process seemed to take forever. He privately joked that it felt like the longest Series A fund raising cycle in history, but he quickly added how grateful he was to have landed this level of investment, knowing quite well how many promising early-stage companies never get to this stage.

The venture investment put Plant Power Fast Food on an even faster track for expansion, with increased likelihood of future, larger investments, and new options for raising capital. As the vegan restaurant market continues to expand in the US and across the world, investors are looking to make much bigger bets on the companies that have a shot at becoming leading consumer brands—the vision that has inspired Harris and his co-founders from the start.

The Plant Power co-founders and prospective vegan fast-food investors are well aware that the original animal-based fast-food market is far larger than the still very niche market for plant-based food overall, and vegan fast food as a subset of that sector. Revenues in the entire fast-food meat and plant-based sectors were estimated to be $278.6 billion in 2020 (Thi 2021).

With total sales of plant-based food in the US (including through grocery stores) estimated at just $5 billion in 2019 (Statista), the vegan fast-food sector where Plant Power operates is still just a tiny dot in the fast-food universe. Nevertheless, market trends indicate strong potential for rapid growth, fueled by consumers embracing healthier, more sustainable eating and an overall increase in the number of consumers who describe themselves as vegetarian or flexitarian eaters. Plant-based food sales from all sources (grocery stores as well as restaurants of all types) are projected to grow over 11% annually, compared to a 2% growth rate for all food sales. Capturing even a fraction of the $278 billion-dollar fast food annual revenue stream would give Plant Power a prominent place on the vegan fast food competitive landscape. One trend in their favor is reflected in a report from Statista that when consumers were asked if they would be interested in ordering plant-based food in restaurants if it tasted as good or better than real meat options, 67.3% of respondents answered "Yes" (Lock 2020).

With billions of dollars at stake, it's no surprise that competition is increasing at a rapid pace. Well-established fast-food brands that became famous for selling billions of burgers each year are busy adding plant-based options to their menus. Inevitably, Plant Power Fast Food is by no means the only new entrant competing for customers and investors in the vegan fast-food sector. At this point however, it's a fairly open competitive landscape, with a lot of opportunity for multiple new entrants and no single dominant brand. The United States Department of Agriculture estimates that in 2021 Americans will consume about fifty billion burgers and over two billion servings of fast-food chicken nuggets. Vegan fast-food restaurants aspiring to become national brands can establish their business capturing just a small share of that seemingly insatiable consumer appetite for burgers and related fast-food items.

Sharing the Value with all Stakeholders

Harris and his partners are mindful that any definition of success must take into account all of the company's stakeholders. The larger circle of Plant Power stakeholders includes the restaurant's guests (Plant Power nomenclature for customers), the communities within which they operate, the planet all humans share, and the animals they share it with. Harris knows that without what he calls the "internal stakeholders" Plant Power would not exist at all. Those are, according to Harris, the passionate team members who are the very lifeblood of the organization and also the individuals, groups, and funds who have demonstrated their support of Plant Power's revolutionary vision with capital investment. "It takes a village," said Harris.

Making Diversity, Equity, and Inclusion a Priority

Harris points out that as the company has grown, its mission has evolved as well. Mindful of the impact that the consumption of animal products has on the environment, on human health, and on the animals themselves, Plant Power's founding vision was laser focused on its goal to increase the popularity of cruelty-free, sustainable, and healthier alternatives in the fast-food market segment. However, in recent years, the company has expanded its scope to focus on the development of a supportive and transformational company culture. Culture was part of the bedrock of the company from the very beginning, but it has become increasingly apparent that to do it right, the company must allocate the time, resources, and attention to make continual improvements. Harris notes that if working at Plant Power isn't fun and rewarding, if people don't feel respected and valued, then the company has failed to achieve its mission.

Meeting these expanded goals is a challenge, and an ongoing process. Harris believes that in building the kind of corporate culture that people want to be part of, it's increasingly important to be mindful of the larger cultural context, both its history and ongoing evolution:

> There are wounds and trauma that so many members of our society have dealt with for so many years. Those of us who may have been born into more privileged circumstances often fail to understand the pain that our culture has inflicted on women, people of color, and those with non-traditional sexual orientations. Creating a culture that is truly diverse and welcoming requires attention. It doesn't just happen because we say we want it to happen.

Along those lines, the company has recently embarked upon a journey to incorporate the principles of Diversity, Equity, and Inclusion into the company culture. In 2020 its senior leaders all participated in a comprehensive training led by a minority owned consultancy that focused on helping companies to build work-cultures based on these principles. Harris characterizes himself and his co-founder Mitch Wallis as sharing a kind of nostalgia for the 1960s, even though they are too young to be original hippies (they are currently sixty-one). They both grew up imagining the 1960s as the era of peace and love, where everyone was willing to hug it out, and people could say things like, "Don't worry, we're all in this together. Just trust us."

At the same time, Harris is very aware that the nostalgic image was never a reality. In past decades, as well as today, society is experiencing political and social divisions, frequent conflict, and embedded economic, racial, ethnic, and gender injustices. Trust has to be earned. Acknowledging that, the Plant Power co-founders and management team are taking responsibility for getting trained in diversity, equity, and inclusion best practices and very consciously working to create a culture and a climate that is welcoming for everyone, where everyone can really feel a sense of belonging.

Sharing value extends to investors as well. Harris, having been the lead fundraiser for Plant Power since its launch, realizes that the company's survival depends on shareholders and investors. He also notes that the early investors were far from being big, faceless Wall Street entities. He knows every single investor personally, and is grateful that they made the choice to trust the Plant Power founders and their vision. Those investors took a risk, and they are counting on Plant Power to use their funds to build a successful business, and to come through in the long run. That creates an obligation to operate profitably, and ultimately to distribute profits back to people who invested in the company at its early stage. If Plant Power doesn't keep trust with its investors, the enterprise can't stay in business. That would mean no more jobs for anyone on the team.

As Harris acknowledges, shared value is a constant balancing act:

> There's an equally real situation that we have to address as a responsible, mission-focused company. People who earn the average fast-food sector salary are struggling to pay their rent, or even to buy food, especially with California's high cost of living. We had done a pretty good job of starting people at minimum wage, and then elevating them as quickly as possible beyond that, based on them qualifying for new positions in the restaurant. You could go from dishwasher to food prep, and then to line cook and as you became validated for each new position, your wage would increase. Even so, we were still getting a lot of young people who, understandably and

appropriately, didn't understand the pressures we were going through, and actually thought we were all rich guys. It didn't matter that we had taken a huge risk to start the company, or that I had worked for free for five years for Plant Power.

We realized that we had to look at our team in a new way. What if we started people above whatever that local minimum wage was, and won employee loyalty and trust with a more inclusive, participatory culture? If the net result was that we had lower turnover, that would reduce our costs in the long run. Staff turnover is expensive, especially when you include the costs of recruiting and training. High turnover also takes a toll on customer service and satisfaction. Even though the upfront cost was daunting, we decided to try a more equitable, less spreadsheet-oriented strategy. On the surface raising salaries would blow our labor costs off the spreadsheet, and it wouldn't work. But we decided to take the risk, in hope of saving some of that money invested in higher wages by reducing turnover and training costs over time. We told our team members what we were going to do and why. So far, it seems to be working. Employee turnover has gone down. Team members feel more valued.

So, we actually saw some evidence of what I had been hoping from the start, that there are innovative ways to keep within our financial constraints and still move toward an out-come that demonstrates value for everyone. Even with that progress, Plant Power is still a fast-food restaurant and no-body's making $100 an hour, or even $50 an hour, including the founders. We can't change our structure enough to make those higher hourly numbers a reality. So, we have to find other ways to make Plant Power a better, more rewarding place to work. We've made a lot of changes to improve overall work-ing conditions and to open up communications, listen to learn what matters and how to do better, and give team members more control over things. These are big changes and they re-quire management to make some leaps of faith. When we can manage to do it well, we will have a much happier culture.

Our other important commitment to all Plant Power team members is to take diversity, equity, and inclusion more seriously— to make it a priority in our operations, in hiring, and in our organizational culture training. To make that happen we found an excellent team of consultants called Critical Diversity Solutions. They developed a formal curriculum and presented ideas and techniques for change. All the senior leaders took part in that training program to clarify our understanding of the issues and get started mapping out the specific changes that we needed to make. At the end of the training sessions, we put together a list of action items that we wanted to do. Importantly, we created a diversity, equity, and inclusion council, the Plant Power Council, made up of a variety of people from our team. Now this council meets on a regular basis with our Director of HR, to provide feedback and hold us accountable for ongoing improvements.

Harris understands that creating a channel for regular feedback from Plant Power employees is critical, especially as the company gets bigger and its geographic reach expands across North America. In the midst of rapid growth, the management team and board are paying attention to everything from customer experience to financial projections and results, to shareholder return, and developing new franchise agreements and locations. Harris says they are committed to keeping shared value, open communication, culture, and diversity high on the list:

The creation of a Diversity Equity Inclusion Council made up of employees in the restaurants puts the concerns and ideas of our team members front and center. We're now getting important input from team members with various cultural, racial, and economic backgrounds, as well as with different sexual orientations. So that's a big, big help in keeping us focused on creating a culture that is truly welcoming and authentically inclusive.

The other thing that Plant Power is consciously trying to do is expand our scope when we're recruiting. We've learned that a key strategy in achieving diversity is to broaden our search process. Whether we are recruiting team members at the restaurant level, or recruiting at the corporate level, we're making more of an effort to seek out talent in diverse communities. When the talent pool we're connecting with is more diverse, it's more likely that over time, that diversity will begin to emerge in our culture and workplace.

Location-Based Sustainability

Planet-friendly, sustainable ingredients are intrinsic to the vegan menu at Plant Power, giving the company a clear sustainability advantage over the comparable meat-based hamburgers and nuggets. As its website declares, "On average, Americans eat three hamburgers each week. If each of us switched just one of those beef burgers to a plant-based burger for a year, it would be like taking twelve million cars off the road for an entire year." In addition to the built-in environmental advantages of plant-based ingredients, Plant Power has made a commitment to restaurant furnishing made from renewable bamboo and reclaimed wood fiber, and the use of compostable take-out packaging. Plant Power is also implementing solar power and other energy saving measures at corporate-owned restaurant locations, documenting the savings, and using this data to encourage its franchise-owned restaurants to make similar changes. Harris had hoped to do even more to reduce waste, with a circular economy model including composting of food waste and reusing certain types of food containers after sterilization. Some of those ideas have been put on hold in the face of restrictive municipal sanitary codes and restaurant food composting regulations. Plant Power's reuse of food containers in their distribution network has been limited by their partnership with a national distributor that could only handle packaging that was compatible with their cold storage facilities. Figuring out more innovative approaches to reducing food waste is on the company's to-do list and Harris envisions bringing on an experienced Chief Sustainability Officer at some point.

Envisioning the Future

From Harris's personal perspective, the next big challenge for Plant Power is managing rapid growth and expansion, while staying true to the vision that motivated him and his co-founders. Part of that will mean sharing power, both with the senior team leaders who are increasingly taking on enterprise level responsibility and also with an expanding Board of Directors. From his perspective, it's a healthy next step:

> The more that Plant Power grows toward becoming a national brand, the more we all have to learn about letting go of running everything the way we used to, and how best to delegate more and more responsibilities to the growing team of senior leaders. We also understand that as we're able to attract the capital required to really accelerate growth, we'll be working more closely with an expanding Board of Directors. Growth requires change and that means being flexible. That doesn't mean being flexible about our vision and our mission. It means being open to new, creative, and inclusive ways to achieve it.

Harris readily acknowledges that the key to his own success is the partnership he has forged with his co-founders Mitch Wallis and Zach Vouga:

> I could not have lived this vision, and built Plant Power without my partners. They're definitely brilliant geniuses. We've learned about ourselves and each other throughout this journey. We came into this partnership with some different goals and ideas for our personal futures, and how we might work together in the long term. As much as we love each other and as much as we support each other, like any partnership, we've had a few challenging moments. But the vision that brought us together acts as a sort of cosmic glue to hold us together. Each of us had this vision before we ever met and magically, the universe brought us together to make it real. Honestly, I'm

still inspired every day by how much intelligence, hard work, and devotion my partners bring to this work. It's an amazing thing to witness and to be part of.

As the company has grown, each of the founders has had to focus more and more on areas where they have the most expertise in order to increase overall efficiency. Harris talks about the contributions that he'd like to make to the team and the future of Plant Power as it continues to grow:

> One contribution I would like to make over the next two to three to four years, is supporting Plant Power's move to becoming professionally managed at a high level. That includes our having a very strong, diverse, and experienced Board of Directors. The faster we grow, and the higher we aim, the more essential this becomes. It's an aspect of company growth that I never really understood before. We need the help of experienced professionals who have actually led companies through this kind of growth. Mitch, Zach, and I serve on the board together and of course lead the way, but I'm more excited than ever about expanding that board to include members who are experts in fields as diverse as global finance, supply chain, and enterprise level operations.
>
> We're also excited about including people with diverse backgrounds and perspectives. Creating that strategic and visionary governing body of the board is an important part of our future, and I want to be intimately involved with helping my partners to build that.

Looking into the longer-term future, Harris wants to ensure that the "investor family" who placed their faith and trust in Plant Power are rewarded for the risk that they've taken. Similarly, he says that he and his partners are deeply committed to the team members who have breathed life into the company, "Those early investors and team members have gotten us to where we are now and we're just getting started."

What's next? Harris is committed to staying the course for as long as it takes to become a successful national vegan fast-food brand. Beyond that horizon however, he isn't wedded to being a permanent chief executive with day-to-day operating responsibility forever. In the long term, he sees himself playing a role on the Plant Power board of directors, helping to shape and guide the company's growth strategy and its implementation of his founding vision. As Harris looks ahead, he feels this transition is part of the wisdom that comes with being an older founder:

> As long as Plant Power continues on the path of being kind and respectful, as long as it's vegan and sustainable, as long as all our basic founding principles are safeguarded, I don't need to be in charge of it forever. I wanted to bring something like this to the world and watch it grow.
>
> This feeling is different from what I would have felt at a younger age. When we're younger, it seems like we want to make our mark in the world in a very personal, and often competitive way. We want the admiration of others for our accomplishments, and there's this desire to be a big deal in society. Honestly, I believe that my intention and vision for the business that became Plant Power was always about saving the planet, stopping animal slaughter, and helping people eat better. But if I'm being totally honest, I think that there was always a little ego in it for me as well; a sense of doing something really great for the world and maybe being noticed for it. You know, being the cool vegan guy. Seeking the approval of our clan is baked into our DNA and I'm no exception. At this point in my life, however, I really believe that kind of impulse isn't helpful. It doesn't lead to love and healing, and it certainly isn't the basis for inspired leadership or team building. That ego trip just doesn't matter as much to me in my sixties. Letting go of all that and focusing on something higher seems like a pretty good plan, both in life and in business.
>
> I'd like to think my willingness to eventually transition to a different role in the company is a combination of the wisdom of

age and the insight from my meditation and reflection. Keep to the intention, live your principles, and let go of your ego. It's a work in progress.

References

Thi Le (2021) Fast Food Restaurants: US Industry Report 72221A. *IBIS World*. https://my.ibisworld.com/us/en/industry/72221a/about. Accessed 14 Oct 2021.

Lock S. (2020) Interest in ordering plant-based meats if tastier than real meat in the U.S. 2019. *Statista*. https://www.statista.com/statistics/1056338/ plant-based-meat-vs-real-meat-taste-in-the-us. Accessed 14 Oct 2021.

About Jeffrey Harris

Jeffrey Harris is the co-founder and co-CEO of Plant Power Fast Foods, a restaurant firm he launched with Mitch Wallis and Zach Vouga in 2016. At Plant Power, Harris focuses on marketing and communication, including responsibility for the essential role of investor relations and fundraising. He describes his mission at Plant Power as "Revolutionizing the fast-food industry by offering plant-based,  cruelty-free, environmentally sustainable, healthier options to the lovely citizens of Earth."

Prior to embarking on his long-term vision to make a positive impact on the environment and society through plant-based food, Harris worked for over twenty years in the corporate world in the professional equipment side of the music and video industry. He held positions in marketing and sales management for progressively larger companies, with responsibilities ranging from developing dealer agreements and sales policies, cooperative marketing programs, national account training, and merchandising strategies. He joined the Harman Music Group in 2001 as the Western Regional Sales Manager and advanced to a position with Harman International in 2014, which he held until his responsibilities at Plant Power demanded his full-time attention.

About the Company

Company	The Plant Power Restaurant Group, LLC
Website	plantpowerfastfood.com
Founding Year	2016
Co-Founders	Jeffrey Harris Zach Vouga Mitch Wallis
Industry Sector	Vegetarian and Vegan Restaurants (Fast Food)
Address	411 Santa Fe Drive Encinitas, California, 92024

Chapter 7

Glanris: The Future of Filtration

When Bryan Eagle agreed to meet with a Memphis area startup team in 2017, he wasn't expecting that the discussion would land him in a co-founder position in a new industry sector. A familiar figure in the Memphis business and startup community, Eagle was well known for his personal entrepreneurial success and his willingness to support new founders. He had a decades-long track record of launching startups and leading them through their fund-raising and growth stages to a profitable exit. Meeting with aspiring entrepreneurs was just one of the many ways he supported the Memphis startup community.

To promote new business formation in his hometown, in 1999 Eagle created Emerge Memphis, a nonprofit incubator that helped early-stage, technology-based companies succeed. Twenty years later, Emerge Memphis joined with two other Memphis organizations, Epicenter and Innova, to establish a $5 million Formation Fund, a nonprofit evergreen fund for innovative companies in industries such as logistics, home services, medical, and agricultural technology. During this time, Eagle also founded and managed Memphis Ventures, his own consulting and investment firm.

Eagle recalls that his 2017 introduction to the Glanris startup team came from AC Wharton, a former Memphis mayor and long-time proponent of business innovation. Wharton wanted to stimulate Eagle's interest in Glanris and its filtration technology in part because Glanris team member Tom Volinchak was also a leader in the Blue Stream Task Force that Wharton had set up. Blue Stream's goal was to explore business opportunities and protect the environmental benefits of the Memphis Sands Aquifer. It struck Eagle as a promising, visionary project for Memphis. As he recalls:

Wharton had put together a strong working group with community leaders from different backgrounds to talk about the future of water, how our community will deal with water related issues in the future, and what business opportunities could be developed based on our geographic location along the Mississippi River. We're very lucky here in Memphis, because we sit on top of one of the largest freshwater aquifers in the United States. Many US aquifers, especially in the west and southwest, are being depleted so rapidly that water scarcity is already becoming a major issue in those regions. Fortunately for Memphis, our aquifer is being constantly replenished. It sits right under the Mississippi River, and a constant flow of water is moving underground through the clay and sand that serves to keep it fresh and abundant. The aquifer is a tremendous natural resource for our area, a resource that will become more and more valuable in the context of water scarcity elsewhere in the US and around the world. So it was very forward-looking for the mayor and the Memphis community to begin thinking strategically about this resource, and the value of water.

That first meeting with Tom Volinchak and his Glanris co-founder Louie Yu Lin was an eye-opener for Eagle. Looking back on it, he remembers:

Tom was an experienced professional in the water filtration sector, having worked for years for leading companies in that sector. His partner Louie, who was a professor in environmental engineering at Christian Brothers University here in Memphis, had developed a really interesting way of filtering water using the agricultural waste from rice hulls as the filtration medium. He had already filed for a patent on this innovation. Their new process had the potential to transform the whole water filtration industry. What's more, it would reduce carbon emissions by converting tons of rice hulls, a predominant form of agricultural waste across the planet, from trash to a powerful filtration medium.

They were very open with me about wanting an experienced founder to join the team. Tom and Louie made a convincing case that the Glanris filtration innovation represented a major business opportunity, but they were struggling a bit with how to put everything together to actually launch the company, attract customers, and raise some funding. They were hoping I would join them as co-founder, and become the business leader as the CEO of Glanris.

Eagle was impressed with what he learned about Glanris at the meeting. As far as he could tell, the company's technology had the potential to revolutionize current methods of water filtration. That would indeed be a big opportunity. Even though he was intrigued, however, Eagle was not convinced that Glanris would be the best fit for him, and vice versa. There were two reasons. The first one he shared right away with Volinchak and Yu Lin:

> My first response was, thanks, but I'm not the right person to take the role of co-founder and CEO of this company. As I told them, I'm not a water guy. My whole career, all of my companies, have been in a different area. I don't have any expertise in water filtration, and that's the background you should be looking for in a chief executive and co-founder.

The second reason that Eagle wasn't ready to join Glanris was more personal. He was already pretty far along in discussions about another opportunity, one that would involve relocation to Europe. This opportunity was with a company and a technology that seemed like a much better match for his experience and expertise. That company was also much further along in its growth curve. It had already demonstrated the value of its technology and its ability to generate revenues. In fact, its management team was looking for an executive to help accelerate growth and prepare the company for going public. Eagle was excited about this opportunity, making him even more inclined to take a pass on working with Glanris. He discovered, however, that it wasn't easy to discourage the Glanris team.

Volinchak and Yu Lin weren't willing to take that first no for an answer. They believed that Eagle was the best person for the CEO role, and were optimistic that he could lead the growth of Glanris all the way from an innovative technology, to a successful high-impact startup, and on to a major force in the filtration industry. To help convince him, they shared more details about the patent pending Glanris filtration process, explained all the ways it outperformed the current solutions for water filtration, and asked him to spend a little more time learning about the whole opportunity before making up his mind.

Eagle agreed to take the time delving into the details about Glanris— both the business opportunity and the positive environmental impact it represented. He remembers that the more he learned about the limitations of current water purification and filtration products, and the urgent global challenges of water depletion and scarcity issues, the more interested he became:

> They made a compelling case for how Glanris would have a competitive advantage in building a business by tackling two major environmental problems. So I started reading, and the more I understood about the problems that Glanris was poised to address, the more I thought, wow, this is such an impactful and much-needed technology. I got excited about the potential of this locally developed innovation to revolutionize the economics and efficiency of the water filtration sector, and eventually other filtration processes. It was so ingenious to create a new filtration media from discarded rice husks. Glanris was poised to commercialize a process that actually takes the biggest global source of agricultural waste out of the waste stream and processes it in an energy-efficient, nonpolluting way to convert it into a filtration media. On top of that, the processed rice husks turned into an active carbon filtration media that outperformed existing water purification systems. I realized that this company could become a major, change-the-world level force in the industry.

That's what hooked me in the end. I wanted to be part of that kind of transformation. I'm at the age where I wanted to be involved with a company that was making an impact on the world, as well as being part of a significant business opportunity. Even though I was by no means a water resources expert at that point, I was well aware of climate change, and future water scarcity, and how that is affecting everything that we do. So once I understood the scope of the Glanris opportunity and the power of its technology to impact water resources worldwide, I really wanted to support that effort.

Just as Volinchak and Yu Lin had hoped, Eagle was hooked on the opportunity to help solve one of the biggest resource challenges of the twenty-first century: the increasing demand for clean water in a world of widespread water scarcity. That convinced him to join Glanris as a co-founder and the company's CEO.

Clean Water for the 21st Century

The Glanris team didn't have to search far to find data confirming the urgent need for innovations in water filtration technology. Dozens of organizations, from the United Nations and the World Bank, to the US Corps of Engineers, and McKinsey Consulting have highlighted the burgeoning global water crisis that impacts the health and livelihood of billions of people around the world.

The United Nations Sustainable Development Goals (SDGs) were adopted in 2015 as a guide to the world's most critical problems. The SDGs serve as a call for government, corporate, and nonprofit leaders to commit to implementing solutions by 2030. Not surprisingly, the global water crisis is high on their list of goals. Access to water and sanitation for all is Goal Six of the seventeen SDGs that the United Nations has identified as essential for the future survival of earth's people and ecosystems. More effective and affordable water filtration is only a part of the solution to global water challenges. However, improvements in water recycling and safe reuse through filtration are two of the major steps recommended by the United Nations in its description of the strategies that will help to "improve water quality by reducing pollution, eliminating dumping, and minimizing release of hazardous chemicals and materials, with a 2030 objective of halving the proportion of untreated wastewater, and increasing water recycling and safe reuse through filtration."

In a 2021 update on the progress towards achieving this goal, the United Nations reported some modest progress, including a global increase of 9% in water use efficiency since 2015. However, most of the data demonstrates the increasing urgency for water recycling and safe reuse. Over two billion people, 26% of the world's population, are still without regular access to safely managed drinking water services, and 44% of household wastewater globally is not safely treated. Water stress is also increasing around the world, with over 700 million people living in critically water-stressed areas (United Nations 2021).

Access to clean, safe water for drinking and residential use is not just a global problem. More than 1.6 million Americans did not have regular access to safe drinking water in 2020 (Riggs E 2017). This lack of access shows every sign of worsening in the coming decade. An estimated twenty-one of the thirty-seven largest aquifers in the United States are currently using water faster than it can be replenished. According to a 2017 study, the combination of aging municipal and regional water infrastructure, climate change impacts such as flooding and fire, and increased industrial and agricultural water use, could leave up to 40.9 million American households unable to afford clean water access and wastewater services in the coming decade (Mack E and Wrase S 2017).

Lack of confidence in the health and safety of tap water is already driving the majority of US residents to adopt alternatives for drinking water—often at considerable cost. Only about a third of US households rely primarily on tap water for drinking, due to widespread concern about potential levels of contamination of local water, and a dislike of tap water taste and color. About a third of households use some kind of water filtration, and the remaining third buy bottled water for drinking. IBISWorld reports that over $7.8 billion in bottled water will be purchased in the US during 2021 (IBISWorld 2021).

Concerns about water safety and scarcity are also rising in the corporate sector. In its 2009 report, The Global Corporate Water Footprint, McKinsey & Company notes that:

> Water, an increasingly scarce commodity subject to the growing pressures of a globalized economy, is capturing ever more attention from business leaders, politicians, and the general public. Many multinational companies, particularly in consumer packaged goods and manufacturing firms, have water footprints that span the globe—and value chains that expose them to local and national water challenges from Atlanta to Beijing. To be sure, businesses of all kinds face risks to their operations and reputations as they use scarce water resources. But understanding trends and using water wisely can help companies differentiate themselves and gain competitive advantage too.

The filtration technology that Glanris has developed is significantly more effective than currently used filtration media at removing metals such as lead from household water supplies, and restoring water to the level of cleanliness that would make it safe for residential use. Its filtration media can also handle the kind of oily, sludgy contamination that industrial processes generate, giving corporate customers more options to reuse the water deployed during manufacturing processes instead of discarding it as wastewater. Importantly, the Glanris technology will also make water filtration and removal of contaminants more affordable for residential and industrial users. That's because the Glanris process is based on using rice husks, or hulls, one of the largest sources of agricultural waste in the world. Because of their composition, the rice hulls can be transformed into a high-performance filtration media that works better than traditional carbon or chemical filtration methods.

A Circular Economy Model for Transforming Waste into Clean Water

In essence, the Glanris technology is a sustainability grand slam, in the form of a circular economy model. The circular model starts by removing rice production agricultural waste that would otherwise become a source of pollution and turning it into a valuable new product. Rice hulls, or husks, are the hard outer coating of the rice grains, making up about 25% of the harvested rice. These hulls are made of silica and lignin, tough substances that are too hard to chew and basically indigestible to humans. They have to be removed by rice producers to create an edible food product. Every year, approximately 218 billion pounds of rice hulls are stripped off of the rice grains harvested in the rice-growing regions around the world. Today, these rice hulls are often burned near the fields where the rice is grown, creating dense smog and accelerating climate change. The rice hulls that are not burned are considered waste and are typically dumped into landfills.

Glanris treats rice hulls with a patented process that converts this waste product into active biochar, a water filtration medium that is highly effective in removing all major contaminants from water. In addition to transforming an agricultural waste substance into a valuable new filtration solution, the Glanris process is itself environmentally friendly, since it needs less heat than carbonization processes used to produce traditional water filters, and requires no added chemicals. Glanris estimates that its clean-tech production uses 98% less energy than competing processes.

The Glanris filtration media can be used in popular residential water filtration systems, as well as in large industrial filtration systems. The filtered water it produces is safe for residential use, including drinking water. It is also effective at cleaning the water that has been contaminated during industrial manufacturing so that this water can be reused by manufacturing firms after it is filtered, cutting back on their overall water consumption.

To close the circle, when the Glanris processed rice hulls are at the end of their useful life in filtration systems, the carbon they still contain can be safely discarded since the contaminants are bound into the filtration media, rendering them harmless. It will take thousands of years for the filtration media to break down, so the process effectively prevents thousands of tons of carbon from entering the atmosphere each year.

The following bullet points from the presentation slide deck that Eagle has used for investor pitches summarize the main advantages for potential customers of the Glanris filtration solution.

Glanris Advantages

Glanris filtration media is more than simply a green solution. Glanris $901x$ Biocarbon^{TM} filtration media has the dual functionality to remove both organic contaminants and dissolved metals in one media. Glanris' Biocarbon is also a fraction of the cost of ion-exchange.

Better Glanris' Biocarbon filtration media has the dual-functionality to remove both metals and organics. It operates in a wide pH range and uses no harsh chemicals or microplastics.

Fast Its structure gives it rapid kinetics. It can achieve in a single pass what others require multiple passes through mixed media to achieve.

Economical Glanris is a fraction of the price of ion-exchange with the added benefit of organics

1. Effective metal removal in the presence of oils, grease and organics
2. Low-cost, lightweight media
3. Economical replacement for ion-exchange with the added benefit of organics removal
4. Drop in replacement for existing filtration tanks
5. Faster kinetics than activated carbon
6. Green and sustainably sourced and produced

7. As or more effective in a single pass vs. multiple passes through competing media

8. Effective in a wider pH range

To protect its technology innovations, Glanris has patented its core production process. The text of the Glanris patent, issued by the United States Patent and Trademark Office in 2019, explains why the new filtration method is such an important advancement for water treatment. Even in the somewhat stilted legal language of patent application writing, the urgent need for a better solution comes through clearly.

Removal of toxic compounds, such as heavy metals, volatile organic compounds (VOCs), semi-volatile organic compounds (SVOCs), pesticides and herbicides, is one of the most difficult challenges in water treatment. Removal of these toxic compounds from wastewater for proper disposal is important for ensuring adequate environmental and public health protective measures are undertaken in order to avoid costly remediation measures as a result of inadequate wastewater treatment processes.

Currently known and utilized processes and materials are limited in their ability to remove the priority pollutants. Additionally, these current solutions are costly, energy intensive, both in the filter media itself and in pumping the contaminated water through the filter media. These current solutions also take up valuable landfill space when the filtration media needs to be disposed of after reaching the end of its useful life. The currently prevailing treatment technologies used in treatment of wastewater for heavy metal removal include reverse osmosis (RO), ion exchange resin, activated carbon adsorption, and chemical coagulation and flocculation. However, as will be described further herein below, each of these known technological solutions have many limitations that are addressed by the inventive subject matter disclosed herein.. . .

Reverse osmosis filtration systems use a semipermeable membrane to remove contaminants from the liquid being filtered. However, reverse osmosis cannot tolerate the presence of, and is ineffective at removing oil, grease, dissolved dirt and/or silt, and heavy organic materials (e.g., algae, phytoplankton, vegetation debris, and chlorine) from the liquid being processed. In fact, oil, grease, dissolved dirt and/or silt and heavy organic materials will block the reverse osmosis material, such that reverse osmosis would not work when sufficient concentrations of such contaminants are present in a wastewater source. Additionally, reverse osmosis has the additional disadvantage in that it generates twenty-five percent more in wastewater, for the water that is filtered, such that this wastewater generated must be further processed in some manner.

Another known wastewater treatment technology is ion exchange resin (IER), however this technology has the disadvantage that it also cannot tolerate and is ineffective at removing oils, grease, and organic materials. Additionally, IER must, in order to be effective, be operated at very low flow rates in order to remove the limited contaminants that it is capable of removing. As a result, IER requires a very large volume for effective processing on any sort of industrial scale and requires longer retention time of the water for effective processing. IER also has an extremely high cost associated with its implementation, is dependent on fossil fuels for the raw material for manufacturing the filtration media and has a high cost for disposal of the filtration media, with marginal ability to further process the filtration media for reuse in many applications.

Additionally, IER must be regenerated (e.g., refreshed) using toxic acids and chemicals, thereby generating additional wastewater during the clean-up process. As such, the safe disposal and clean-up from an IER filtration system is itself a secondary source of environmental pollution.

Conventional Granular Activated Carbon (GAC) is the most commonly employed filter media in heavy metal removal from wastewater. While the ability of GAC to remove heavy metals has been shown to be only marginally, if at all, successful, GAC is nevertheless widely considered to be the best media for their removal. However, GAC cannot be used to remove oil or grease but is effective to remove organic and inorganic chemicals from wastewater. As is already known, GAC is typically manufactured from a source material of rice husk, coconut shells, animal bones, and/or clam shells. This source material is first pulverized and then incinerated into ash (e.g., small particles) before final treatment with toxic chemicals in order to produce the resultant GAC product. The small particle size is easily clogged by pollutants, thus making this approach unsuccessful. Due to the energy consumption and time required to produce GAC for use in a filter media, GAC is also a very costly media. Additionally, the manufacturing process used in making GAC remains expensive and the cost is actually becoming higher over time because of the inflation of raw material costs....

As such, there exists a strong commercial, as well as environmental, need to develop improved and alternate filtration media, filtration systems, and filtration methods, having improved efficacy and lower associated costs in removing toxic contaminants from wastewater.

The alternative filtration methods using the Glanris process for processing rice hulls are further described in the patents that are at the core of the Glanris filtration solution. Eagle notes that the goal of obtaining patents is to defend Glanris and its innovations against the possible future claim that it copied another company's idea. Having a patent on a core innovation is a great asset for any startup since it creates opportunities to license the technology to other companies. That's the revenue-generation option. In theory, patents can also be used to block other companies from copying intellectual property through litigation. However, as Eagle notes, it's not realistic or even desirable for a small company like Glanris to wield patents in that way:

We didn't pursue patents because we thought we could block competitors with similar ideas, because there's just too much activity in this sector. At this point, the general idea of carbon-based filtration, and even different ways to use rice hulls and other agricultural waste are out in the public. To the extent that activated carbon was ever patented, those patents are old and expired, and have become prior art that everyone is free to use. Still, patents do have an important value as a defensive mechanism. And that's really what motivated us, to create a clear defense in case a competitor decided to claim we were infringing on their intellectual property. Now we can say we are operating inside our own patent, that we own this intellectual property related to treating rice hulls to produce our biochar™ filtration media. So we don't have to worry about our rights to that process being challenged. When it comes to new intellectual property for Glanris, we're actually keeping a lot of the details of our production process as trade secrets, rather than patenting it.

From Technical Innovation to Business Growth

As an experienced entrepreneur, Bryan Eagle knows all too well that developing an innovative technology, even one that outperforms its competition and addresses a critical worldwide environmental issue, doesn't guarantee that a startup will succeed in the market. As the CEO, he is responsible for leading the business planning and market entry strategies, winning early customers, ramping up revenue, and attracting investors. It's a daunting task for Eagle and his small team in Memphis.

The market entry strategy was straightforward, at least in terms of the order in which Glanris would proceed. There are three major market sectors for water filtration solutions in the US: industrial, residential, and the public sector, such as municipal wastewater treatment systems. All of these markets would benefit from adopting the high performance, lower priced filtration media that Glanris would produce from rice hulls in place of the traditional activated carbon media.

After surveying the full market opportunity, Eagle concluded that the first entry point for Glanris should be the industrial sector, in particular manufacturing firms that used water in their production process. An important selling point to early adopters was that the Glanris filtration media was ready to use in a company's existing gravity filters, exchange tanks, and pressure filters. No new equipment or system modifications would be needed. In addition to removing more water contamination at a faster rate than competing filters, the Glanris filtration media is lighter and faster drying, reducing the cost of disposal. Manufacturers that were heavy water users and needed to clean up their water either for reuse or for disposal would see a clear ROI from the lower costs and higher filtration capabilities that Glanris provided. The sustainability factor would be a bonus for customers.

Proof of Concept: Glanris Implementation for Modine Manufacturing

To demonstrate their value proposition to industrial clients, the Glanris team worked on a proof of concept implementation with Modine Manufacturing, a major US producer of integrated heating and cooling solutions for the HVAC industry. Modine was searching for a more effective approach to cleaning the water in the tanks they used for testing the compressor coils in their HVAC systems. Testing the coils for leaks involved submerging them in a large tank of clear water and watching for bubbles. The resulting contamination issues proved to be a perfect test case for the Glanris solution.

Because the coils are covered in oil and other lubricants when they come off the Modine manufacturing line, the water in the test tanks is quickly clouded, and the oily substances start to accumulate, interfering with the testing process. Other filtration methods that Modine had tried were not effective in dealing with oils and lubricants, so the company had resorted to time-consuming manual cleaning of its tanks. Manual cleaning required draining the tank of the dirty water, scrubbing it with chemicals, and refilling the tank. This manual process was not only a time consuming, expensive use of labor, it was wasting thousands of gallons of water and adding caustic chemicals to the tanks. As described in a case study on the Glanris website:

> Glanris, in partnership with a regional water services company, designed the GESO 2P mobile skid filtration system that skimmed the contaminants off the water surface, and then passed them through exchange tanks containing Glanris $901x$ media. The media did not foul in the presence of the dirt, oils, and solvents contaminants. Within a few minutes, the clarity of the water began to improve and within two hours, the water surface was clear and virtually free of visible debris. Over the course of daily operation, the accumulation of debris on the bottom of the tank was also eliminated. The portable design of the skid allows it to be used on multiple pools within the plant.
>
> In addition to the process improvements, the implementation of Glanris technology eliminated the need of twenty man-hours per month to clean and refill the test ponds. It also eliminated the discarding of 5,000 gallons of water to drain. These were the savings for one pond [testing tank]. The customer now uses this unit on multiple ponds.
>
> According to Michael Franklin, Plant Manager, Modine Manufacturing Company, "The Glanris Filtration Skid has provided clear water, facilitated a more efficient quality assurance process, minimized maintenance costs and allows us to reuse, instead of dumping our wastewater."

The Modine Manufacturing installation provided a convincing demonstration that the Glanris filtration solution would live up to claims of better performance, even in a challenging industrial application. Modine's early adoption paved the way for additional firms to consider switching to Glanris filtration, helping the startup to build its pipeline of industrial customers.

Another attractive entry point for Glanris is the residential filtration market, a fast-growing sector with increased adoption spurred by consumer concerns surrounding water safety and purity. As in the industrial sector, Glanris is pursuing a business-to-business sales strategy. Instead of selling directly to consumers, the company is working to establish partnerships with water filtration manufacturers and vendors. Leading brands in this sector include companies such as A.O. Smith Corporation, Brita, Pentair, and Culligan International.

In summer 2021, Glanris received NSF/ANSI/CAN 61 certification of its $901x$ Biocarbon filtration media by the International Association of Plumbing and Mechanical Officials. This certification was a major milestone in the company's ability to expand its sales efforts beyond the manufacturing sector. It opened the door to the adoption of the Glanris filtration media for products designed for residential drinking water filtration including the ubiquitous filtered water pitchers and refrigerators with built-in water dispensers.

According to Eagle, the municipal wastewater treatment market is the most challenging and slow moving of the three water filtration markets, so it will be a somewhat later target for sales after the company has established a foothold in the industrial and residential sectors. That said, treatment of municipal wastewater is a huge market with ever-growing filtration needs. The NSF/ANSI/CAN 61 certification of Glanris media means that its solution can now be sold in bulk for municipal water treatment systems and for testing in applications ranging from point-of-entry to point-of-use.

After several years of building up a market reputation for high-performance filtration, establishing business partnerships, and delivering proof of concept installations such as the one for Modine Manufacturing, 2021 has been a breakthrough year for the company's growth, customer acquisitions, and revenues.

In March 2021, Glanris announced two major milestones, a $2 million Series A venture investment that included funding from Riceland, Pittco Capital, Innova, and Sage as well as the opening of its first local production facility just across the Mississippi River from Memphis in Olive Branch, MI. This facility will allow Glanris to produce up to three tons of filtration media per day using its patented processes.

There is reason for optimism that the plant will soon be at capacity. Glanris attracted five new customers in the first half of 2021, including a major international distributor with the potential to generate over $2.5 million in business during 2022. Glanris is sending out proposals to interested prospects every week, with over $2 million in new proposals under consideration by prospects large enough to fill its customer pipeline for 2022.

Eagle acknowledges that raising investor capital for Glanris took longer and was a lot harder than he had anticipated when he became CEO. Being an older founder was one among several challenges he faced in getting investors to commit to the new venture. As a long-time entrepreneur with a series of profitable company exits in the communications and telecom space, he had been confident that he could attract the attention of a number of past investors. Attention, however, didn't convert into dollars in the case of Glanris. The company's focus on the water filtration sector, combined with its location in Memphis, turned out to be disincentives for many of Eagle's former investors. As Eagle remembers, even solving a global environmental challenge with a patented technology didn't overcome an ingrained reluctance among many investors to look outside their comfort zone:

> It turns out that a lot of investors don't grasp the importance and potential of water purification as a growth sector. It may seem like investors are always talking about their commitment to socially responsible investing, climate tech solutions, ESG and impact investing. But that's not really where they are putting their money right now. Some funds just want to invest in a sector that they already know, something with a

thin veneer of social impact. When I presented the Glanris opportunity, I realized that investors were just not willing to think about branching out into the water and filtration sector. They would say, "Bryan, I love you, and I'd invest in you heading up a telecom company any time. But I don't know anything about water. So I have to pass on Glanris."

That was pretty much the same thing I had said after my first meeting with the Glanris co-founders. So I tried to convince these investors with all the data about the global water crisis, and how Glanris had developed a transformational approach to filtration, a technology that was more effective than the competition and also cut back on agricultural waste. But in the end, a lot of the investors I approached just wouldn't budge. They wanted more telecom deals, and that was all they would consider.

Location was also a deterrent to investors who were focused on expanding their portfolio of startups in the Bay Area, where almost 80% of venture money still originates. The remaining funds are scattered around the west and the east coasts, with a bit in Austin, Portland, and Chicago. Memphis was a stretch too far for most VCs.

As Eagle notes, all startup companies are well advised to seek out local investors. Ultimately, Glanris was lucky in that regard. In part because of his own work supporting the technology and startup community in Memphis, the city had an established agricultural technology fund, which was a great match for the Glanris solution. There were also a few local family offices that were very interested in both climate change and in making ESG and impact investments, particularly ones that were located in Memphis so that the company could help to create knowledge-based jobs and pull knowledge-based employees into Memphis.

In positioning Glanris for future growth, Eagle believes the company has compelling competitive advantages. In an early implementation at an automotive parts manufacturing plant, the Glanris filters proved to be up to

20% more effective in removing the target contaminants, and achieved these results in one third of the time and at one tenth of the cost of competing filtration methods. In addition to its high performance, it has the advantage of being a local source of filtration media for the North American market:

> We're the only manufacturer of activated carbon in the United States for drinking water applications. The other filtration media either comes from China, India or Sri Lanka, where they use coconut shells. Currently, there are lots of delivery issues and challenges in moving containers of this media across the ocean. So I think we're uniquely positioned on that front to have an advantage selling in North America for the near term. We are working hard to leverage our 'made locally' component.

Eagle expects to be fully occupied with establishing a strong pipeline and customer base in the industrial, residential, and eventually municipal wastewater filtration sectors for the next few years. At the same time, he is already thinking about opportunities for international expansion. Not only is Asia a major rice-growing location, it's a region already suffering from the impact of water scarcity and pollution. For that international expansion, he hopes to create an ecosystem of partnerships and joint venture opportunities possibly based on licensing the Glanris process.

His long-term business goal is to build Glanris as fast as possible, to achieve its first $100 million dollars in revenue, and keep on growing the company from there. Eagle is optimistic about future growth:

> With Glanris, I think we've got an opportunity to create a multi-billion-dollar company. The need for high-performing filtration is enormous, across the industrial, residential, and wastewater sectors in the US to start. We are also planning to expand our reach internationally through partnering and licensing. Finally, in the long run we will work on expanding the classes of contaminants that we can deal with, in water

and even beyond to address air filtration. All these steps will become the foundation for expanding our market reach and increasing revenues.

Historically, there hasn't been a lot of innovation in the water filtration space. Today, the pressure is on water sector leaders to figure out how to enable water reuse by removing contamination more effectively. Effective in terms of actually removing the toxic chemicals, and in terms of doing that at realistic price points for market adoption. Glanris can offer both of those advantages. So there might be acquisition offers from some of the industry giants, but there's no rush to the exit—that's in the future, after we have grown a lot more.

Reflections on Being an Entrepreneur Over 50

As Eagle reflects on his decision to join Glanris as a co-founder, he thinks about the advantages and the challenges that an older entrepreneur brings to a startup, as well what attracts him and other serial entrepreneurs to companies that are aiming to change the world for the better:

> One advantage of having decades of startup experience is that you develop an instinct about how and when to pivot, whether due to a positive opening, or to a setback. When an unexpected opportunity appears, experienced founders have some history to analyze the pros and cons before deciding to jump right on it. And you have probably learned to keep away from the type of jumps that put the whole business at risk. Conversely, when you hit a brick wall, as every startup will, you know that it's possible to pivot your way around it and keep on going. And you can assure your team and your investors that the company will survive and become stronger.

Eagle also has learned that there are downsides to being an older entrepreneur. It is a lot harder to convince investors to support your ideas, especially when it comes to the VC funds, as most of them are not interested in entrepreneurs over a certain age. VC funds gravitate toward founders in their twenties and thirties, reflecting the widespread belief that innovation and high energy are characteristic of that age cohort. Eagle agrees that founders need to be infused with energy; he just doesn't see that as being an exclusive quality of the young.

> I've definitely met people who are younger than me, and who can't keep up the pace I'm used to setting as a CEO. One thing I enjoy about being an entrepreneur is the challenge to move faster, and accomplish more, than managers working in established companies. It would drive me crazy to do the same thing every day. I knew that by agreeing to become CEO at Glanris, I had signed on to wake up every morning, and so to speak, eat nails for breakfast, and be ready to accomplish whatever needs to be done to keep the company on course from day to day. That level of energy level is a personal element, and age is only one factor that impacts it.
>
> That said, I still run into the widespread misconception that energy and ambition are exclusive to younger founders and entrepreneurs. Seeing the age of Glanris' founding team, a lot of people ask me outright, "When are you going to bring some young people into your team?" Of course, we're hiring young people, we're bringing young people into the team, and we are working hard to diversify our ranks as we grow here, and that's very important to us.
>
> At the same time, frankly, we are happy to hire some very experienced older talent who know how to steer Glanris to the next stage of growth. That expertise is a real asset to a fast-growing company.

Eagle is a firm believer that building up the collective talent of the management team, and hiring smart, is essential for success. As a founder, he knows when to get out of the way of the experts he hires, and how to take charge of executing on the core ideas:

I've never seen any single founder, no matter how experienced an entrepreneur, who could do everything on their own. Some founders may take credit for their company's success after the fact, but in reality, growth always takes a team approach. That means recruiting the most talented people, ideally the folks who know more than you do, and who are willing to help steer the company. Honestly, when I find myself in any organization where I'm the smartest person in the room, I don't want to be there. That's not a formula for success. It's not a secret strategy by any means. I've heard that John Houston, the director, was asked once, what's the secret to making a good movie, and he said, hiring the right actors. It's basically the same, with startups—you have to get the right people into the team because every startup is going to hit the wall at many points in its evolution. Sometimes you hit that wall multiple times a day, multiple times a week, and when that happens to inexperienced founders, it will be crushing. Every founder, no matter how smart and seasoned, has to have a team that can figure out how to overcome recurring obstacles.

I didn't come up with the Glanris filtration technology innovations, or work out the original production details. I know that in this field, I need support from the best water filtration experts we can hire. My role is to manage the execution. In the long run, execution is the dividing line between outstanding success and failure to achieve the company's potential. There are so many great technical solutions that don't turn into billion-dollar, or even $100 million-dollar businesses because of team limitations and problems with execution.

Three years after deciding to join Glanris as co-founder and CEO, Bryan Eagle is still hooked on the company's potential to provide cleaner water and reduce pollution around the world. He has no regrets about stepping off his previous path to entrepreneurial success in telecom and communications to take on a whole new set of challenges. In fact, as an older entrepreneur, he can't imagine being in a better place:

You know, founders don't start new companies to do the same old thing. There's a drive to create change, to be a change agent. I realized that everything that I've done in my career, and every new company I've helped to grow was founded to make something better. There aren't many technology innovations out there that can make a massive impact on essential resources like water and clean air, something that 100% of every living thing on the planet needs daily, right? And there aren't many opportunities to tackle such urgent global issues with solutions that are so powerful and so affordable. If Glanris is adopted worldwide, it will help to transform water availability, water security, and remove massive amounts of carbon from the environment. That's a transformation to be proud of.

References

IBISWorld (2021) Bottled Water Production in the US–Market Size 2002–2027. IBISWorld Industry Statistics.

Mack E A, Wrase S (2017) A Burgeoning Crisis? A Nationwide Assessment of the Geography of Water Affordability in the United States. *PLoS ONE* 12(1): e0169488. pmid:28076374.

Riggs E (2017) An Overview of Clean Water Access Challenges in the United States. Environmental Finance Center at the University of North Carolina, Chapel Hill School of Government.
https://efc.sog.unc.edu/sites/default/files/2018/
An%20Overview%20of%20Clean%20Water%20Access%20
Challenges%20in%20the%20United%20States.Final.pdf.
Accessed on October 15, 2021.

United Nations (2021) Summary Progress Update 2021: SDG 6 Water and sanitation for all. https://www.unwater.org/publications/summary-progress-update-2021-sdg-6-water-and-sanitation-for-all.
Accessed on October 15, 2021.

About the Bryan Eagle III

Bryan Eagle III

Bryan Eagle joined Glanris in 2018 as CEO and co-founder. He is a seasoned entrepreneur and an award-winning strategic planning and business development leader with over twenty-five years of experience. He has led multiple companies toward successful exits, including the acquisition of his own startups by global corporations.

Eagle learned to love startup ventures in his twenties, when he became the twelfth employee at the Discovery Channel in 1985 to help launch the fledgling cable network. He left Discovery Channel in 1987 to join Cylix Communications Corporation, a specialized provider of satellite and fiber managed data networks. Eagle was part of the team that led the management buyout of Cylix from GE. After a successful turnaround of the business, Cylix was sold to France Telecom in 1993.

That experience sparked another business passion—growing and selling companies that leveraged digital technology, wireless networks, and data. In 1993, he founded Skywire, an early Internet of Things company, raising over $12 million in venture funding to accelerate its growth. Skywire attracted a customer roster that included Coca-Cola Company, Federal Express, and Pepsi Cola, before selling Skywire in 1998 to a British conglomerate. After Skywire, he joined Media4, a pioneer in delivering Internet content over direct broadcast satellite networks, and helped to sell it to EchoStar in

1999. Following that exit, Eagle founded Memphis Ventures, a consulting and investment firm, and launched Emerge Memphis, a nonprofit startup incubator and accelerator.

About the Company

Company	Glanris, Inc.
Website	glanris.com
Founding Year	2018
Co-Founders	Bryan Eagle, III Thomas Volinchak L. Yu Lin
Industry Sector	Filtration
Address	3955 Vantech Drive, #15 Memphis, TN 38115

Part II

Changing the Future

Chapter 8

Co-Generating a Better World: A Framework for Action

by Mary J. Cronin

The urgent issues confronting our society and our planet add up to a compelling case for change. Amid the myriad opinions and debates about how to solve specific problems, *Starting Up Smarter* is focused on a particularly promising but still under-appreciated opportunity for building a better future. Let's work together to realize the potential of older entrepreneurs as they tackle some of our most formidable social and environmental challenges. Our society has much to gain, and nothing to lose, from more actively supporting the strong inclination of founders over 50 to prioritize social impact, shared value, and regenerative sustainability in their companies.

How can we make founders over 50, together with all social impact entrepreneurs, more effective? This book recommends developing an intentional, collaborative framework of entrepreneurial and stakeholder co-generation. As described below, a co-generation approach is ideally suited to harness the social impact mission of millions of founders over 50. By connecting entrepreneurs of all ages with their stakeholders, a co-generation framework can scale to become a powerful spark for a more diverse, cross-generational, and successful cohort of founders, startups, and stakeholders.

A Framework for Action

As we have seen in Part I, older entrepreneurs exhibit a number of traits that expand the value of their businesses for the benefit of employees and customers, and for all other stakeholders. The passion for solving social problems, the skillsets needed to accomplish transformative goals, and the desire to work collaboratively do not expire at a certain age. In fact, the opposite is true. By virtue of their age, older founders are more likely to have experience working in multigenerational teams with younger colleagues. They have also learned to value the expertise and skills of their peers. As a result, founders over 50 recruit employees of all ages, based on shared purpose, willingness to learn new skills, and a commitment to excellence, rather than a rigid algorithm that relies on years of experience in specific types of roles. They work to foster inclusive diversity and cross-generational cohesion, and prioritizing sharing the value that their companies generate with employees and stakeholders.

The intrinsic characteristics of founders over 50, described in Chapter 1 as the entrepreneurial imperatives, and explored in more detail by Doug Dickson in Chapter 10, Leading with Purpose, underscore how programs that empower and support older entrepreneurs are an effective strategy for expanding economic opportunities across the workforce and into the community.

In developing a framework for action to build a better world, it's counterproductive to think in terms of how to divide up a fixed number of resources among various competing stakeholders. That approach will just pit different ages and interest groups against each other in a zero-sum game. Instead of proposing a series of programs and resources that will exclusively engage with older entrepreneurs, I believe that a strategy of co-generation is the most effective path to creating a better collective future. As the next section discusses, in the contexts where a co-generation strategy has been implemented to date, it has demonstrated system-wide benefits for multiple stakeholders, including features that are critically important for any framework that aims to reach millions of entrepreneurs.

What Is Co-generation?

Recently the term co-generation has been adopted by nonprofit organizations, such as Encore.org, to describe programs that bring multiple generations together for a common cause. The concept of co-generation is not new; in fact, it has been applied for many years as a technical strategy in the energy sector.

COGEN Europe, the European Association for the Promotion of Cogeneration, defines cogeneration [without a hyphen] as an efficient technology to generate electricity and heat. It is also called Combined Heat and Power (CHP) since a cogeneration implementation produces heat and electricity simultaneously (COGEN Europe 2021).

As we consider adopting the concept of cogeneration within the context of older entrepreneurs and social impact startups, it's interesting to note that the COGEN Europe website lists multiple cogeneration benefits in addition to increased energy efficiency, lower emissions, and energy costs. These benefits include enhanced system resilience, scalability, and the flexibility to meet the needs of all types of users, from a single household to a large industrial complex or entire town, resulting in more empowered businesses and citizens.

The US Department of Energy website at energy.gov adds that cogeneration and CHP technology can be deployed quickly, cost-effectively, and with few geographic limitations. CHP can use a variety of fuels, both fossil-based and renewable-based. It has been employed for many years, mostly in industrial, large commercial, and institutional applications.

The 2017 book, *Design as Democracy*, describes how a co-generating strategy works for stakeholders in a community context. The authors of the "Co-generating" chapter are urban planners, environmental designers, and landscape architects. They discuss using a co-generating process to meet the challenges of urban design and collaborative community planning as follows:

Co-generating is the process by which community members and various stakeholders generate designs through active collaboration and critical exchanges. Everyone brings their ideas, knowledge, and skills to the table, and rather than simply soliciting inputs to inform a design, co-generating guides the community and designers through the negotiation of form alternatives and solutions that embody multiple perspectives and values. ...When truly shared, co-generating simultaneously builds and reinforces community as one outcome and defines environmental intervention as another (de la Pena D et al. 2017).

Change the lens on this *Design as Democracy* description of co-generation from urban design and community planning to entrepreneurs, stakeholders, and social impact startups, and this process provides an excellent model for productively bringing together entrepreneurs of all ages, with potential team members and customers, community members, and all interested stakeholders to craft powerful, shared value strategies for starting and growing companies.

To avoid confusion in overlapping terminology between the energy sector, urban design, and the application of 'co-generation' to a variety of multigenerational programs, the framework for action proposed in this chapter will be referred to as entrepreneur+stakeholder co-generation and defined as follows:

A co-generation initiative that connects entrepreneurs who want to make a positive social impact through their companies with stakeholders who want to shape and support their efforts with the mutual goal of generating value for society.

Granted, appreciating the power of co-generation models in other sectors is one thing, while actually implementing practical, on-the-ground co-generation programs to unleash the world-changing potential of older entrepreneurs is quite another. Fortunately, the core characteristics of cost effectiveness, speedy deployment, geographic reach, and scalability make it feasible for multiple organizations to try out the entrepreneur+stakeholder co-generation model in experimental or pilot mode. Pilot implementations that meet the organization's objectives and demonstrate generative value can be expanded to benefit an ever-widening circle of entrepreneurs and stakeholders. Public sector, educational, and nonprofit organizations that are already providing services and resources to entrepreneurs across the age spectrum can integrate co-generation elements into their existing programs.

For example, college and university entrepreneurship centers and courses that are traditionally limited to students can provide meaningful opportunities for co-generation by intentionally inviting older, experienced entrepreneurs and community stakeholders to participate along with potential business partners. Nonprofit, corporate, and public sector services geared to older employees, aspiring entrepreneurs, and small business owners can reach out to younger stakeholders to facilitate intergenerational co-generation initiatives. All of these organizations can work with private equity and venture firms to sponsor programs that support intergenerational entrepreneurs moving from ideation, to team formation, to business model development, and to implementation plans.

Connecting Millions of Entrepreneurs

A brief review of how many entrepreneurs are starting new companies each year, including older founders focused on positive social impact, spotlights the critical importance of a scalable framework for action and the advantages of an entrepreneur+stakeholder co-generation model.

"The diversity of interest in later-life entrepreneurship" study by Halvorsen and Chen estimates that more than thirty-one million Americans between the ages of fifty and seventy have an interest in entrepreneurship and founding a business. The authors note that the economic and social benefits of supporting the entrepreneurial aspirations of older adults include boosting overall economic activity, employment, and growth as well as potentially providing an extended period of income and financial security later in life.

These benefits apply to all types of startups, regardless of whether the founder has a social impact mission. The study also reports on the most important motivations for those highly interested in entrepreneurship. An estimated 6.5 million older adults prioritize a positive social impact when planning to found a company, with over 20% stating that their primary reason for starting a new company would be to meet a social challenge or to help others. (Halvorsen C and Chen Y 2019).

The findings of the *Global Entrepreneurship Monitor (GEM) 2020/2021 Global Report*, based on interviews with nearly 140,000 people ages eighteen to sixty-four from forty-six economies by a global team of researchers, underscore the increasing numbers of older founders. Across all the economies studied, the authors noted that interest in founding new businesses (Total early-stage Entrepreneurial Activity, or TEA rate in the parlance of the report) had increased significantly among older entrepreneurs in the past two years, in contrast to their younger counterparts:

> Interestingly, GEM data for 2020 show that, for the oldest age-group, ages fifty-five to sixty-four, levels of TEA had actually increased compared to 2019 in many more economies than it had decreased, while the opposite is the case for all other age groups. While the pandemic has certainly impacted the health of older people more than younger people, the evidence tells us that many seniors are still starting new businesses (Bosma N et al. 2021).

This finding coincides with the age of entrepreneurship data in the 2021 Kauffman Indicators of Entrepreneurship report on early-stage entrepreneurship in the United States, concluding that older adults represent a growing segment of the US entrepreneurial population (Fairlie R and Desai S 2021).

The US section of the GEM report notes that more than thirty million Americans of all ages were starting or operating newly founded businesses during 2020, while an additional 19.5 million entrepreneurs were running established businesses. According to the Business Formation Statistics tracked by the United States Census Bureau, a record-breaking number of applications were filed during the first six months of 2021 to form new businesses. Almost one million of these companies were classified as likely to hire employees in 2021. Even in the midst of a pandemic, the entrepreneurial urge remains strong.

However, the US GEM study also reported more sobering data on startup trends in the past two years: over 8.5 million existing businesses had to shut down during 2020, often because of the disruptions caused by the global pandemic. This represented a 50% increase in closure rates compared to 2019. Among new entrepreneurs in the US surveyed by the GEM researchers, 82% responded that starting a business in 2020 was more difficult than it had been in the past.

The US GEM study also reported on the interest (intention) in starting a company among black and women entrepreneurs. Notably, black entrepreneurs expressed twice as much interest and intention as white respondents in starting a new business. However, black entrepreneurs who had already started companies reported a higher rate of business closures in the past year, and black entrepreneurs were only half as likely as white entrepreneurs to be running an established business. Early stage entrepreneurial activity was also lower among women than men, a pattern that is consistent with previous years world-wide and in the US. The GEM data underscores the need for strategies to increase diversity among founders of all ages, as well as the importance of helping entrepreneurs to connect with stakeholders during the often precarious early years of business operation.

Clearly, there is an unmet need to support the goals of entrepreneurs of all ages and backgrounds who share a mission to change the world through business. Notwithstanding the success of the founders over 50 featured in Part I, and the research documenting that older founders consistently outperform their younger counter parts, the harsh reality is that almost half of all companies started in the US will not survive more than five years. For all the inspiring stories celebrated in this and other studies of older entrepreneurs who are focused on solving the most urgent issues—climate change, water scarcity, health care costs, senior caregiving and companionship, and more—there are literally millions of aspiring entrepreneurs with transformational ideas waiting to launch, searching for co-founders, team members, investors, suppliers, or other resources that will enable them to move from vision to startup implementation. These millions represent essential resources for changing the future.

As Bryan Eagle of Glanris notes in Chapter 7, entrepreneurs are natural drivers of change, and older founders are especially motivated to make the world a better place:

> You know, founders don't start new companies to do the same old thing. There's a drive to create change, to be a change agent. I realized that everything that I've done in my career, and every new company I've helped to grow was founded to make something better.

Change Agents with a Mission

The four contributed chapters in Part II provide expert insights on the many roles that older entrepreneurs and innovators play as change agents. These chapters amplify and complement Part I and validate that far from being uncommon, the social impact accomplishments of the founders and companies described in Part I represent a widespread and recurring pattern. The Part II authors provide strong evidence that older entrepreneurs are already hard at work creating new value, often while addressing today's most challenging issues. In the process they are developing solutions and resources that will help us all to live more equitable, sustainable, and productive lives in harmony with each other and the planet we all share.

In Chapter 9, "Highlights for Children: Across the Generations," Kent Johnson, the company's fourth-generation CEO, reflects on his great-grandparent's world-changing goals for *Highlights Magazine*, how their founding vision has impacted the lives of millions of children and their families, and steered the company through its seventy-five years of operation. Notably, long before the popularity of corporate social responsibility and stakeholder expectations for shared value, the *Highlights* founders pioneered a focus on social mission and purpose rather than profits. One example: as child development experts, founders Caroline and Garry Myers took a stand against bombarding children with ads to bring in revenues for their magazine. That principled stand is still in effect at *Highlights*. Most print publications depended heavily on advertising to balance their budgets in the past century, and that dependence has only increased over time. Today's digital media giants have built billion-dollar revenue streams based on advertising, often slanting their content to boost these revenues. *Highlights*, in contrast, has become a digital publishing leader and maintains a high subscriber base for its print publications, while abiding by the founders' vision of putting children first.

In Chapter 10, "Leading with Purpose," Doug Dickson analyzes stage of life research to explore the impetus to solve urgent social problems and to design durability and long-term impact into their organizations that is a predominant characteristic of older founders. As Dickson notes:

> This research suggests that people over 50 are more likely, simply because of their age and life stage, to be generous in thinking about or responding to the needs of others, more open to new opportunities they may have missed or sidestepped earlier in life, more positive in their outlook, and more focused in the face of challenges. These attributes suggest that older adults are, in many ways, primed for entrepreneurship. When added to deep business and related experience accumulated during earlier stages of life, this helps to explain their success as founders.

In Chapter 11, "Inventing Over 50," Scott Guthery analyzes data derived from over seven million patents granted in the US between 1976 and 2020 to demonstrate that far from experiencing a decrease in innovative drive or ability, older inventors are highly productive. Inventors frequently receive multiple new patents after the age of fifty. A particularly interesting finding refutes the misconception that older employees are less likely to contribute new technical ideas to multigenerational teams. In summarizing his analysis of all patents with multiple inventors, compared to the set of patents with multiple inventors in which at least one inventor is over 50, Guthery notes:

> What runs counter to given wisdom is that the presence of an over-50-inventor on the patent increases the probability that the patent was a team effort by about 40%...Whatever the cause, the data on patents with multiple inventors combined with the estimated age of the inventors contradicts the view that older inventors are not as likely as their younger colleagues to collaborate or to work effectively in teams that are focused on innovation. To the contrary, this data points to the conclusion that older inventors are important catalysts for innovation within teams.

In Chapter 12, "Models for Regenerative Sustainability," Rick Terrien discusses the affinity of older entrepreneurs for prioritizing sustainability goals and implementing circular economy models. Terrien emphasizes the far-reaching impact that even small startups and their founders can make as they join sustainability-focused, cross-generational business ecosystems. As Terrien notes:

> Increasing sustainability within one organization creates increasing sustainability within their broader ecosystems, from suppliers to buyers. This virtuous circle means that even small startups that focus on sustainable solutions can be positively leveraged as part of broader, interconnected business networks. As these networks grow in numbers, and spring up in different industry sectors, their participants have access to shared experience, new innovations, strategic skills, and increased capacity so that each network grows more valuable for everyone involved.

Terrien's observations about the multiplier effect of circular economy and sustainability ecosystems reinforce the natural synergy between models for regenerative sustainability and a framework for action based on entrepreneurial+stakeholder co-generation.

What Next?

There are many organizations in the US and around the globe working to change the world for the better. But there are not nearly enough groups or resources dedicated to connecting the millions of entrepreneurs of all ages who have already founded, or aspire to start, social impact focused companies. The possibilities for productive entrepreneurial+stakeholder co-generation are limitless. Perhaps the most straightforward co-generation stimulus is providing opportunities for entrepreneurs to find each other and coalesce into the kinds of partnerships, teams, and short-term intersectional groupings that will help them at particular points on their path to social impact and company maturation.

Whether deployed on a small, grassroots scale, by informal collectives, or by national organizations, every new entrepreneur+stakeholder co-generation initiative will increase the chances of startup success, and contribute to a transformational change in our shared future.

I hope that the following Part II chapters, together with the founder stories highlighted in Part I of *Starting Up Smarter*, will motivate and inspire stakeholders and entrepreneurs of all ages to join forces in co-generating world-changing solutions for the twenty-first century.

References

Bosma N et al. (2021) 2020/2021 *Global Report Global Entrepreneurship Monitor (GEM)*.

COGEN Europe (2021) Website accessed online on October 20, 2021 https://www.cogeneurope.eu/knowledge-centre/what-is-cogeneration.

Fairlie, R. and Desai, S (2021) *National Report on Early-Stage Entrepreneurship in the United States: 2020. Kaufmann Indicators of Entrepreneurship*.

Halvorsen C and Chen YC (2019) The diversity of interest in later-life entrepreneurship: Results from a nationally representative survey of Americans aged 50 to 70. *PLoS One.* 2019;14(6):e0217971.

Pena, D et al. (2017) "Co-generating" pp. 165–194 in *Design as Democracy: Techniques for Collective Creativity*, Island Press.

US Department of Energy 2021. Website Accessed online on October 20, 2021 https://www.energy.gov/eere/amo/combined-heat-and-power-basics.

About the Author

Mary J. Cronin, Ph.D. is a Research Professor at the Carroll School of Management, Boston College and the President of 4Q Catalyst. Her research and teaching focuses on corporate social impact, entrepreneurship, the future of work, and business transformation. She designed an interdisciplinary minor in Managing for Social Impact and the Public Good for undergraduates at Boston College.

Mary offers consulting services to social entrepreneurs and purpose-oriented companies. She is a nonprofit director for the Center for Ageless Entrepreneurship and the Encore Boston Network, and a co-founder of the Founders Over 55 Collective at the Cambridge Innovation Center AGENCY hub. Her research, consulting, and nonprofit work combined with her entrepreneurial advising to inspire *Starting Up Smarter: Why Founders Over 50 Build Better Companies*.

Mary has authored or edited ten prior books including Managing for Social Impact: Innovations in Responsible Enterprise with Tiziana Dearing (Springer, 2017); *Top Down Innovation* (Springer 2014); *Smart Products, Smarter Services* (Cambridge University Press 2010). Earlier books include the international best sellers *Doing Business on the Internet* and *The Internet Strategy Handbook*, as well as *Unchained Value: The New Logic of Digital Business*; *Banking and Finance on the Internet*; *Mobile Application Development* with Scott Guthery, and numerous entrepreneurship, management, social impact, and digital strategy articles.

Chapter 9

Highlights for Children: Across the Generations

by Kent Johnson

Fun with a Purpose: Founding Highlights

On a March day in 1946, a middle-aged couple, married over thirty years, prepared to take the stage in rural Bradford, PA, to give a talk on child development and family life. They'd been on the lecture circuit for years now, traveling across America by car and train, living out of suitcases for months at a time. In 1944 and 1945 alone, the pair's popular lectures, delivered in a crowd-pleasing town hall style, had reached some 64,000 people, kids and adults, in 119 cities.

But before they could inform and entertain the group assembled in Bradford, someone handed them an imperiously worded telegram from their boss, publisher of the kids' magazine *Children's Activities*.

"Information of your proposed publishing venture has reached me," it began. "If true, your resignation effective March thirty-first after completing your present itinerary is demanded. If not true, present proof at once."

Leaving aside the impossibility of proving a negative, the proposed publishing venture was true. At sixty-one and fifty-eight, respectively, Garry and Caroline Myers—my great-grandparents—topped the masthead at *Chil-*

dren's Activities. The publisher had deployed their reputations and considerable energies as a marketing juggernaut for the magazine, but he refused to grant them authority over what would appear in its pages. In their long hours on the road, Garry and Caroline had talked about just what a kids' periodical would look like if they had their way. That January, they, together with a handful of other couples working for *Children's Activities*, had pledged to make this vision a reality. The boss's telegram merely accelerated their timeline.

Garry and Caroline were supremely confident about the ways in which their new publication would nourish the growth of children and the well-being of families. Still, they had little inkling of how their fledgling publishing company would itself adapt, grow, and thrive, becoming, seventy-five years later, a multi-product, multi-platform family-owned brand reaching millions of children in the U.S. and around the world, with more than 500 employees, and their own great-grandson as CEO.

These forebears—we at Highlights are apt to call them simply "the founders"—thought of their magazine as a capstone project—a "memorial," Garry said, reflecting their life-long experience and careers as experts in education, child psychology, and family life. So who were these two people, born in the nineteenth century, whose legacy persists so palpably in the twenty-first?

My great-grandparents both grew up in close-knit rural communities of Pennsylvania, surrounded by kin. Their families encouraged hard work and learning, shunned ostentation, and instilled an everyday ethic that called on each person to consider their words and actions. The two met at Ursinus College northwest of Philadelphia, beginning their habit of far-ranging conversation on their long walks together. They married in 1912 in Caroline's hometown church in Boyds Mills, Pennsylvania, which her Sunday school class had decked out with masses of local rhododendrons.

Caroline and Garry launched an extraordinary partnership in which the personal and professional were fully intertwined. In its equality, their marriage was ahead of its time. Garry was a generative, imaginative thinker,

Caroline a highly organized and pragmatic one. Each valued and needed the other's contributions to the work they shared.

They both pursued formal education, Garry earning a PhD in psychology from Columbia University not long after their wedding and Caroline, while in her early forties during the 1930s, undertaking grant-supported studies in early childhood education at Detroit's Merrill Palmer School and Columbia University Teachers College.

They were accomplished educators. To earn their way through college, they instructed children in country schools. They taught literacy to World War I recruits. For twenty years Garry was a psychology professor at the Cleveland School of Education of Western Reserve University (later Case Western Reserve University). In Cleveland, Caroline taught some of the country's first prenatal and parenting classes, helping to ignite a movement that brought a humane, scientifically enlightened approach to child rearing. Garry devised a curriculum and inaugurated the Department of Parent Education at Western Reserve.

The couple's editorial output was prodigious. They published a series on teaching literacy, workbooks for school children, and a number of books for popular audiences on childhood and family life. From 1929 until his death forty years later, Garry penned a six-days-a-week syndicated newspaper column, "The Parent Problem," which addressed, in a warm, intimate tone, concerns and queries from the parent letters that poured into the Myers household for all those years. In the 1920s and 1930s, Garry became editorial advisor and sometimes editor-writer for some of America's first children's periodicals, including *Child Play*, *Babyhood* (for mothers), and *Junior Home*, which went bankrupt in the Depression and reemerged as *Children's Activities*.

Garry and Caroline were also gifted and practiced speakers. "The United States is their laboratory—its people their source material," said a flier for their lecture series in the 1940s. That was a fair statement. They knew their audiences, whether child or adult, general or professional, and understood, by the eager crowds that came to hear them, that there was appetite for the sensitive exploration of child development they had to give.

Finally—and this was important for the company that would become their late-in-life "dream child," as Garry once put it—they were loving, fascinated parents themselves. By the time they founded Highlights in 1946, they'd raised three kids to adulthood: Jack (born in 1913), Betty (1915), and Garry Jr. (1922). The couple took an ordinary parental delight in watching each unique child's development unfold, but their observations were unusually close and scientific. It entered family lore that as a little boy, firstborn Jack (who would later become a molecular chemist) joined in his parents' studies. After creating a picture or story of note, he'd call out buoyantly, "Take a record!"

So the Meyerses had a lot going for them when they started Highlights, including a reputation and platform, a wide network of personal and professional allies, deep experience, and a variety of finely honed skills. But their most important asset was an enormous zest for pouring all their talents into a single product for children—one that would cleave to their philosophy, encapsulated in the tagline that appeared on the very first issue of *Highlights*: "Fun with a Purpose."

Their "great treasure book of fun" for ages two to twelve would be full of stories, puzzles, articles, jokes, activities, and drawings carefully designed to call forth each child's natural curiosity, creativity, and empathy. Garry and Caroline passionately believed that, whatever their ability level, all kids are thinkers who can learn and grow while taking pleasure in the process. They thought kids would learn values through gentle, affirmative suggestion, build social skills by exploring just what it is that makes people laugh, and stretch their limits as readers in order to decipher the few words under a particularly charming illustration or pick up enticing details in a scientifically accurate piece on bugs. The pair wanted to bring families together around their treasure book, convinced that positive human bonds (not rote reward and correction) are the greatest motivators on earth. They wanted to show their young audience a world at once endlessly fascinating and blessedly safe. Caroline and Garry took care that everything appearing in Highlights, including Garry's editor's notes directly addressing kids, modeled and encouraged moral courage (standing up for what's right, even when it's hard), civility and kindness, nonviolence, respect for nature, and celebration of human diversity in all its forms.

What the Myerses didn't have as they embarked on this venture: much capital, business know-how, or indeed interest in business per se. They saw these things as the means to an end—their publication and its positive influence on children, of course. This bifurcation in their mission was symbolized and reinforced by a physical separation between the Highlights "business side," headquartered in Columbus, Ohio, where they'd located a printer, and the "editorial side," located in Honesdale, Pennsylvania, near Boyds Mills, where the pair had settled in the renovated homestead founded in 1867 by Caroline's grandparents.

With the Myerses' insistence on high-quality content, printing, and paper amid post-war shortages, the magazine was expensive to produce. There were no newsstand sales and no revenue from advertising, which Garry and Caroline banned as inappropriate for a children's periodical. Income came only from subscriptions, which were sold by independent salespeople who fanned out in neighborhoods to call on mothers at home. Door-to-door was the dominant mode of selling magazines at the time, and some Highlights salespeople were talented pitch-people enthusiastic about the product. But recruiting and training them was laborious, and it was tough for sales reps to earn a good living without leads to make their legwork efficient.

The Early Years

If Highlights' first years out of the gate were creatively exciting, they were little short of harrowing from a business perspective. There was rising tension with the tiny company's head of sales, who, along with his wife and the Myerses, had invested his savings in Highlights, but who proved less than effective at ramping up subscriptions fast enough to keep up with costs. After 1948, when the Myerses moved to an even more expensive printing company in Indianapolis, there was mounting debt. This resulted in repeated scrounging for cash in order to get the magazine out and the threat of closure when the printer balked at running the presses before his bill was settled. By early 1950, Highlights owed their printer $32,000 for three issues. Garry borrowed $7,500 against his life insurance, and the next issue went forward.

This was hardly a sustainable business plan. Garry and Caroline were sending brave but unmistakably doleful letters to their children, and these adult offspring were worried. In March 1950, their youngest, twenty-seven-year-old Garry Jr., decided to investigate the books, talk to relevant parties, and perhaps help his folks wind down their beloved but troubled enterprise.

What happened next was tantamount to a second founding for Highlights. Garry Jr. and his wife, Mary, leapt into the breach, dedicating their own lives to putting the wobbly startup on its feet. Garry Jr. left his stable, high-paying job as an aeronautics engineer for McDonnell Aircraft Corp., and with their four small children, the couple pulled up stakes in their home of St. Louis and moved to Columbus. Jack, Garry Jr.'s older brother, wrote to him about the move with a sibling's candor. "My first reaction, Garry, was that you are crazy as hell," he observed. "On sober reflection, however, it becomes clear that you are probably the one guy who maybe can pull this off."

Indeed, Garry Jr. had become convinced Highlights was a truly outstanding product that, with perspicacious management, could be sold into the "gigantic" (his word) market represented by America's historic Baby Boom. He became committed not only to the product, but to the mission and philosophy it represented, developed through his parents' life work.

The first job was to raise capital to keep the leaky vessel afloat. Garry Jr. pitched his heart out with help from other family members and staff. His uncle and cousin came through with loans. Top sales and marketing leader Cyril Ewart and his wife, Arlene, mortgaged their lake cabin and gave $1,000. Garry Jr. and Mary took out a loan on their car—their sole asset. Donors opened their pocketbooks—most notably Rollett Carson, a Cleveland surgeon and acquaintance of Garry Jr.'s sister Betty, and the Cleveland philanthropist Dudly Blossom, Jr., who in 1951, agreed to substantially bankroll the struggling Highlights with flexible repayment terms—a role he would play for the next several years.

Just as importantly, Garry Jr. sought advice far and wide, hunting for ways to unlock the magazine's market potential. These efforts yielded the techniques that would introduce Fun with a Purpose to millions of American children. The first breakthrough was the introductory offer through teachers. Each teacher got a sample magazine with an order form to send home with pupils offering a discounted, five-issue introductory subscription. Mary shaped and ran this enormously successful initiative from the Myers home. The second watershed innovation was the reception room program. Here, copies of *Highlights* containing tear-out "inquiry cards" were mailed to kids' doctors and dentists, who would place the magazines in their waiting rooms.

Both of these sales methods linked the magazine with trusted figures who were invested in children's development. By the late 50s these programs were generating hundreds of thousands of solid-gold leads for sales reps, who could follow up with families that already had expressed interest by filling out an inquiry card or buying a short-term subscription. The Highlights salesforce swelled. Subscriptions soared.

To everything there is a season, and the year 1960 dawned as an exuberantly joyful time for Highlights. Garry Jr. no longer labored alone in Highlights' modest, untidy executive office. In 1956, he hired Dick Bell, a powerhouse salesman for Encyclopedia Britannica, who was a friend and neighbor, as director of sales. In April 1960, he rehired Cy Ewart (who'd had to take another job in a particularly lean year) as Vice President for mail sales and public relations, and brought on longtime Highlights counsel Howard Crown as full-time counsel and Vice President of operations. Meanwhile, a new corporate headquarters with room to grow was under construction in Columbus. Financed without debt (lesson learned), this new home opened in May 1960 with an emotional dedication that brought together the entire Highlights family. By this point, that group included the extended Myers clan and many others who, like Garry Jr. himself, had taken up the Highlights mission as their own. They all embraced the dedication Garry Jr. and his folks had recently formulated for Highlights, and that now appeared in every issue. Each issue closed with the words, "for CHILDREN are the world's most important people."

That year concluded with an abrupt and terrible turn. The morning of December 16, 1960, Garry Jr., Mary, and Cy Ewart boarded a flight from Columbus bound for New York City to investigate newsstand sales among other things. They never landed. In the largest air disaster to that date, their plane collided with another jet over New York City. All aboard perished. The catastrophe deeply marked the lives of Garry Jr. and Mary's orphaned children, nieces and nephews, siblings and in-laws. The founders of Highlights, now in their seventies, were utterly stricken. All those who'd worked alongside the three fun, infectiously ardent young leaders grieved at their loss.

Their memory became a guidestar. It led to what might be called a third founding for Highlights. Everyone doubled down on the mission to which the lost had so wholeheartedly given themselves. Dick Bell rebuilt the leadership team to take the company forward, and, working in an airy new headquarters, they collectively put shoulder to the plow. In the 1960s, they began the painstaking task of computerizing operations, which allowed them to fine-tune direct-mail marketing using rented lists (with the help of talented consultants). In 1973, they launched telemarketing as an important complement to mail and door-to-door marketing.

Garry and Caroline never really retired. Instead, they decanted the balance of their years into Highlights; Garry writing prodigiously as ever, Caroline curating contributions, editing, and assembling pages. They watched over the development of successors. Garry died in 1971 at his desk in the Highlights editorial offices in Honesdale. Caroline continued as managing editor until her strength gave out in the late 70s. She passed away in 1980 at nearly ninety-three.

Highlights After the Founders: Transitions and New Business Challenges

Highlights of the 1980s was not too different from Highlights of the 1940s. The company still existed to create one product, the magazine, still marketed by door-to-door salespeople, with direct mail and telemarketing as synergistic adjuncts. It was different, though, in this respect: the business model had come together, and it was working—and working well.

The strength of this developing model drove circulation from 100,000 when Garry Jr. came on in 1950 to half a million at the time of his death a decade later. By 1971, circulation topped a million; the Highlights salesforce numbered 700. Circulation climbed to 2 million by 1980, and even briefly topped three million by 1989. Roughly a century after the founders' births, their "dream child" magazine was the most-read children's periodical on the planet. Kids and adults alike fondly and instantly recognized the special sauce we call Fun with a Purpose. Certain long-running features of the magazine—Hidden Pictures puzzles, for example, and the twin-like characters Goofus and Gallant—constituted brands within the brand. Long apprenticeships and gradual, considered leadership transitions in Honesdale and Columbus made for a steady-as-she-goes corporate culture at the turn of the twentieth century.

Caroline and Garry had mentored Walter Barbe, an educational psychologist specializing in literacy as well as learning disabilities, as editor. He joined the Honesdale team in 1963 and retired in 1986. Along with Caroline, Barbe mentored his successor, Kent Brown Jr. Kent Brown was the son of Garry and Caroline's daughter Betty. He led a redesign of the magazine and created the nonprofit Highlights Foundation to nurture the specialized crafts of writing and illustrating for children. Brown joined in 1971 and retired in 2007. He in turn hired Christine French Cully, who was already a seasoned editor of children's magazines, in 1994. She became editor in chief for the Highlights consumer business in 2007. Today, as chief purpose officer, Cully is a key executive leader, author, podcast host, thought leader, and voice for the Highlights brand.

At Columbus corporate headquarters, President Dick Bell operational-ized and refined marketing approaches. In 1976, he hired Garry Myers III, an MBA with sales experience at Alcoa, as an information analyst in di-rect mail. Under Bell's mentorship, Garry III rose to lead the company, with unerring business ethics and a keen instinct for new opportunities. He served as chief executive from 1981 until his death in 2005 from complica-tions of cancer at the age of fifty-nine.

Garry III began a cautious diversification of Highlights products, plat-forms, and marketing channels. That diversification grew more confident and urgent as changes in technology and society made transformation at Highlights a do-or-die proposition. "No one should make the mistake of thinking profit isn't important," he wrote in our company newsletter, The Purpose, in 1990. A reminder that making money is a goal would have been ludicrously redundant at most corporations. But he went on: "At least as important are such issues as quality and conformance with our philosophy."

This philosophy initially guarded the magazine against the development of new products that, it was feared, would draw off customers from the flagship product and dilute the founders' ideals. This is perhaps why it wasn't until the early 1990s that Highlights launched its first subscription "clubs," offering kids an extra helping of a particular type of Highlights material. This was an idea both Garry Jr. and Dick Bell had championed. The Original Highlights clubs featured content packaged as books or activity kits and provided in a series. Puzzlemania and other clubs surged off the starting blocks and have since delivered over one hundred million shipments to children. This has been a business triumph, and proof that non-magazine products, far from diluting our mission, can powerfully advance it.

The pattern of experimenting with new products, and building on suc-cessful options repeated. Reacting to new challenges may feel like grasping a nettle at first because change is hard. But often, once the work was underway, we've found that what seemed risky at first was opening a door.

As a great-grandson of the founders I, like other Myers relatives, grew up in the atmosphere of Highlights, but without any intention to ever work for the company. I had earned a PhD in physics and was working for a biotech startup in technology development and business operations when I joined the Highlights board of directors in 2002. In the next couple of years, as Garry III's health grew uncertain, I was becoming a father and thinking about what was most important in life. I was also contemplating the interesting, complex challenges facing the Highlights business. Garry III, my mother's first cousin, brought me on board as Vice President of strategic planning in 2004; at his untimely death, I became CEO.

Digital and Business Innovations

Notwithstanding the company's apparent stability and success, we faced the need to invent and adapt as we entered a new century. Our business challenges included sharpening competition, growing costs, the closing off of traditional marketing channels, and revenue limitations inherent in a mass-market magazine with thin margins. More fundamentally, we had to find new vehicles for bringing the Highlights experience to children and families. The idea that kids from toddlers to 'tweens would get everything from holiday recipes to brain teasers in a single print magazine? It doesn't take an atomic physicist to see that this model doesn't fit in our present century.

The seemingly inexorable rise of online and mobile communications spurred the development of Highlights' first websites in the 1990s and early 2000s, and our first mobile app for kids, called Hidden Pictures, in 2009. This transition, full of trial and error, laid open a path to reaching our audience in all kinds of creative ways off the printed page. We've now got podcasts for parents and kids sharing everything from crafts to field trip ideas to animated stories through YouTube and other platforms. We have original audio shows for children now available on Audible. We're even exploring partnerships with traditional TV and streaming partners to bring quality, growth-promoting programming to small screens everywhere.

In a more diverse America and increasingly globalized world, we've worked hard to broaden access to Highlights products and content—as a way to grow the business, of course, but also as a matter of equity, because we believe what we're offering enriches that universal season of life known as childhood. We launched our first bilingual (English to Spanish) kids' magazine in the US in 2014. We've also initiated social-impact partnerships with curriculum companies and other organizations that can bring Fun with a Purpose to children—preschoolers in Head Starts, for example—who may be underserved by a direct-to-consumer model.

In the 1990s, we took our first steps toward forging publishing partnerships outside the US. Like the "laboratory" that informed Garry and Caroline's layered philosophy, this move presented a steep learning curve. The point wasn't just to get into, for instance, the Chinese market, but to engage in a genuine cross-cultural collaboration creating products that would be distinctive to the Highlights brand and speak to Chinese kids and families within their own social and language traditions. We're getting better and better at finding the right partners and working with them effectively. Today, through these content partnerships, we're able to reach millions of children in more than forty countries around the world.

Finally, yes, it's been a challenge to modernize the founders' notion of a "treasure book" that would address the whole child at every stage. Twelve-year-olds these days are more apt to identify with adolescent concerns than those of preliterate two-year-olds. A great body of research has put into actionable terms something Garry and Caroline certainly understood: the very first years of life deserve special attention as the critical time for cognitive and social-emotional growth.

Here, Chris Cully has been instrumental in paving the road for Highlights. In the early 2000s, with much study and consultation, she developed the prototype for *High Five!*, a Highlights magazine specifically for preschoolers that launched in 2007. At the same time, she led a recasting of Highlights for an audience of children ages six and above. Chris was thinking hard about what a periodical for infants might look like when, at a dinner get-together, she met an architect who talked to her about Tyvek, a breathable but waterproof polyethylene-fiber material used in construction. That's when the idea of using a non-toxic synthetic "paper" was born. In

2013, we introduced this first-of-its-kind monthly magazine for babies—a soft, wipeable book meant to be manipulated by tiny hands and enjoyed in the lap of an adult, bathed in the warm bonds that accelerate infant learning and open a child's mind to the pleasure of words and images. High Five! and Hello, our baby magazine, quickly garnered critical accolades and huge sales far outpacing their competitors.

Segmenting our magazine business into three age pillars (birth to two, three to five, and six and above) was, in the context of our history, a radical move for Highlights. It laid the groundwork for us to create a host of products and experiences that match the particular needs of today's families, from the newborn (even expectant-parent) stage to the brink of adolescence. That expanding brand permission is obviously important for the business. It expresses what Highlights is all about in a way that's deeply gratifying.

Naturally we've had to adapt our marketing techniques for the twenty-first century, too. By the early 1990s, when the last of Highlights' door-to-door salespeople folded their tents, hoofing around to would-be customers' homes had become so inefficient as to be obsolete. For one thing, nobody answered the knock—mothers were increasingly at work.

We still use direct-mail and telephone marketing, but these techniques have faced regulatory hurdles to curb deceptive mail pitches, unscrupulous use of customer data, and incessant or scamming phone calls. Highlights has not been an offender, but rather a contributor to industry self-regulation. Indeed, Garry III was selected to chair the ethics committee of the Direct Marketing Association in the late 1990s and the Better Business Bureau had singled out Highlights with a Torch Award for marketplace ethics. Even so, the regulations are costly to comply with and reduce sales effectiveness.

What has become critical is a marketing channel that didn't exist in the founders' lifetimes: e-commerce. Even before the Covid-19 pandemic, the internet was our fastest-growing and most important channel, in terms of both customer acquisition and customer engagement through Highlights.com. During the pandemic, this channel exploded. Our Amazon orders more than doubled in volume. We expect this trend to shape the foreseeable future.

Retail sales—something akin to the newsstand sales Garry Jr. was looking into on the day he died—have also become important. Highlights has taken several runs at this over our history, meeting with meaningful success only in the last five years. Highlights' Fun-with-a-Purpose products can now be found at Target, Walmart, and Amazon, among other retail outlets. We started by assembling the right talent, individuals who really understand retail commerce, along with an open-minded curiosity about what retail shoppers want and need, including appropriate price-points that, like our social-impact partnerships, can expand access to Highlights material. At the outset, we concentrated on our strongest brand suits—Hidden Pictures, puzzles, activities, and humor, across the High Five! and Highlights age ranges. From there, we've responded to the feedback of outlet buyers and end-customers, investing in developing products for particular retail shelves.

One concerted effort in this area has been to build a suite of Highlights Learning products, including content, books, and other products designed to promote school readiness and success. These are well-spiced with the Highlights special sauce, integrating belly laughs, brain-teasing puzzles, and overall engagement with rigorous educational goals informed by curriculum standards and teacher review. Sales were promising before the pandemic of 2020. When Covid-19 transformed parents the world over into accidental but fervently committed homeschoolers, our products were there. More than ever, moms and dads turned to Highlights as a resource.

On the strength of this new success, we've recently engaged a licensing agent in a partnership that can help us bring the Highlights brand to life in new, off-the-printed-page categories. The sky's the limit, really. We imagine plush toys and apparel representing favorite Highlights characters, puzzles on the backs of cereal boxes, and thrilling, Fun-with-a-Purpose activities kids can encounter on tray liners at quick-serve restaurants.

We've come a long way from the analog, localized world my great-grandparents inhabited. But at Highlights we always come full circle to the mission they began and the basic values they enacted. The founders abhorred the idea of advertising to children, by which they meant the print ads and blaring TV commercials hawking stuff and more stuff to minds of tender age. Garry once remarked drily that ads in a competing magazine encouraged children "to enjoy more gum." "Quite an educational angle," he added. We recognize that kids today are involved, to an almost astonishing degree, in consumer decisions. They help their parents select new cars, for goodness sake, and also express their appetites while trawling the internet or the aisles of Target and Walmart. We understand that. But here's the ball we keep our eyes on: Kids are not a market. The adults who care about them are the most appropriate recipients of our marketing messages. Children, on the other hand, are our audience, our inspiration, our reason for being. They're the most important people in the world.

Highlights Now:
A Company, A Brand, a Voice for Children

Our founders chose a magazine to be the instrument of their deeply felt mission. Magazines have been and continue to be critical to the Highlights business. We believe in and take every opportunity to champion the value of the printed page. It's pretty clear that if we hadn't diversified, Highlights and all it stood for would be a faded memory by now. Our work to express the brand through a variety of products, platforms, sales channels, and global cultural traditions has brought us to a liberating insight: we are not and never have been primarily a magazine business.

The founders weren't media people; at their core, they were children and families people. Their magazine asked editors and contributors to internalize and iterate, in myriad forms, a particular approach to nurturing the growth of children and, by extension, a vision of the world those children would bring about together. Our job today is likewise to create experiences for children that will nourish them as thinking, social, emotional, and moral beings. In doing so, audacious as this may sound, we believe we're contributing to the creation of a better world.

One reason Garry and Caroline's philosophy endures so many years after their deaths is that, frankly, it's a good doctrine, the product of their maturity and depth of knowledge. In many ways, their approach anticipated the cutting-edge concerns of the twenty-first century, just using different words.

The very fact there is a philosophy—that we've always been guided by a social mission—made Highlights an outlier among for-profit companies for most of its history. As evidenced by Garry III's 1990 comments in our company newsletter citing philosophy and quality as "at least as important" as profits, we wrestled with how to define ourselves and operate as a mission-driven, for-profit organization when there wasn't a map. For the last fifty years or so, the prevailing theory of a corporation, at least in the world of business and investing, was that it exists to maximize wealth for its shareholders, period.

In recent years, though, we've seen an outcry over the manifold failures of this model, which favors short-term gains over investment in the future and concentrates the benefits of economic growth in the hands of a few while externalizing costs (damage to the environment, for example) to the larger society. From the World Economic Forum to the Business Roundtable, chief executives today are embracing the idea that a corporation ought to benefit an array of stakeholders, including shareholders but also customers, employees, partners, local communities, and society as a whole. At Highlights, we've watched these developments with great interest. Family-owned and privately held businesses like ours have always been more apt to value multiple stakeholders. Among today's "conscious capitalists," we have found an exhilarating opportunity to exchange ideas with many like-minded organizations.

We feel we have much to contribute to these forums. Highlights leaders today wear our company mission very comfortably, more so than ever, but we're equally at home with making money. In fact, we deeply believe that earning a fair profit is what puts wheels on our mission, empowering

Highlights to achieve scale in its impact. We must earn a fair return on our efforts in order to continue investing in our people, our products, and our company's capacity to serve children and society for many years to come.

The mission itself also anticipated today's most pressing issues. That's because in their approach to children Garry and Caroline were concerned with social, psychological, and moral sustainability, though they didn't use that word. Patient and extremely thoughtful investment in how a child would spend a rainy afternoon was their way of building a better future. They laid down a basic goal of exposing kids to the breadth and beauty of the human family, one we've updated but not fundamentally altered as we seek new ways to represent and celebrate differences in race, age, gender and gender expression, cultural and geographic background, religion, and mental and physical ability. We've always tried to show kids that people matter more than things, and that the greatest value lies in trying and doing, not winning a prize or beating the competition. Kids, Garry and Caroline readily acknowledged, may be excited by images of violence and entertained by cheap laughs at somebody's expense—but at a steep cost to themselves and society. The founders taught us to engage, but never abuse, children's attention. They understood that children learn best when they feel appreciated and encouraged as the human beings they are right now. Highlights has always sought to make a "safe space" for kids.

Some things don't change about children and families, about people. Our mission, based on these deep truths, is not a matter of virtue-signaling in response to a moment. It is our brand—powerful, trusted, and indeed beloved. It takes a long time and a lot of consistent work to build trust, but just a short time to lose it. Our trusted brand, the essence of our business success, is not an inheritance that allows us to coast, but a relationship that charges us with responsibility each and every day. With awe and gratitude, we've seen over our seventy-five years that when we do things right, Highlights kids become parents and grandparents who want the Highlights experience for the children they care about.

While certain things about kids never change, the world does change, sometimes in head-spinning ways. As much as our business depends on the perpetuation of our brand, it also depends on entrepreneurial alertness and response, rigor and hustle. It's important to note that the foregoing sketch of our company history leaves out a lot of initiatives that didn't work. In the 1990s, for example, marketing people would send boxes of pogo sticks from Columbus to editors in Honesdale who gamely tested them in the driveway and dispatched a review, all for a toy catalogue that consistently lost money. We tried parent parties (think Tupperware) as a marketing tool three times, and also made a failed attempt at selling in kiosks at malls. In the early 2000s, we bought a fulfillment system that nightmarishly dropped nearly half our orders and lost us millions, which we recovered only through protracted litigation. Challenges and failures are inevitable, but what's important is how well, and how quickly, you respond and adapt.

Meeting 21st Century Challenges with Mission, Organization, and Communication

Entrepreneurs over the age of fifty may recognize in themselves many of the assets Garry and Caroline possessed in the 1940s—maturity and conviction, a focused mission and related vision of the world, a well-developed network of friends and colleagues. The better-prepared among them won't have to tap their life insurance to capitalize their endeavor. But they're launching their dreams into a different environment. Probably the biggest difference is the hugely accelerated pace of change in knowledge, technology, communications, culture, and society. This requires nimbleness, testing the mettle of all entrepreneurs. On the other hand, today's environment offers an ecosystem of technologies and potential partners that may allow mature entrepreneurs to focus on the strengths that inform their mission and, as practiced learners, reach out to other people and systems for help in areas where they're not experts.

At Highlights, the way we meet today's agility challenge while maintaining a consistent social mission boils down to two things: how we work together as an organization and how we communicate as a brand.

How we work together, in a nutshell, is that we're a family-owned business that insists on professional management, whether family or not, and relies on objective, expert advice and governance.

Family ownership gives Highlights independence. We are not beholden to purely market-based and profit-motivated interests. We think in terms of generations. But family proprietorship is no guarantee of mission consistency, much less of business success. A mere ten percent of family businesses survive into a third generation. To address this issue, in 1993, we established a Myers Family Council that promotes fair and orderly family decision-making. A few years later, the third family generation (Garry and Caroline's thirteen grandchildren) signed a mission statement pledging, among other things, to operate Highlights as a family-owned business "forever." The fourth generation (my own) developed and signed its own mission statement in 2010. In all this, we engaged consultants and studied best practices to shape policies that would help us reap the benefits of family ownership while avoiding common pitfalls.

Our board of directors has transformed over the years, again as a result of study and consulting. Once dominated by family members and filled out by company executives (sometimes these were one and the same), the board brought on its first independent director in 1991. The board now consists of five independent experts and three fourth-generation family members including myself. In addition, we cycle family members through an eighteen-month non-voting board fellowship experience that educates them about the company and its governance.

For many years, our mission consistency rested on very long learning phases in which employees would marinate slowly and deeply in the company philosophy. Leadership tenures were equally extended. As our company has grown (and the pace of change picked up), we've realized that a few fragile human bridges are not sturdy enough planks to carry our company into the future. Instead, we focus on hiring the right people—people who not only have the requisite skills but also demonstrate simpatico with our values and approach to kids. We invest time and money into helping these folks understand our brand so they can express it in new ways on their own, even after Chris Cully and I have exited the scene.

In just about everything we do at Highlights, we're quick to recognize when we need another set of eyes to solve a particular business puzzle. The ability to identify and engage the person or organization that can best help us meet a specific challenge is a very real form of capacity, a force multiplier every company needs. Our belief in our mission gives us courage to pick up the phone; on a human level, it helps us recruit all manner of for-profit and nonprofit partners who warm to the notion of being part of something worthwhile.

When I became CEO over fifteen years ago, a first priority was to mend a historic divide between the Highlights editorial or "creative" side, long considered the keeper of our mission, and the business and marketing side. This firewall may well have been useful in sheltering the Highlights philosophy during its formative years, but in a rapidly changing world, it became unduly constraining. Silos by their nature slow things down; they create operational bottlenecks—situations in which marketers await the judgment of editors valiantly testing pogo sticks, and in the meantime have little idea what the heck they're selling and why. Part of our effort to dissolve institutional barriers has been to reorganize our management structure, including, most recently, establishing Chris Cully in her company-wide role as chief purpose officer, a voice for our brand internally and externally. We want to empower our business teams to own the company philosophy as much as product developers do, thus eliminating layers of review. Indeed, we want employees across our multiple divisions to see themselves as part of one Highlights consumer business team.

As a scientist I've also tried to encourage a data-driven thinking and learning environment at Highlights. Commitment to success can paradoxically yield a stubborn refusal to see that an initiative isn't working, and to cut losses and move on expeditiously. Those opportunity costs clip our wings. If, on the other hand, we look at our business as a process of continuous experimentation with rigorous evaluation at every level, product developers and marketing teams alike are freed to try new things, and failure is just a prelude to the next, adapted effort. This requires communication across the company about how each product, division, and initiative is performing, along with company-wide transparency about strategic planning. Everyone needs to know how we're doing and where we're headed.

This brings us to the second way Highlights adjusts to the twenty-first century's roiling currents of change while advancing a mission founded in 1946: communication. Today's proliferation of platforms means our customers and larger audience face a bombardment of chatter, voices, images, and ideas. Amid this competition for attention and credibility, basic communications aptitudes become all the more important.

Happily, communication is a foundational strength of Highlights, beginning with Garry and Caroline and the communication skills they honed for decades before starting the company. We've long understood the power of narrative to engage the emotions, the importance of tuning our communications to the ears of different audiences, the significance of choices we make about representation and focus (e.g. give oxygen to kindness, not rancor), and the indispensability of facts, truth, and clarity for communications that are both ethical and effective.

We tell our own story, in a number of ways and for various audiences. We dedicate substantial effort to communicating within the company about our history, our principles, and our brand. Our goal is to develop the shared self-understanding that allows an organization to navigate the most difficult decisions efficiently and wisely, guided by the North Star of common purpose. We also want partners, parents, and kids to understand what they'll find (and won't find) in the Highlights space, and we create messages for these external audiences, too. Chris is a principal shaper and keeper of these communications; she on-boards and mentors employees and presents the brand to the entire complement of external audiences. Along the way, we've produced materials, sometimes just snippets of verbiage, that capture what's important in our story. They help prompt our conversations and guide our business.

We've been fortunate to have a family and company archivist in Patricia Myers Mikelson, daughter of Garry Jr. and Mary, who also worked at Highlights in various business-leadership roles. In the 1980s, Pat began opening rusty file drawers and interviewing company "old timers." Over time she discovered a mountain of records, including such valuable primary sources as her dad's weekly diaries from 1952 until his death in 1960. In 1996, in a company warehouse, she came upon a vast pile her CEO brother had labeled "Garry's DO NOT DESTROY Wall"—hundreds of pallets of records. Pat gathered and organized this enormous volume of information into a rather complete archive. This made it possible to create, in 2015, two full-length books mostly for internal use. One is a narrative recounting the company's history, sketching its highs, its lows, and the characters who drove the plot forward. The other, The Highlights Way, details the company's special approach to children using examples spanning seven decades.

For external audiences, we've developed pithier, plainer ways to describe what we're about. When Chris was building High Five! we began talking about childhood as "a short, sweet season." At our sixtieth anniversary, we encapsulated the brand as one aiming to help children grow into "their best selves," people who are "curious, creative, caring, and confident." These are our "4Cs." More recently, we've spoken of the need to "lean in and listen" to kids, another way of saying they're the most important people in the world. A couple years ago, a handful of us at Highlights worked with a branding and storytelling consultant to pick out the most important elements of our mission and vision and cobble them into an accessible PowerPoint presentation we call "Our Meaningful Story."

As Chris attests, this brainstorming gave us a lucid, engaging "elevator speech" and a flash of realization: The most impactful way to express our brand is not, in fact, to talk about us, our founding, our history, our people, our family, a message clothed in a tale of the mid-twentieth century. It is instead to connect with parents and others on ground we share—the values that underpin our hopes for all children (those 4Cs) and for the world. Told this way, Our Meaningful Story is also meaningful to a wide spectrum of folks in the contemporary context.

Most often, when we communicate with parents and other adults who care (and buy stuff) for children, "our" story is just the internalized map that orients us. We speak with these adults via content that addresses their concerns and meets their everyday needs—a tradition going back to Garry's daily "Parent Problem" column answering parent letters. Our parent website offers free articles, activities, and how-tos from experts. Chris authors a blog, "Highlights Aha," in a personal, up-close voice. Lately she has written about why Highlights has chosen to depict kids wearing masks in our magazines, the need for calm and kindness in the nasty aftermath of our recent presidential election, and the exhaustion and sorrow we all feel as the Covid-19 pandemic grinds on. There's an underlying theme: Kids are watching us grown-ups. They can deal with life's tougher moments, but they need to feel heard and have hope. So let's set the tone.

Our most vital channel of communication is with children themselves. We communicate with children through all our content and products, of course, but we also address them very directly in *Highlights* magazine's "Dear Reader" message. Though Chris has stepped away from hands-on content and product development, she still composes this message as the voice for our authentic dialogue with kids. It is a dialogue, because we hear from kids, too. Since 1946, hundreds of thousands of children have sent us their stories, jokes, poems, drawings—and letters (or emails). In these notes, kids share with us their worries and joys, their searching questions, quirky enthusiasms, and serious thoughts. They introduce us to their families, friends, teachers, and pets. It is a sacred trust. From our founding to today, we've answered every single letter from a child, directly and personally. We send our young correspondents encouragement and reassurance, thoughts on their queries, or suggestions about grown-ups who may be able to help with a problem. It's a practice that sets Highlights apart from every other organization we know of, for-profit or nonprofit, and represents perhaps the deepest emotional through-line of the Highlights "way."

Finally, we use the Highlights voice to speak for and about children to a larger public. Children truly are the world's most important people (humanity's present and future, too) but they are not, as a rule, holders of societal power. We want to give them a platform. The trust that generations of kids have invested in us, we believe, gives us the authority, the insight, and in fact the responsibility to do so. In some ways, this stepping up into public discourse is part of our company DNA. Our founders spent their lives speaking both to and for kids. On the other hand, it's our full seventy-five-year track record and success as a company that embolden us to enter the fray. It feels new, exciting and a little scary, especially when we wade into controversial topics.

An early example is our State of the Kid survey, begun in 2009. Each year Highlights polls children aged six to twelve on roughly ten questions about aspects of their experience and perspective. Results have attracted coverage by major news outlets including USA Today, National Public Radio, *Real Simple* magazine, the Washington Post parenting blog, *Fox & Friends*, and NBC's *The Today Show*. In 2018 we shared the result that kids increasingly rank teachers and celebrities as top influencers in their lives. This summer we are listening to children regarding their feelings about returning to school in the wake of pandemic.

In the summer of 2019, we published a company statement about family separations occurring on the US-Mexico border. I knew speaking up carried short-term costs; there might be complaints and cancellations. I also knew in my gut how I would feel if my own kids were deprived of family care in a frightening environment. Not making peep would be a statement in itself, with the long-term cost of losing our integrity as a brand that advocates for all children. If Highlights couldn't talk about this, who could? "This is a plea for recognition that these children are not simply the children of strangers for whom others are accountable," I wrote in the statement. "This is an appeal to elevate the inalienable right of all children to feel safe and to have the opportunity to be their best selves."

Our statement was featured by the *Washington Post*, CBS News, CNN, and USA Today, among other mass-media outlets; it lit up social media. We did see cancelled orders and angry comments. But mostly what Highlights received was an outpouring of love and thanks for drawing attention, in our cacophonous communications environment, to the simple practice of kindness and empathy. I was asked to give a TEDx talk in Columbus explaining the genesis of the statement and how it emerged from the

Highlights philosophy.

Shortly after the 2020 election (but before the storming of the U.S. Capitol), a reporter for *The Atlantic* reached out to Chris for guidance in helping kids become engaged citizens and at the same time dwell in the comfort of a "short, sweet season." America's discourse was aflame with partisan rage, and the reporter had seen Chris's blog on the subject. The resulting Q&A appeared November 22, 2020, under the headline "How to Keep Your Kids Out of the Culture War." The *Atlantic* interviewer asked Chris, "What, in particular, have you heard from parents and kids as they've struggled through this era?" Here was where our conversation with children could be given play. "Kids are watching us," Chris replied. "Often what they see playing out on television and in their families and communities is also playing out in their worlds, with friends and classmates. We were reminded of this when we received a letter from a child who self-described as a die-hard Republican, and he asked for help because he was being bullied. His friends were accusing him of being a racist, which he vehemently denied."

Highlights is soon to publish its first book for an adult general audience, *Dear Highlights: What Adults Can Learn from 75 Years of Letters and Conversations with Kids*. In it, we share correspondence we've received from children over our history, along with our responses. Chris has authored introductory and thematic essays on basic issues the letters raise—school, friendship, family, feelings and self-esteem, self-improvement, hopes and dreams, societal concerns and events, biases and exclusion, Covid-19, "really hard things," and adults. This is both delightful and heavy stuff that grown-ups need to hear. We see Dear Highlights as more than a book. We see it as no less than an attempt to seed a movement that, not unlike the humane parenting movement Caroline and Garry spearheaded in the 1920s, encourages adults to "lean in and listen" to the children in their lives.

Highlights has a fingerprint that no one can duplicate. Including the founders' lifetimes of experience, our company is the product of more than a century's evolution. The brand promise we settled on as the culmination of Our Meaningful Story applies to all people, maybe especially to that class of seasoned, over 50 grown-ups working to actualize their own mission-driven, for-profit companies in the twenty-first century.

Our brand promise is simply to nurture optimism. By optimism, we don't mean a blithe expectation that the road will always rise to meet you. Such naive optimism is the stuff of inexperience and overconfidence. When we talk about optimism, we're talking about the self-assurance that comes from trying, and failing, and succeeding sometimes, too, while finding ultimate meaning and pleasure in the effort. That's the kind of experience we try to create for kids. That's the kind of optimism that carried Highlights through trials and losses onto higher ground. It's the way we want to work together. It's a strong foundation for any company. To those who stand at the beginning of this road, we at Highlights wish you well on the journey.

About the Author

In his role as CEO of Highlights for Children, Kent Johnson is responsible for leading Highlights and its family of companies and works closely with the senior leadership team on long-term strategic planning. His key focuses include evolving Highlights' offerings to best serve a growing audience of parents and caregivers and evaluating opportunities to make a greater impact on a global scale—all while keeping Highlights' mission at the center of everything the company does. He is also a member of the board of directors, and previously served as a corporate vice president of strategic management.

Johnson is proud to serve as the CEO of the company which his great-grandparents, Garry Cleveland Myers, Ph.D., and Caroline Clark Myers, founded in 1946. While he initially had no aspirations to work in the family business, he officially joined the company in 2005 and continues to be inspired by the higher purpose of the company. He is committed to the company mission of helping children become their best selves—curious, creative, caring, and confident—and is motivated by the challenge of carrying that philosophy to more children and families in homes, at schools and all the places in between.

Johnson received his bachelor's degree from Amherst College and his doctorate in physics from Harvard University. Before joining Highlights, he served in various roles in scientific research and development, manufacturing and operations in the medical diagnostics industry.

About the Company

Company	Highlights for Children, Inc.
Website	highlights.com
Founding Year	1946
Co-Founders	Caroline Myers and Garry Myers
Industry Sector	Publishing, Education, Retail
Address	1800 Watermark Drive Columbus, OH 43215

Chapter 10

Leading with Purpose
by Doug Dickson

Introduction

People over 50 are uniquely positioned for successful entrepreneurship. In fact, data shows they start businesses at a rate greater than any other age group (Fairlee R and Desai S 2021) and that their businesses are significantly more likely to succeed (Azoulay P et al. 2019). In this chapter, I will show how attributes specific to stage of life, combined with changes in the business climate, are not only propelling greater numbers of people over 50 in the direction of encore entrepreneurship, but positioning them for higher levels of success.

The contributions of stage of life and business climate to encore entrepreneurship are all the more powerful because they share a common theme—social impact and purpose are foundational for business success. Understanding how they have converged to form a novel context for older founders helps to explain the trends toward encore entrepreneurship and validates their prevalence and success. It should also open the door to greater support for people over 50 whose future might include business startup. As illustrated in Figure 1, the decisions of purpose-driven encore entrepreneurs are influenced by a combination of classic business success factors, the expectations of various stakeholders, emerging social impact drivers, and their own strengths, motivations and values shaped by stage of life and life experience. This convergence is a significant element in the success of companies that are headed by older founders.

Figure 1: Convergence of factors driving the success of founders over 50

Like all entrepreneurs starting a company today, older business founders must take into account traditional business success factors, stakeholder expectations, and to some extent social impact drivers. These factors create guideposts for business planning and decision making. What differentiates older founders in their response to these common factors are the personal and professional attributes that older adults bring to the startup process. Older founders typically have years of experience and professional connections, often leading to a jump start in acquiring customers, supply sources, talent, and capital. In addition, they bring a level of commitment and motivation that is grounded in an outlook unique to their stage of life. Values, priorities, and interests shaped by age and life experience take center stage and align in remarkable ways with stakeholder, social impact, and other demands on the business. Such alignment can equip older founders with a ready-made, built-in toolkit for business success.

The Language of Purpose

The word "purpose" is used so widely and in so many ways that its meaning is not always clear. Indeed, dictionaries include a dozen or more ways in which the word is commonly used. Even in the context of business and entrepreneurship, its use can vary from expressing a concrete objective, to conveying a high-minded intention.

In this chapter, purpose is defined as "a resolve to follow a chosen direction that generates a clear benefit for others in addition to ourselves." Clarity about purpose can come as a result of a carefully structured process, designed to bring contributing factors into focus, or from recognition after it has been enacted intuitively or through trial and error. How we get to a purpose is less important than its capacity to drive a set of decisions about a business startup that creates coherence, direction, and benefit. This definition is illustrated in Figure 2.

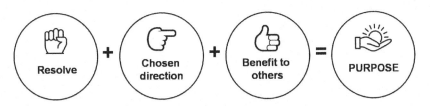

Figure 2: Purpose defined

Other words are commonly used as synonyms of purpose. "Passion" is sometimes used as an equivalent term, but I use it in this chapter to indicate a contributor to purpose, specifically related to an emotional or empathetic response. "Calling" is often used interchangeably with purpose, though it is commonly applied in a religious or spiritual context. "Energy," "in the zone," or "flow," are terms used to describe the feeling of engagement in purposeful activity. "Meaning" is thought of as synonymous with purpose, but I use it in this chapter to describe an outcome of purpose. We achieve meaning, including feelings of significance, satisfaction, pride and contribution, from purposeful activity.

Purpose, along with these related terms, describes the motivations of individuals, including business founders. But purpose can also be used to characterize the overarching goal or goals of a business, as the next section suggests. In this context, I think the above definition works as well when applied to business purpose as it does to individual purpose.

Business Climate

Purpose is a longstanding topic and trend in business; in fact, it has been gathering momentum over the past twenty to twenty-five years. It reached a crescendo in 2018, when Laurence Fink, Chairman of Blackrock, stated in an influential letter to CEOs that the time had come for companies to reach beyond financial performance to demonstrate their commitment to employees, customers, communities, and society. Breaking with fifty years of orthodoxy, his letter stated that "Without a sense of purpose, no company, either public or private, can achieve its full potential" (Fink L 2018).

Then in August 2019, the Business Roundtable signaled a tipping point with its adoption of a statement on the "Purpose of a Corporation" (Business Roundtable 2019). In addition to shareholder value, long thought of as the sole measure of business success, companies would now be expected to deliver value to customers, invest in employees, deal fairly and ethically with suppliers, and support the communities in which they work, including a focus on environmental protection and sustainable practices.

In the run-up to these declarations, public companies have been pressured from the outside and convinced from the inside that corporate social responsibility (CSR) and environmental, social and governance (ESG) practices not only enhance the reputation of their brands, but also yield a substantial return on investment (Cronin M and Dearing T 2017). More recently, research has shown that embracing diversity, equity, and inclusion (DEI) leads to greater productivity, innovation, and profitability (Dixon-Fyle et al. 2020). So what may appear as an enlightened view by business leaders is still driven, in large part, by a continuing focus on the financial bottom line. Now the shift in expectations about corporate behavior and its impact on both society and the economy is becoming firmly established, with those that fail to adapt to this new priority at risk of falling behind.

What these developments in the world of big business overshadow is that smaller businesses have historically looked beyond financial performance as their sole measure of success. Small business owners typically live in the communities they serve. They hire as well as sell to their neighbors. Their customers are often people they know on a personal level. These owners recognize that their success depends largely on the support of their friends and neighbors and are therefore more likely to balance social and financial goals. The result has generally been a pattern of business support for community activities (youth sports and fund drives) and employee engagement (scholarships, gatherings, holiday bonuses), along with fair business policies and practices (credit, returns, and service based on trust). Small businesses achieve this balance between social and financial goals because their business purpose is aligned with the personal sense of purpose and accountability of their owners. In a local setting, business decisions reflect the honor, integrity, and character of the individual making the decisions as much as the entity, and the reputation of the two are intertwined.

While reputation has always played a role in business decisions, for many larger companies, as they grew and moved away from their local communities, reputation was often left to public relations staff or agencies to "manage." This was achieved by promoting the things a company wanted us to know, or concealing the things they didn't. In this way, purpose ceased to function as a primary driver of decisions. The advent of the internet and social media has begun to change that calculation once again. Online reviews and unmediated public comments require all businesses to think and act more like the way their smaller, community-minded siblings always have. What has emerged, while far from perfect, is a broader level of accountability and with it, increasing sensitivity, engagement, and respect for customer experience. This has shifted marketing, pricing, and service policies, and it has also led to a remarkable range of social impact initiatives designed to demonstrate the value created by the business beyond the product or service. These range from products donated to people in need, to responsible product sourcing and testing, and product-related community engagement activities. This convergence of business purpose with social impact is setting a new standard for all businesses.

In this environment, older founders are likely to excel because of their greater business and life experience. But they also bring a perspective uniquely related to their stage of life, which I believe positions them to connect their individual purpose to their businesses and to the impact that can be generated by those businesses.

Stage of Life

There is a substantial and growing body of research about the aging process and how it manifests in older adults. Much of what we have learned from this research refutes our common assumptions about the ability and capacity of people over 50. Some of our misunderstandings about the impacts of growing older stem from a deep fear of, and bias against, aging that is embedded in our youth-oriented culture. Some grow out of the medicalization of aging and the belief that disease and dependency are inevitable attributes of aging. And some arise from the relatively recent cultural expectation that a retirement of leisure is the just reward for a life well lived. Nonetheless, there have always been exceptions to these normative beliefs and biases, and now the research is making it clear that, when it comes to people over 50, the exception is the rule.

As public health and medical advances over the past century have contributed to longer lives, it has become evident that what is being extended is not old age, but middle age (Carstensen 2019). These added years offer the opportunity, and often the need, for continued work and contribution, as the alternative is a retirement that could last a quarter or more of the life span. With a third of the population now qualifying as "older," we live in a society in which there are as many generations over the age of fifty as there are under. One implication of this shift is that we can no longer talk about "older adults" with precision. We need to qualify them by stage: are they working, are they active and contributing in other ways, are they retired, and so on. In this way, stage of life is a more accurate way to think about and describe the motivations and abilities of older people.

Life stages have been a focus of psychology since its inception as an academic discipline. Erik Erikson, a developmental psychologist at Harvard, whose revolutionary theory of psychosocial development was first published in 1950, was the first to systematically address adult development. He suggested that in midlife, people begin to shift from a focus on themselves—developing relationships, beginning families, and building careers—to a concern for others. He coined the term "generativity" to convey a growing concern and care for the next generation (Wikipedia 2021). In this conception, generativity can apply to one's own children, but it also includes care for others in society and for future generations.

Gene Cohen, a student of Erikson's, who further delineated the stages of later adult life, added to the idea of generativity a quest for meaning at midlife. People become more thoughtful about where they've been and more open to taking a new direction. They are motivated by a desire to make a difference in the lives of others (Cohen G 2005). This leads to a life stage Cohen calls "liberation," which occurs roughly between the ages of fifty and seventy. The liberation stage is characterized by innovation and a willingness to take risks. According to Cohen, the questions "Why not?," "If not now, when?" and "What can they do to me?" respond to an "inner push" towards new possibilities (Cohen G 2005).

In addition to the inner push towards action, this stage of life is characterized by a shift in the perception of time. Research by Laura Carstensen at Stanford examined how perceptions shift as people see the horizons of their lives coming more clearly into focus. She found that as people begin to recognize their time as limited, their motivations shift to goals and activities that are emotionally positive. This isn't limited to just looking on the bright side, but includes actively filtering out the negative (Carstensen L and DeLiema M 2018). This "positivity effect" is coupled with changes in the aging brain that appear to reduce the brain's response to negative stimuli (Nashiro K et al. 2011). These findings suggest that older adults are better equipped to manage their emotional responses, remain optimistic in the face of challenges, and focus on the things that matter, without needless distraction or becoming hopelessly sidetracked by negative results.

In summary, this research suggests that people over 50 are more likely, simply because of their age and life stage, to be generous in thinking about or responding to the needs of others, more open to new opportunities they may have missed or sidestepped earlier in life, more positive in their outlook, and more focused in the face of challenges. These attributes suggest that older adults are, in many ways, primed for entrepreneurship. When added to deep business and related experience accumulated during earlier stages of life, this helps to explain their success as founders. But how does this latent readiness get triggered into a response that leads to recognition of a business opportunity? As the next section shows, that too can develop and improve with age.

Founder Motivation

For purpose-driven entrepreneurs to be moved from opportunity to action, three kinds of engagement are needed. First, they must become passionate about a defined need or problem. Second, this passion must align with their beliefs about their obligation to address this need or problem for the benefit of others. And third, they must see a path forward to take action, usually related to their own experience and skill. Often, they don't set out to find such an opportunity, but a random event or connection brings it to their attention and the circumstances of time and place make it possible for them to respond. They may be receptive because of a relevant life experience, an empathetic impulse, or the encouragement of others and they may have the time, resources and knowledge needed to act. These elements come together with a force strong enough to motivate action, which may come as a surprise even to those involved but when it happens, it helps to build a sense of momentum and confidence.

Richard Leider, bestselling author and executive coach, who has written extensively about purpose, uses this formula as a way to help people understand purpose: Gifts + Passions + Values = Calling (Leider R and Webber A 2013). He defines Gifts as strengths and talents—what you're good at and what you love to do. Passions are the things you care deeply about, or feel a strong sense of curiosity about. Values are the non-negotiable anchors that define what you believe is important in life. Leider uses calling interchangeably with purpose to mean an active commitment to others through personal contribution that gives meaning to life.

Determinants of purpose...	STRENGTHS	PASSIONS	VALUES
Characterized by...	What we know and do well	What we feel strongly about	What we believe is important
Entrepreneurship drivers...	Proficiency	Empathy	Justice
Entrepreneurial priority...	Finding a better way to do things	Meeting a human or societal need	Responding in an equitable manner
Outcomes...	Improved effectiveness	Improved quality of life	Improved fairness

Table 1: Leider's determinants of purpose in an entrepreneurial context

Table 1 adapts Leider's determinants of purpose and relates them to a business context, connecting the drivers and priorities of purpose-driven entrepreneurs and the outcomes they generate. The strengths, passions, and values of encore entrepreneurs are linked to drivers, which give rise to priorities that lead to predictable outcomes. The prominence we give to these attributes of purpose determines the focus of the business. Purpose-driven founders engage all three attributes, but one of the three can play a larger role in moving a person to action.

Purpose-driven entrepreneurs use their strengths, passions, and values to achieve improved effectiveness, better quality of life, and greater integrity by acting on the motivations and priorities emanating from their purpose. For example, by leading with their strengths, older entrepreneurs find a better way to do things, improving the effectiveness of a product, process, or project. Similarly, by leading with passion, entrepreneurs meet human or societal needs that improve quality of life. And by leading with values, entrepreneurs respond in a just and equitable manner, achieving greater integrity as a result.

Pathways to Purpose

There are many ways to discover the purpose that motivates action at this stage of life. As noted in the examples below, sometimes it is an experience or an event. Sometimes it's a long-held, but unfulfilled dream. It can arise from an emotional reaction, an intellectual exercise, a feeling in the gut, or the result of a spiritual quest. The path to purpose can be triggered by someone else's decision, as in a layoff, or your own, as in a retirement. Health and other personal circumstances can prompt a change, as can learning about and understanding needs in a new light. Sometimes boredom, loss, or transition can spark a new view of the way forward. All pathways are legitimate, but there are many possibilities. As a result, it is hard to be prescriptive about what steps will lead to purpose, but as Figure 3 illustrates, there are five key phases that founders most often encounter in moving from inspiration to action. These phases are connected by four bridges.

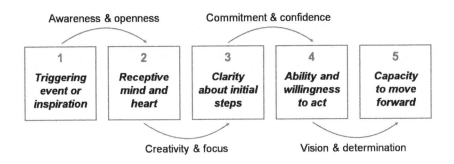

Figure 3: Phases on the path to purpose

Triggering event or inspiration:

An entrepreneurial venture at any age inevitably begins with an event or moment of inspiration, but plenty of events happen without consequence. Responding to the trigger is what gets the ball rolling. As previously noted, stage of life can make people more receptive to certain triggers. Accumulated life experience can enable people to experience events with a keener understanding or in a broader context, but this is not likely to become anything more than an insightful moment until an intentional step is taken. To reach beyond the ordinary, triggers must lead to a conscious awareness of need or opportunity that gives rise to an openness about the possibility of doing something about it. This state of receptivity is the bridge that crosses from the moment of inspiration to the next key phase.

Receptive mind and heart:

For the triggering event or inspiration to be consequential, it must land in a place that puts it into contact with one or more of the three determinants of purpose—strengths, passions, and values. Does empathy lead to recognition of a human or societal need that ignites a passion for making a difference? Maybe circumstances illuminate injustice or an ethical breach that sparks an impulse for advocacy or reform. Or perhaps, using your strengths and skills, you see a more effective and efficient way to do things. These connections, through both the mind and the heart, activate the sense of purpose needed to move from inspiration to action. That raises the next question: what can I do? This reveals the next bridge: creatively considering options and focusing on those most likely to succeed.

Clarity about initial steps:

The process of considering options for action and narrowing the list is critical to the process of envisioning realistic possibilities, and also for seeing yourself as part of the solution. At this point, the process becomes personal; it's not just someone else's problem. As you understand the challenge and break it down into its component parts, the next steps begin to become clear. A sense of possibility and momentum emerges and you become increasingly committed to moving forward with the confidence that you can make a difference. Another bridge is crossed.

Ability and willingness to act:

There are still questions to be answered and issues to be resolved. What can I achieve alone? What is needed beyond what I have to offer? How can I fill the gaps in my own experience? What resources will be required? Who can I learn from and rely on? Finding answers to these and other questions builds confidence and mitigates hesitation. It can also help inform a vision for what can be accomplished. The vision at this stage is aspirational, as well as being grounded in real-life experience, gained through earlier roles. It also emerges from the insight of others, whose input comes through networks built over time and opens doors to new sources of knowledge and inspiration. The layering of information in support of the emerging vision serves to confirm the opportunity and build a growing determination for next steps. This point in the process is marked by a conviction that there is a way forward and that this direction is aligned with a personal sense of purpose.

Capacity to move forward:

The final phase in the pathway to purpose includes an assessment of what is needed to act and the beginning of a plan to build the capacity for action. This can range from a plunge into immediate action for some service ventures, to a pilot designed to uncover best options in a learn-as-you-go approach, or a prototype product or service. It can also involve a detailed planning process intended to identify the essential ingredients for more complex initiatives. The goal in this phase is to take the early steps that begin to give shape and meaning to the impulse triggered at the outset. That initial moment of insight and inspiration has by now tracked a path to purpose and a new venture is born.

The next section describes the personal paths to purpose that a sample of older entrepreneurs have followed in their founding of new companies and nonprofit organizations.

Passion and Purpose in Action

David Campbell was lunching with a friend shortly after news broke about the devastating tsunami that hit Southeast Asia in 2004. Just ten days earlier, his friend had been in Phuket, Thailand, one of the hardest-hit sites. Deeply affected by the conversation, David began to research the impact of the disaster. Moved to action, he boarded a plane to Thailand to see what he could do to help.

After a successful career as CEO of three technology services companies, David was serving on several public company boards, but had time on his hands. What he found in Thailand was a few other unaffiliated volunteers like himself, together with an urgent need far greater than the initial volunteers could hope to address. That led to a spontaneous insight: he knew the capacity of the internet to connect volunteers to the places in need of their help. So he quickly set up a makeshift website that soon drew 300 volunteers. That's when a second insight came: from his forth years in leadership roles, he knew how to get random people organized into an effective team and that's what he did for much of the next year.

David returned home just in time for Hurricane Katrina, which ravaged coastal communities in Mississippi and Louisiana. Using what he learned in Thailand, he swung into action, recruiting 1,500 volunteers and organizing them into effective disaster relief teams. These two responses demonstrated the value of an internet-based disaster relief and recovery effort. The outcome of David's combined business experience, passion, and purpose was his founding of All Hands and Hearts.

This platform was designed to harness the goodwill of people from all over the world whenever and wherever natural disasters strike. Over its first fifteen years, All Hands has mobilized more than 60,000 volunteers to assist in 125 natural disasters, in twenty countries. David says that All Hands has given his life deeper meaning. Quoted as he accepted a Purpose Prize in 2014, an award started by Encore.org and now operated by AARP Foundation to recognize social entrepreneurs over sixty, he said, "My goal is to remain as highly effective as I can be in this next phase of my life—to live a life that has purpose."

David exemplifies the work of social entrepreneurs who are motivated by their passion for a cause. Note that David's "pathway to purpose" took only a few weeks, moving rapidly through the five phases described above as he recognized the full scope of his opportunity for impact. However, it then took several years to design and operationalize a nonprofit business model that could be replicated many times over in the context of very different disasters. It is also evident that his success drew heavily from his business experience, ranging from his understanding of technology, to building and managing teams, to fundraising. The biggest difference on the fundraising side was that investment capital came more readily from donors and philanthropy than from angels, venture funds, and institutional investors. He had to learn to navigate this new terrain, but much of his previous fundraising experience was still relevant as he shifted from the for-profit to the nonprofit world.

David is not alone in making this shift in response to his passion for a cause. Judy Cockerton read about challenges in the foster care system and became a foster parent. But she didn't stop there: she now leads the Treehouse Foundation, a network of intergenerational communities she has built in which kids and their foster parents get the support they need to be successful. Craig Young was helping his teenage children find summer volunteer roles and discovered the need for better volunteer recruiting platforms. Using his tech background, he founded Inspiring Service, and is building out state-of-the-art platforms in cities and states around the country. Catalino Tapia, a landscape contractor, raised money from his clients and created the Bay Area Gardeners Scholarship Foundation to fund scholarships for Latino youth. In its first ten years, the Purpose Prize recognized nearly 500 social entrepreneurs over age sixty, selected from more than 10,000 applications it received (https://purposeprize.encore.org/), a hint at how much activity there is in this category.

Values and Purpose

When purpose-driven founders lead with values, their goal is to use their businesses to deliver products or services in a more just and ethical way. When David Marshall acquired and built a chain of seven hardware stores, called Neighborhood Hardware Group, he was leveraging his experience in real estate and finance, his fascination with the hardware business, and his conviction that people like himself would opt for the convenience of a neighborhood store to a big box for many hardware purchases. As he explored this option, he saw an even greater opportunity. More than big box stores, the stability of these businesses was threatened by a revolving door of minimum-wage employees, many of them first-generation immigrants, who felt no loyalty to the business. This resulted in higher costs in the form of recruiting, training, and stolen merchandise. As a career financial services executive, David understood how to translate those lost dollars into programs that would retain employees, build loyalty, and return a better bottom line for everyone. So he structured the business to pay living wages and provide benefits, including a profit-sharing plan, for his employees. By resetting the HR policies so they aligned with his own belief in the worth of his employees, he proved that his values-based hunch was right. Instead of a turnstile for entry-level employees, he built trusted teams with low turnover and high productivity that keep the stores profitable, while giving him the time and space to grow the business.

David is one of a multitude of older entrepreneurs who have exemplified their values through their businesses. They may do so by growing food locally to avoid carbon-intensive transportation, demonstrating cosmetic safety without animal testing, or sourcing materials through fair trade practices. A few years back, Jean Proulx and Andrew Dibner were looking for toys for their grandchildren that were safe, durable, and environmentally friendly, meaning among other things, no petroleum-based (plastic) components. After an extensive search, they found only a few that met their criteria, mostly from outside the US. Hearing from friends that they experienced the same frustration, Jean and Andy decided to build an online sales platform dedicated to wooden toys and other safe products for children. Out of their own strong beliefs and personal experience, a business emerged that carried forward the goal of making available for others what they had found of value for themselves. In fact, as these products became more readily available in the US market, they opted to wind down their business, concluding that the need that was triggered by their values was no longer there.

Strengths and Purpose

A third category of purposeful founders lead from the strengths they have cultivated in previous roles. Their motivation is often to find new and better ways to do things using their skills, talents, and experiences. Frederick Quinn, a veteran of the specialty chemicals industry with numerous patents to his credit, saw an opportunity to bring together businesses with complementary technologies to create products that no one could produce alone. As a trusted partner, he leveraged his connections to capital and reputation in the industry to create a new corporate home, Quest Specialty Chemicals, and put together the complementary businesses. Leading the integration, he used his experience to strengthen existing products that helped build revenue and in turn fund the design of new ones. This is an approach favored by some private equity funds that are willing to partner with industry leaders, recognizing they need the deep experience of these industry experts to realize their investment goals.

Sometimes leading from strengths involves developing an idea for which the founder could not previously achieve support in a corporate environment. Rick Miller was working for a mutual fund company when he recognized a gap in the market for younger and less wealthy clients. When he failed to convince his firm to enter this market, he struck out on his own. After acquiring the needed credentials, he built an innovative financial planning practice model using index funds and other low-cost investment products and targeted an untapped market segment. Within a couple of years, his firm, Sensible Financial Planning, became the fastest growing financial advisor in his region and has now expanded to serve a broader range of clients. Working from his knowledge of the industry, he spotted an opportunity to use his skills and experience to meet the needs of an underserved group of clients.

A Virtuous Circle

An overriding sense of purpose is the central feature in each of these examples. These are not people for whom money alone is sufficient motivation; in fact, some older entrepreneurs would work for little or no compensation. Nor is this work designed primarily to build status or wealth, though they sometimes occur as byproducts. In Amy Wrzesniewski's analysis, purpose-driven entrepreneurs have achieved a "calling." A Yale psychologist who studies the role of work in people's lives, Wrzesniewski distinguishes among jobs, careers, and callings. Jobs meet income and other financial needs; careers focus on the need for recognition, status, and growth; callings are associated with purpose, meaning, identity—and greater satisfaction (Wrzesniewski A et al. 1997).

A study conducted by Penn Schoen Berland and Encore.org found that older adults working in social-purpose roles felt greater satisfaction in their work than their peers. They also reported feeling worthwhile, a sense of pride, and greater interest in life (Encore.org 2014). A preliminary finding from research conducted by the Quality of Life Research Center at Claremont Graduate University and Encore.org found that greater investment of time in social-purpose activity led to increasing levels of individual purpose and meaning. The research found that, through their work experience, the study participants felt a stronger connection to others and a higher level of excitement, energy, concentration, and productivity. It also revealed that, even when faced with challenges and required to make sacrifices, these individuals remained committed to and motivated by their work (Nakamura J et al. 2020). In other words, the more purposeful your activity, the better you feel about it, and the greater your ability is to deal with adversity.

These findings parallel research on intensive social-purpose volunteer work done by older adults. These studies show that, in addition to greater job satisfaction, social-purpose work improves health, reduces disability, and improves the ability to manage stress. A meta-analysis of fourteen such studies found a twenty-four percent lower risk of mortality for those engaged in social-purpose activity. This longevity effect holds true regardless of medical history, age, socio-economic status, social support network, marital status, or physical and emotional health (Okun M 2013). So purposeful engagement is a virtuous circle: those motivated to help others also help themselves and the more committed they are, the greater the benefit.

Conclusion

According to research, older entrepreneurs are significantly more likely to succeed than their younger counterparts (Azoulay P et al. 2019). As we have seen, they bring skills, experience, connections, and many other advantages to their efforts. In starting their businesses, founders need a set of guideposts to help them understand where they are, where they have been, and what comes next. With an effective roadmap, they are better equipped to anticipate challenges and to avoid missteps. With this idea in mind, I have identified six successive phases that most businesses move through as they develop from initial conception to maturity (see Figure 4).

They include Planning, Launch, Market Entry, Early Growth, Expansion and Maturity (or Exit).

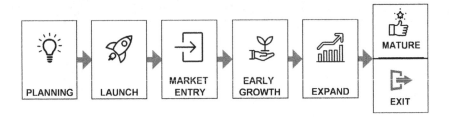

Figure 4: Typical business phases

Each of these phases carries associated tasks, calls upon certain skills, and anticipates different outcomes. They require various plans and resources. When these aspects of the growth and development process are arrayed across the six business phases, the resulting Framework for Founders outlined in Table 2 offers a business planning roadmap for everyone associated with the business. This offers founders both a roadmap for their startup over time, and a set of guideposts for gauging progress. Every business is different and for that reason many organizations will deviate from the typical pattern suggested by this framework. Nonetheless, recognizing and accounting for the ways each business is different can be just as useful as noticing a discrepancy from the pattern that suggests the need for attention.

In this chapter, we have seen that purpose-driven, encore entrepreneurs lead with their strengths, motivations, and values, acquired over years of experience in business and life. We have noted that shifts in the business climate, including the rising influence on business success of stakeholder relationships, social impact factors, and corporate citizenship, play to the attributes of older founders. Having crossed the threshold into mid-life and gained a broader perspective that comes with experience, people over 50 naturally develop a greater generosity toward others and a willingness to see and pursue new possibilities. This sets the stage for triggering events that serve to connect strengths, motivations, and values to identified needs

Phases > Focus v	PLANNING	LAUNCH	MARKET ENTRY	EARLY GROWTH	EXPAND	MATURE	EXIT
Mindset	Exploring, researching, validating	Committing, experimenting, testing	Organizing, positioning, engaging	Proving, marketing, shaping	Expanding, executing, structuring	Managing, tracking, supporting	Concluding
Key skills	Creativity, innovation	Judgment, problem solving	Discipline, persuasion	Sales, perseverance	Customer focus, diligence	Market focus, leadership	Negotiation, transition
Core activities	Target & develop business idea; initial product/service design	Organize; set up initial processes; shape product/service; identify initial customers	Add capacity to support sales; perfect product/service; begin to build market	Determine capital needs for growth; expand capacity & infrastructure; fine-tune product	Set growth goals & scale business to meet them; add new or related products	Set targets for ongoing sales & operations; manage to meet targets	Seek buyer or merger; conduct due diligence; close deal
Planning output	First concept/business plan	Product/service plan	Marketing plan	Funding plan	Growth plan	Ongoing business plan	Succession/exit plan
Professional resources	Informal advisors, mentor	Lawyer, accountant, IP lawyer	Branding consultant, investors	Banker, Investors	Ad, media & marketing agencies	Various	Exit advisor, banker, broker
Sources of capital	Self, friends, family	Self, credit, seed, angel	Self, credit, early venture	Self, credit, venture	Credit, venture, customers	Business	
Product/service	Theoretical, assumed	Prototype, beta, emerging	First generation, market-ready	Adapting to market	Next gen, extensions	Extensions, new products	
Revenue	None	Limited or none	Early sales	Breakeven	Profitable	Continued profitability	

Table 2: Framework for Founders

and opportunities. Increasing numbers of older adults are responding to those needs and opportunities by starting businesses and social ventures.

The significant contributions by encore entrepreneurs to our society and the economy suggest that we should be actively encouraging and supporting more people over 50 to start new businesses. This would take advantage of their unique positioning based on stage of life and overall experience, and would also convey the improvements in health and wellbeing that derive from purposeful engagement, with benefits both to individuals and to society.

References

Azoulay P et al. (2019) Age and High-Growth Entrepreneurship. https://www.kellogg.northwestern.edu/faculty/jones-ben/htm/Age%20and%20High%20Growth%20Entrepreneurship.pdf. Accessed 18 July 2021.

Business Roundtable (2019) Statement on the Purpose of a Corporation. https://opportunity.businessroundtable.org/ourcommitment/. Accessed on 18 July 2021.

Carstensen, L. L., & DeLiema, M. (2018) The positivity effect: a negativity bias in youth fades with age. Current opinion in behavioral sciences, 19, 7–12. https://doi.org/10.1016/j.cobeha.2017.07.009.

Carstensen L (2019) Opinion: We Need a Major Redesign of Life. https://www.washingtonpost.com/opinions/we-need-a-major-redesign-of-life/2019/11/29/a63daab2-1086-11ea-9cd7-a1becbc82f5e_story.html. Accessed 18 July 2021.

Cohen G (2005) *The Mature Mind: The Positive Power of the Aging Brain.* Basic Books, New York.

Cronin MJ, Dearing T (eds) (2017) *Managing for Social Impact: Innovations in Responsible Enterprise.* Springer, Switzerland.

Dixon-Fyle et al. (2020) Diversity Wins, How Inclusion Matters.

https://www.mckinsey.com/featured-insights/diversity-and-inclusion/diversity-wins-how-inclusion-matters. Accessed 18 July 2021.

Encore.org (2014) Working to Make a Difference: Before and During an Encore. https://encore.org/wp-content/uploads/2015/07/AttitudesatWorkv5.pdf. Accessed 18 July 2021.

Fairlee R and Desai S (2021) National Report on Early-Stage Entrepreneurship in the United States: 2020. https://indicators.kauffman.org/wp-content/uploads/sites/2/2021/03/2020_Early-Stage-Entrepreneurship-National-Report.pdf. Accessed 18 July 2021.

Fink L (2018) A Sense of Purpose. https://corpgov.law.harvard.edu/2018/01/17/a-sense-of-purpose. Accessed 18 July 2021.

Leider R and Webber A (2013) *Life Reimagined: Discovering Your New Life Possibilities*. Berrett-Koehler Publishers, San Francisco.

Nakamura J et al. (2020) Quality of Life in Social-Purpose Commitment. Unpublished

Nashiro K et al. (2011) Age Differences in Brain Activity during Emotion Processing: Reflections on Age-Related Decline or Increased Emotional Regulation? https://www.ncbi.nlm.nih.gov/pmc/articles/PMC3388265/. Accessed 18 July 2021.

Okun M et al. 2013 Volunteering By Older Adults and Risk of Mortality: A Meta-analysis. *Psychol Aging* 28(2), pp. 564–77.

Wikipedia (2021) Generativity. https://en.wikipedia.org/wiki/Generativity. Accessed 18 July 2021.

Wrzesniewski A et al. (1997) Jobs, Careers and Callings: People's Relations to Their Work. *Journal of Research in Personality* 31(1), pp. 21–33.

About the Author

After twenty-five years as a business executive, Doug Dickson began a new chapter counseling other midlife professionals through their work and life transitions. As vice president of New Directions, he developed an entrepreneurship program, helping numerous clients start, buy, join, or invest in new or early-stage businesses. While at New Directions, he also helped develop Life Portfolio, a pioneering, holistic framework for retirement planning. As president of Discovering What's Next, Doug helped people design retirement alternatives, including social-purpose careers.  He helped found and lead the Life Planning Network, a community of advisers, coaches and counselors who focus their practices on the needs of people over 50, and the Encore Network, which connects organizations in the US and abroad that support the work and life interests of people over 50.

Most recently, Doug co-founded the Encore Boston Network to accelerate the growth of meaningful work and service options for older adults. Doug has also run micro-businesses of his own and helped to launch a number of municipal commissions and advocacy organizations. He has contributed to several books and journals and presented at conferences on encore careers, over 50 entrepreneurship, and related topics.

Chapter 11

Inventing over 50
by Scott Guthery

New, Useful, and Non-Obvious

The first patent granted in the United States was issued on July 31, 1790 to Samuel Hopkins of Philadelphia. The subject of his invention was a method for making potash and pearl ash by means of a new apparatus and process. Since potash and pearl ash were essential ingredients for producing soap, gunpowder, and glass back in 1790, Hopkins likely had some very practical applications in mind for his invention. The Hopkins patent, and the two other patents granted in 1790, were signed by then President George Washington, Secretary of State Thomas Jefferson, and Attorney General Edmund Randolph to make them official.

A lot has changed in the US patenting landscape since 1790. For one thing, the President, Secretary of State, and Attorney General no longer personally review and sign each patent application that is granted. That's the responsibility of a staff of over 10,000 people at the United States Patent and Trademark Office (USPTO). Another change is the sheer number of patent applications that flow through the USPTO every year, from applicants around the world. In 2020, the USPTO reported receiving 597,175 utility patent applications, 47,838 design patent applications, and 976 plant applications, and issuing a total of 352,066 other types.

The three requirements for obtaining a US patent, however, have not changed much since Hopkins' day. In order to be granted a patent by the

USPTO, an invention is required to be new, useful, and non-obvious. Of these three criteria for receiving a patent, being new is the hardest to meet and, perhaps surprisingly, being useful is the easiest. You might wonder if an electric jump rope, for example, would qualify as useful, but if you want to jump rope without swinging your arms you might regard the invention as being very useful.[1]

In practical terms, being new means that the invention hasn't already been patented, appeared in published literature, or is sitting on the shelves at the local shopping mall. With regards to existing patents, more than ten million have been issued by the USPTO and many millions more have been issued by other patent offices around the world. The innovations proposed in these millions of inventions, having already been described in their patent applications, are no longer considered to be new. The same is true of ideas that have been written about in scholarly articles and in the popular press. Simply put, if your idea for a patent application has already been invented it's not new.

It is, however, critical to note that to qualify as being new from the USPTO perspective, an invention does not have to be based on break-through scientific principles or significantly advance human knowledge. It simply means that the idea underpinning the utility of an invention, what makes it useful, hasn't been turned into a product or published before. The very first US patent is a good example. Issued on July 31, 1790, the patent begins:

> Whereas Samuel Hopkins of the city of Philadelphia and the State of Pennsylvania hath discovered an Improvement, not known or used before, such Discovery, in the making of Pot ash and Pearl ash by a new Apparatus and process. . .

---

[1]US 4,192,501, "Electric jump rope," issued to John R. Peoples on March 11, 1980. There was, I suspect, little doubt in the patent examiner's mind that Mr. Peoples' electric jump rope was new and non-obvious.

People had been making potash out of wood ash for centuries so Hopkins didn't invent pot ash. What he invented and patented was a new, non-obvious, and useful method for doing so.

The mention of a patent often brings to mind the type of innovations that have changed the way we do things or enabled us to do something never before possible—the cotton gin, the telephone, and the means to edit genes come easily to mind—but the reality is quite different. Out of those millions of patents that have been issued in the United States and other countries, very, very few of these inventions ever become widely adopted commercial products. The patents that do make it into the marketplace (whose patent numbers appear in small type on the label) are most often incremental and largely invisible improvements on processes that are already familiar. They enable us to do something we're already doing just a little bit faster or cheaper or better. And importantly for this discussion, they are grounded in and stem from a deep practical understanding of the context of the invention just as much as they do on the mechanism of the invention itself. Necessity may be the mother of invention but experience is the father.

Despite the critical role of practical experience in inventing, there is a widely held view that even though experience grows with age, somehow the ability to invent declines with age. This contradictory view may be at least partially due to often-repeated stories of early-career scientists making breakthrough discoveries or the youth of some mathematical geniuses. Albert Einstein was only twenty-six when he published his ground-breaking papers on relativity. He reputedly said in later years that "a person who has not made his great contribution to science before the age of thirty will never do so" (Simonton 2004).[2] A number of studies have documented the frequency of early-career science achievements, along with a decline in scientific prowess with age (Zuckerman 1972).

As the three requirements make clear, a scientific discovery is not a precondition to be granted a patent. The day-to-day reality is that scientific research is conducted without explicit consideration of its utility, and much

---

[2] Einstein's friend, Max Planck, was forty-two when he started the quantum revolution.

invention is done without explicit consideration of the science that underpins it. Fundamental scientific discoveries may eventually give rise to world-changing technology, but this forward linkage is not hard and fast. In fact, inventions can be precursors of scientific discovery just as readily scientific discoveries can be precursors of inventions (Jewkes 1969).

The conflation of science and technology may help explain the line of reasoning that most patents are granted to young inventors because most science is done by young scientists. While the numbers do not support this line of reasoning, it still leaves open the question of whether or not there is any evidence that inventiveness declines with age. This question is quite different from whether or not there are more young inventors than old ones.

This chapter explores the relationship between inventor age and granted patents. The findings are based on an analysis of the seven million patents issued by the USPTO from 1976 to the present. The primary finding is that contrary to popularly held belief, inventiveness increases with age rather than decreases. This finding is consistent with the view that inventiveness relies more on experience with technology than on knowledge of the fron-tiers of science. Simply put, people over 50 have more experience with technological contexts and can spot opportunities for their improvement more readily than people under fifty.

Identifying Inventors Over 50 in the USPTO Patent Data

The United States Patent and Trademark Office makes available the full text of all granted patents from January 1976 to the present on their bulk data website, bulkdata.uspto.gov. My analysis of this data is the basis of the tables and figures in this chapter, particularly the 7,856,109 patents granted to 4,736,105 inventors from the beginning of January 1976 to the end of July 2021. Figure 1 is a plot of the number of patents issued each week during this period.

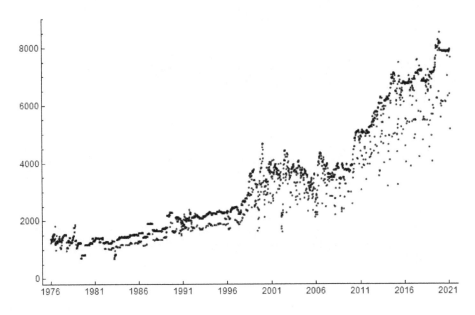

Figure 1: Patents issued per week

A patent application includes the name and current address of the inventor, but it does not include the inventor's date of birth. If one is interested in the history of transformational inventions or the inventions of Nobel laureates, data about the inventor's date of birth can be derived from other sources. However, if one is interested in broader questions about all patents and all inventors such as how many patents are granted to individuals over 50, looking up birth dates isn't feasible. The alternative is to rely on statistical estimates about the age of inventors.

In a widely quoted 2005 paper (Jones 2005a), Benjamin Jones tracked down the birthdays of 56,281 holders of US patents and came up with an estimate of an inventor's age that will be useful in the following analysis: the average age at which individuals are granted their first patent is around thirty-one. Jones has additionally noted that "the age at first patent is rising at a rate of six years per century" (Jones 2010) and thus could be approaching thirty-two today. However, for our purposes, it suffices that

Jones' age proxy is not decreasing so we'll conservatively use thirty-one.

For example, if an individual was granted their first patent in 1986 and their most recent patent in 2016, we will estimate that the individual was thirty-one years old in 1986 when they received their first patent and thus sixty-one in 2016 when they received their most recent patent. Of the 4,736,105 inventors in the full data set, 1,955,102 (44%) were granted more than one patent during the timespan of our data and thus can be given an imputed age. This imputed age is the primary data set for the analysis of the number of inventors over 50.

Figure 2 is a histogram of the age of inventors when they received their most recent patent based on Jones' estimate of being thirty-one years old when they received their first patent. Fairly obviously, inventors continue to invent as they age. Said another way around, once an inventor always an inventor.

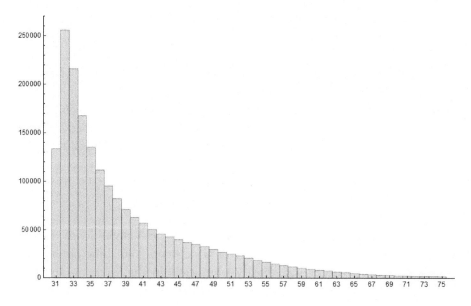

Figure 2: Age at most recent patent

There are a number of limitations in this method of estimating an inventor's age when they receive a patent that should be noted. First, because the USPTO patent database is not available for earlier years, we have not included patents that were issued before 1976. Such patents would potentially identify additional older inventors, or increase the estimated age of an inventor since the number of years between their first patent and their latest patent would be greater.

Second, an individual who was, say, sixty when they received their first patent in 2010 would be taken to be thirty-one in 2010 based on the current age estimation method. As with the growth of Jones' estimate of the first-patent age over time, both of these shortcomings serve to underestimate the age of inventors when they are granted a patent and make them appear to be younger than they actually were in our analysis. On the other hand, the most-recent-patent age of an inventor who received their first patent when they were less than thirty-one will be overestimated so the histogram is suggestive but not definitive.

Another caveat is that the patent data provided by the USPTO contains inventor names but not unique inventor identifiers. That is, there is no guarantee that the Sally Green listed as an inventor on one patent is the same individual as the Sally Green listed on another patent. The Harvard Patent Project[3] and American Institutes for Research (Monath 2020) have considerably augmented the value of the USPTO data by disambiguating inventor names so that if the two Sally Greens were two different human beings, one would be effectively known as Sally Green_1 and the other as Sally Green_2.[4] For our analysis, we chose to use the American Institutes for Research data since it is more current than the Harvard Patent Project.[5]

---

[3]dataverse.harvard.edu/dataverse/patent

[4]In actual fact, each inventor is given an unique identifier and this identifier is then associated with each of the inventor's patents. The inventor's name as it appears on the patents is also associated with the identifier.

[5]As of this writing the AIR data stops in October 2020 so all of our results that concern the age of the inventors are only valid up to this date too.

We are thus dealing with three populations of inventors:

All Inventors Inventor names on plant and utility patents[6] granted between the beginning of 1976 and the end of July 2021.

Disambiguated Inventors Inventors on listed on the above patents whose names could be disambiguated.

Inventors Over 50 Disambiguated inventors who were granted at least one patent nineteen years or more after their first patent.[7]

Each population is clearly a subset of the previous one. Furthermore, since the disambiguation data only runs to October 2020, patents that (disambiguated) inventors received after this date cannot be included in the analysis. For inventors over 50 this means we may not have a fully accounting of all their patents so tabulations based on the inventors' patents will err on the low side.

Table 1 lists the number of inventors in each of these three populations. While it is not counterintuitive that older inventors would hold more patents by simple dint of having been around longer, the 5.6 ratio of patents per inventor over 50 says that not only have they been around longer but they go on inventing at a significant pace.[8]

---

[6]Excluded are design patents, re-examination and reissued patents, defensive publications, and statutory invention registrations.

[7]The term "over 50" will henceforth refer to inventors whose estimated age when a patent was granted was 50 or more.

[8]In the cases of disambiguated inventors and inventors over 50, a patent is tallied if at least one of the inventors could be disambiguated or was over 50 respectively. As noted above, disambiguation was only applied to inventors on patents issued before the November of 2020. No inventors who received their first patent after this cutoff are included in the disambiguated tallies and no inventors over 50 who received their second patent after this cutoff will are included in the inventors over 50 tallies.

Population	Inventors	Patents	Patents/ Inventor
All Inventors	4,648,640	7,856,109	1.7
Disambiguated Inventors	4,058,006	7,618,062	1.9
Inventors over 50	350,196	1,981,311	5.6

Table 1: Three populations of inventors

Figure 3 is a histogram of the percent of patents received after the age of fifty for the inventors who received at least one patent after they were fifty. Over half of these individuals—71% of them to be exact—received most of their patents after they were fifty. This is a rather surprising statistic. It says that after an individual receives their first patent after they reached the age of fifty—not their very first patent, but their first patent after turning fifty—it is highly likely that they will receive at least as many patents in the future as they have received in the past.

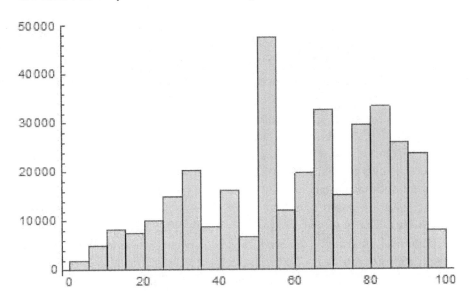

Figure 3: Percent of patents granted after 50

Due to the way we estimate age, we are unable to identify inventors who were granted all of their patents after they turned fifty. Table 2 lists top inventors based on the total number of patents that have received and the percentage of those patents received after inventors turned fifty.

Name	Total	% After 50
Yamazaki, Shunpei	5,807	91%
Wood, Jr., Lowell L.	1,952	99%
Koyama, Jun	1,449	60%
Yu, Chen-hua	1,243	82%
Gaal, Peter	1,128	99%
Suzuki, Takashi	1,107	81%
Sullivan, Michael J.	1,017	96%
Weder, Donald E.	1,000	80%
Kare, Jordin T.	978	99%
Myhrvold, Nathan P.	888	70%
Hall, David R.	850	95%
Kimura, Hajime	773	98%
Whetsel, Lee D.	767	80%
Ando, Hideo	745	92%

Table 2: Top inventors receiving most of their patents after 50

Using our estimate of age and keeping in mind that disambiguation stops in October 2020, the oldest an inventor can be when they are issued a patent is seventy-five. This is an individual who was awarded a patent in 1976 and another patent in 2020. There are 4,065 such individuals, 3,217 of whom were granted half or more of their patents after they were fifty. Robert Paul Morris received patent US 3,964,059, "Method and apparatus for statistical counting," on June 15, 1976, when he was working for Bell Telephone Laboratories. According to his website, he also received US 10,862,791, "DNS methods, systems, and computer program products," on December 8, 2020, working for Sitting Man LLC.[9]

---

[9]Sitting Man, LLC, is in fact the assignee on over sixty patents.

Alexander Graham Bell

Alexander Graham Bell got his first patent at age twenty-eight for an harmonic telegraph. He was granted his last patent at age seventy-four for a seaplane. He is most well-known for the patent that has been called the most valuable patent ever issued, the one for the telephone: US 174,465 IMPROVEMENT IN TELEGRAPHY. Bell is so well-known for the telephone patent we might not stop to wonder if he invented anything else. Table 3 is a list of all of Bell's US patents. He also holds British and French patents corresponding to some of his US patents.

One might say that when Bell invented the telephone he was just getting going. The lone patent previous to the telephone patent, US 161,739, is for a method of sending multiple telegraph messages down the same telegraph line simultaneously. Bell observes in passing in the patent that "The same arrangement of . . . can be adapted to the chemical telegraph, and the various systems of autograph-telegraph," what we would know today as a FAX machine. Not only was Bell still inventing up to two years before his death at seventy-five but his last patent is with Frederick W. Baldwin, age thirty-nine, and Sydney S. Breese, age thirty-seven. Baldwin went on to get five patents of his own.

Number	Title	Age
US 161,739	Improvement ... for electric telegraphs	28
US 174,465	Improvement in telegraphy	29
US 178,399	Improvement in telephonic telegraph-receivers	29
US 181,553	Improvement in generating electric currents	29
US 186,787	Improvement in electric telegraphy	30
US 201,488	Improvement in speaking-telephones	31
US 213,090	Improvement in electric speaking-telephones	32
US 220,791	Improvement in telephone-circuits	32
US 228,507	Electric telephone transmitter	33
US 238,833	Electric call-bell	33
US 230,168	Automatic short-circuiter for telephones	33
US 235,199	Apparatus for signaling ... called Photophone	33
US 235,496	Photophone transmitter	33
US 235,497	Selenium cell	33
US 235,616	Treating selenium to increase its ... conductivity	33
US 238,833	Electric call bell	33
US 241,184	Telephonic receiver	34
US 241,909	Photophonic receiver	34
US 244,426	Telephone-circuit	34
US 250,704	Speaking telephone	32
US 341,212	Reproducing sounds from phonograph records	38
US 341,213	Transmitting sounds ... by radiant energy	38
US 757,012	Aerial vehicle	56
US 770,626	Aerial vehicle or other structure	56
US 856,838	Connection device for ... aerial vehicles...	59
US 1,011,106	Flying machine	62
US 1,050,601	Flying machine	63
US 1,41,0874	Hydrodrome, hydroaeroplane, and the like	73
US 1,410,875	Hydrodrome, hydroaeroplane, and the like	73
US 1,410,876	Hydrodrome, hydroaeroplane, and the like	73
US 1,410,877	Hydrodrome, hydroaeroplane, and the like	73

Table 3: Patents of Alexander Graham Bell

A Closer Look at the Findings and the Inventors Over 50

Based on patent production then there is no discernable decline of inventiveness with age. The data does not say whether this is due to a constantly accumulating reservoir of experience with an application context or simply because some people are inveterate inventors. But for our purposes, we can reason that someone who has been granted patents before they were fifty is highly likely to be granted more patents after they are fifty.

Applying this finding to the corporate world, it indicates that a good strategy for stimulating inventiveness and creating a patent portfolio in any given company is to hire people who have already been granted patents, including people who are over 50. Hiring younger technical experts who have never received a patent is arguably much less likely to result in an invention.

In the next section, we consider the topics and fields of invention that characterize inventors before and after they turn fifty. The findings indicate that in addition to a long-term pattern of receiving patents over time, the majority of inventors go on inventing in the same field well after they reach fifty. Harking back to our brief science versus technology discussion above, this supports the view that inventiveness is based on concentrated first-hand experience as opposed to making breakthrough scientific discoveries.

Classifying the Field of Invention

When a patent application arrives at the USPTO, it is classified according to its subject matter so that it can be sent to the patent examination department with staff members who are knowledgeable about the application's technology. Applications regarding animal husbandry get one classification and go to one department while applications regarding surgical instruments get another classification and go to another department.

As the patent application moves through the examination process at the USPTO, it acquires more refined classifications as it is compared to other patents that have already been granted. Notice the plural "classifications." It is rare that a patent application is only about one classification topic; for example, think about an application describing a surgical instrument that would be used by a veterinarian for operating on cows; this would eventually be assigned classifications in both animal husbandry and surgical instruments.

While patent classifications can be very useful in doing patent analytics, it should be kept in mind that their actual purpose is to serve patent examiners and today's patent administration process. The classification system used in the US has evolved over time to accommodate the massive increase in the number and scope of applications being filed from year to year.

As the number of patents submitted to the USPTO increased, so did the number of classes in the classification system: 36 in 1868, 145 in 1872, 158 in 1878, 163 in 1880, 186 in 1887, 200 in 1891, 213 in 1895, 226 in 1897, 235 in 1902, 241 in 1908, and finally 243 in 1912. By this time the system had taken on a name: the United States Patent Classification (USPC). In 2013 when the system was retired for utility patents, there were over 450 classes.[10]

Other countries issuing patents went through the same evolution of their national patent classification systems. European countries were the first to understand the need for a classification system that unified their national systems and in 1971 established the International Patent Classification System (IPC) managed by the World Intellectual Property Organization (WIPO). Other countries, including the US, stuck to their national systems, at least for a while. In 2006 WIPO announced a revamping of the IPC that came to be referred to in some circles as IPCR, the R standing for revised. At this time the USPTO began classifying US patents according to both the USPC system and the IPC system.

---

[10]A complete history of the United States patent classification systems can be found in (USPTO 1912).

As trade involving patented products globalized, the need for a world-wide patent classification system became apparent. Work started in 2010 with the United States at the table with the result that the Cooperative Patent Classification (CPC) system was established by an international treaty in 2013. The effort to build the unified CPC system was led by WIPO so it is not surprising that it is a direct descendent of the IPC system. As more patents have IPC classifications than CPC classification codes, at least at the time of this writing, we will use IPC classification codes in the following analysis.

Patent Classifications of Patents Granted to Over 50 Inventors

Table 4 lists the number of patents in the top ten patent classifications of the 2,184,054 patents granted to inventors over 50. No electronic jump ropes here.

Code	Description	Patents
G06F	Electric digital data processing	214,541
H01L	Semiconductor devices; electric solid state devices	184,222
A61K	Preparations for medical, dental, or toilet purposes	89,685
A61B	Diagnosis; surgery; identification	76,030
H04N	Pictorial communication, e.g. television	72,977
H04L	Transmission of digital information	54,257
G01N	Chemical and physical properties of materials	47,260
G02B	Optical Elements, Systems, or Apparatus	46,933
G06K	Recognition of Data; Presentation of Data	43,242
G03G	Electrography; electrophotography; magnetography	43,116

Table 4: Top ten classification IPC codes for over-50 patents

IPC Sections and Classes

The IPC/CPC patent classification coding scheme is hierarchical. The first alphabetic character of the code, the patent's section, is the primary classification. The next two digital characters are the patent's class within its section and the final alphabetic character is the patent's subclass within its class.

Table 5 lists the counts of patents in the major IPC sections of the 2,760,992 patents granted to inventors over 50 that have an IPC classification together with the count of the number of these patents that were granted when the inventor was over 50.

Section	Description	Total	% Over 50
A	Human Necessities	861,535	42%
B	Performing Operations; Transporting	914,542	40%
C	Chemistry; Metallurgy	836,510	34%
D	Textiles; Paper	48,854	32%
E	Fixed Constructions	113,554	45%
F	Mechanical Engineering	421,995	42%
G	Physics	1,704,634	44%
H	Electricity	1,519,928	46%

Table 5: IPC section classifications of patents of inventors over 50

The last classification code tally of interest is the number of different technical fields in which inventors over fifty have received their patents. In particular, we are interested in the number of inventors over 50 all of whose patents are clustered in a small number of technical fields as these are individuals who possess a deep understanding of a technology and a proven record of converting that understanding into intellectual property.

The first three characters of an IPC classification code—G06 of G06F— are called the class of the patent. We will take the primary class of a patent to be a proxy for its technical field. Table 6 lists the number of inventors over 50 all of whose patents were in one, two, or three IPC classes. Roughly, one half of the inventors over 50 got all of the patents in three or fewer patent classifications.

Classes	Inventors	Percent
1 Class	18,594	5.3%
2 Classes	74,078	21.1%
3 Classes	70,493	20.1%
Total	163,165	46.5%

Table 6: Number of classes of patents of inventors over 50

Table 7 lists the ten most popular IPC classification classes for inventors over 50 all of whose patents were of a single class.

Class	Description	Inventors	Patents
A61	Medical or veterinary science; hygiene	4,045	49,341
G06	Computing; calculating; counting	2,225	23,278
H01	Basic electric elements	1,827	1,6777
G01	Measuring; testing	1,211	6,020
H04	Electric communication technique	1,033	7,510
C07	Organic chemistry	608	3,940
F16	Engineering elements and units	594	3,512
A01	Agriculture; forestry; animal husbandry	457	7,242
B65	Conveying; packing; storing	448	2,422
C08	Organic macromolecular compounds	430	2,881
C12	Biochemistry; beer; spirits; wine	321	1,832

Table 7: Top Ten IPC classes of single class inventors over 50

Based on the USPTO patent data, inventors don't typically turn to inventing in completely different areas when they pass fifty. They go right on inventing in the field in which they received their first patents. Again, this finding reinforces the hypothesis that depth of experience in a field, boosted by practical knowledge accumulated over the years, is an important advantage in obtaining patents. For companies and startup founders seeking to foster innovation and build an intellectual property portfolio protected by patents, this is a factor that might lead to preferential hiring of older employees with a track record of successful patenting in the company's area of work.

Collaboration and Working in Teams

Researchers of trends in invention have observed that the number of inventors on patents is trending upwards; that patents are awarded to teams as opposed to lone inventors more frequently now than in the past. As older employees are mistakenly perceived as finding it difficult to collaborate with younger employees and to work in teams one would expect that there would be fewer and fewer inventors over 50 on team patents and that this, in turn, would reinforce the misperception that inventiveness declines with age.

While the patent data doesn't speak directly to this concern, we can inquire about the degree to which inventors over 50 are listed as co-inventors with inventors under fifty with this later population serving as a proxy for younger employees.

Figure 4 plots the percent of patents with more than one inventor for two populations of patents: all patents (the dotted line) and patents for which one or more of the inventors was over 50 at the time the patent was granted (the solid line). Both series support the widely held view that teams are increasingly likely to create patentable innovations as compared to lone inventors. What runs counter to given wisdom is that the presence of an over 50 inventor on the patent multiplies the probability that the patent was a team effort by a factor of about 1.4.

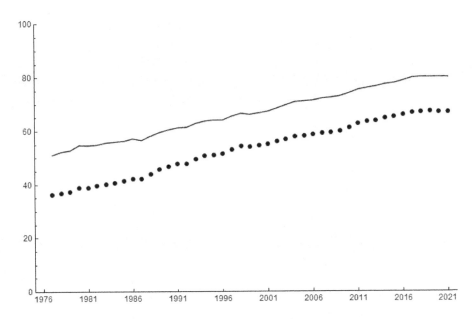

Figure 4: Percent of Patents with more than one Inventor

One can bring to mind several reasons for the persistence of inventors over 50 in lists of co-inventors. For example, one reason would be the inclination of older experts to mentor their younger colleagues; another would be that companies often include older experts in groups responsible for innovation within the organization. Whatever the cause, the data on patents with multiple inventors combined with the estimated age of the inventors contradicts the view that older inventors are not as likely as their younger colleagues to collaborate or to work effectively in teams focused on innovation. On the contrary, this data suggests that older inventors are contributors to successful team innovation. The usual statistical caveats regarding sample size, time horizons, age estimation, and so forth apply to this analysis, but at least one can conclude that the patent data do not support the view that over 50 inventors are most likely to be solo inventors or lone wolves.

To finish this section on a personal note, I am a co-inventor on many of the sixty-five patents I have received. My first patent was the only patent I was granted before I turned fifty. On all of these patents, I am also the oldest inventor. In a number of cases—US 6,676,022, "Smart card system with command queuing," with Perry Sperro and US 8,447,969, "Transfer device for sensitive material such as a cryptographic key," with Mark Robinton and Scott Haigh, for example—the patent was the first for my co-inventors. Setting aside the apportionment of technical contributions, what I recall bringing to the table was recognizing a potentially patentable idea. This is not, of course, to say that Perry or Mark or Scott could not have just as easily come to this realization. Rather, my experience and the track records of many other inventors with multiple patents show that recognizing patent potential comes more readily to somebody who has already been granted a patent. Once the potential is recognized, what is "new, useful, and non-obvious" can be isolated and elaborated on the way to writing and filing a patent application. In addition to the years of experience with a technology, these older inventors develop an eye for patentability which is almost as important.

Conclusion

Data on United States patents between 1976 and 2021 does not support the commonly held view that the ability and will to invent decreases with age. Inventors over 50 continue to receive patents at a rate equal to if not slightly greater than the rate at which they received patents before turning fifty. If, as I content, invention depends primarily on experience, this is not at all surprising. In addition, older inventors are willing and able to pass along the inventive spirit to younger employee since one of the experiences that older inventors have had is spotting an invention and a getting patent.

References

USPTO, U.S. Patent Activity Calendar Years 1790 to the Present, online at: https://www.uspto.gov/web/offices/ac/ido/oeip/taf/h_counts.html.

Benjamin Jones, E.J. Reedy, and Bruce A. Weinberg. Age and Scientific Genius in *The Wiley Handbook of Genius*, Dean Keith Simonton, ed. (2014).

Benjamin F. Jones. Age and great invention. The Review of Economics and Statistics, 42(1):1–14, February 2010.

John Jewkes, David Sawers, and Richard Stillerman. *The Sources of Invention*. W. W. Norton & Co., New York, 2 edition, 1969.

Nicholas Monath, Christina Jones, and Sarvo Madhaven. Disambiguating inventors, assignees, and locations. Technical report, American Institutes for Research, 2020.

President's Commission on Economy and Efficiency. Report of the Investigation of the United States Patent Office. U.S. Government, Washington, D.C., 1912.

Harriet Zuckerman and Robert K. Merton. Age, aging and age structure in science, volume III of *Aging and Society*, Chapter 8, pages 292–356. Russell Sage Foundation, New York, 1972.

About the Author

Scott B. Guthery, Ph.D., is an inventor, software system architect, and serial entrepreneur. He is the inventor on over sixty U.S. patents that represent innovations in smart card and wireless security, natural language processing, and conversational programming. He currently provides patent landscape and intellectual property analysis and advisory services to enterprise and public sector clients.

In his forty-year career as a developer and systems architect, Scott has contributed to major technology projects at global corporations such as Schlumberger, Microsoft, and HID Global, and led small engineering and product teams at software startups. As the co-founder and CTO of Mobile-Mind, he managed projects ranging from implementing a multitasking operating system for a chip manufacturer, to the design and implementation of a trusted hard drive encryption and key management system, to developing mobile consumer and corporate applications. He is the founder and director of Docent Press, publishing books in the history of mathematics, science, and technology.

Scott's most recent patent, US 10,311,874, "Methods and systems for voice-based programming of a voice-controlled device," was granted on June 4, 2019, shortly before his 78th birthday. His 2017 book, *Practical Purposes: Readers in Experimental Philosophy at the Boston Athenæum (1827–1850)*, explores the connections between patents awarded to members of the Boston Athenæum and the books they borrowed from the Athenæum's library.

Chapter 12

Models for Regenerative Sustainability

by Rick Terrien

Corporate executives, shareholders, employees, and consumers today share a belief that businesses must adopt more planet-friendly products, services, and ecosystems in order to survive and prosper in the twenty-first century. During the past decade, sustainability has changed from a trendy buzzword for brands to an urgent priority in the boardroom, the consumer market, and executive offices worldwide.

According to "The Next Phase of Business Sustainability," an article in the *Stanford Social Innovation Review*:

> The era of corporations integrating sustainable practices is being surpassed by a new age of corporations actively transforming the market to make it more sustainable... more than ninety percent of CEOs state that sustainability is important to their company's success, and companies develop sustainability strategies, market sustainable products and services, create positions such as chief sustainability officer, and publish sustainability reports for consumers, investors, activists, and the public at large (Hoffman 2018).

In "Signals of Change: Business Futures 2021" Accenture notes that research on responsible leadership demonstrates a correlation between corporate financial performance and a commitment to sustainability. In fact, in its 2021 analysis of business futures, Accenture concludes that:

> In the years ahead, the relationship between financial performance and sustainability is expected to grow. Sustainability sits at the heart of new pathways to growth, from circular business models to virtual environments to innovation in the natural sciences (Accenture 2021).

Consumer behavior and purchasing decisions are also increasingly impacted by sustainability priorities. A *Harvard Business Review* article, "The Comprehensive Business Case for Sustainability," summarizes the importance of sustainability in consumer buying decisions as follows:

> Today's consumers expect more transparency, honesty, and tangible global impact from companies and can choose from a raft of sustainable, competitively priced, high quality products. In fact, one study found that among numerous factors surveyed, the news coverage regarding environmental and social responsibility was the only significant factor that affected respondents' evaluation of a firm and intent to buy.
>
> Nearly two-thirds of consumers across six international markets believe they "have a responsibility to purchase products that are good for the environment and society"—82% in emerging markets and 42% in developed markets. In the food and beverage industry, a growing number of consumers are considering values beyond price and taste in their purchasing decisions, such as safety, social impact, and transparency.
>
> Far from feeling skittish about buying sustainable products, today's consumers perceive a higher level of product performance in products from sustainable companies and sustainability information has a significantly positive impact on consumers' evaluation of a company, which translates into purchase intent (Whelan and Fink 2016).

Employees and in-demand job candidates have also made it clear that they want to work for companies that prioritize sustainability and implement planet-friendly policies across the organization. According to a 2021 article in *PeopleHR*, "More new hires and existing employees insist that their employers adopt sustainability options" (Crowley 2021).

While the increased demand from all stakeholders for the corporate world to invest in smart, sustainable, reproducible solutions is abundantly clear, there is far less recognition of the many contributions that older entrepreneurs make to sustainability innovations and applications. Similarly, the role of older founders in developing sustainability-centered companies has received relatively little attention.

Planet-friendly business models are an ideal pathway for older entrepreneurs to create sustainable change, while adding to their own resiliency and the strength and value of the markets they serve. Older founders recognize that what endures is not the hype or any fame accreting to business formation and growth, but sustainability models designed to regenerate, rather than extract resources. Entrepreneurs of every color, ethnicity, and background are coming to understand that their mission is to leave a better, more sustainable world as a legacy for those who follow.

The knowledge, networks, and know-how associated with older workers—and especially founders in the second half of life—are often hard-won rules of thumb. These pathways may not be readily embedded in business plans or designed to maximize short-term revenue growth. It is intrinsic to sustainability priorities to find solutions that expand, rather than limit ecosystem participation and to grow market opportunities and benefits for all stakeholders. The goal of improving our home planet to ensure survivability and prosperity for future generations is typically implemented in a forward-looking, long-term business strategy.

Older Founders Are Antifragile Leaders

In his 2012 book, *Antifragile: Things That Gain From Disorder*, Nassim Nicholas Taleb defines the term antifragile as characterizing people and organizations that are able to survive and even thrive in the face of social and economic shocks that produce stress, disorder, and volatility. He says, "Some things benefit from shocks; they thrive and grow when exposed to volatility, randomness, disorder, and stressors and love adventure, risk, and uncertainty" (Taleb 2012).

The global pandemic has delivered multiple shocks along with lingering uncertainty and volatility to firms and their founders over the past few years. Unsurprisingly, many companies have not been able to withstand the stress. Business plans can be written with every imaginable contingency covered, yet there are always black swans—unpredictable events that rip apart the best laid plans. If founders don't have the ability to grow through volatility and unexpected change, these market forces will devastate any potential value those organizations represent.

Founders over fifty have often lived through these kinds of market upheavals in the past. They are knowledgeable enough to understand that while the details of these events can't be anticipated, reactions to them can be managed. They also have learned that solutions and strategies that prioritize sustainability are intrinsically more agile and better able to survive any of the future shocks that are bound to come. Sustainable solutions are an essential part of an antifragile business, an organization that is prepared to not only survive volatility, but can thrive on it. Businesses that chart their course down unsustainable pathways will simply not survive.

Older entrepreneurs often have a strong sense of urgency to act, even in the face of uncertainty and risk. The process of creating sustainable change is imperative and immediate. The high stakes for our planet and our responsibility for managing its resources have never been more apparent. As founders leading new organizations, these entrepreneurs design their company around sustainability, resilience, and regenerative business practices.

It is exciting to many of us working to promote sustainable businesses that entrepreneurs in the second half of life largely share this sense of purpose with their peers around the world. This phenomenon is happening just as online tools for communications and collaboration are becoming ubiquitous and largely free or low cost. Identification of key markets, problems, and solutions can be shared among peers worldwide. This presents a novel moment in history. The wisdom of millions of people, drawn from lifetimes of work, can be organized, developed, and deployed to meet pressing needs for the world to become more sustainable.

While projects may focus on local problems, this development towards ageless entrepreneurship will not stay confined within specific markets or geographies. Tools for communicating across cultures, languages, and great distances have made sharing of solutions a global best practice, one that is only accelerating.

Young and old alike can be innovation partners in this new world. While older entrepreneurs have lifetimes of experience and networks to share for the common good, young people have been born into a world where existential threats are a clear and present danger. Young people do not have the luxury of 'kicking the problems down the road'. They feel their timelines for finding solutions are shrinking. There has always been a strong sense of urgency in younger generations to make change happen quickly, but this movement is being magnified by the multiple system failures endemic in the world, including climate change, food systems failures, and rampant pollution endangering health and life.

Founders in the second half of life will find abundant overlap of purpose with younger entrepreneurs. This is a unique time in our cultural and commercial history where these kinds of multigenerational partnerships can be formed around shared causes. Mentoring can and should be multidirectional. We can all learn together as we build more sustainability into business models, companies, and movements. Multigenerational teams and work groups also embody antifragile characteristics in their dynamic decision making and mode of operation.

Building Solutions and Companies to Last

Building robust and sustainable enterprises requires a fresh look at old paradigms. We are not simply building supply chains to get low priced products and services to market; we are developing value chains and collaborative ecosystems that create genuine reciprocal, sustainable value. A planet-friendly value chain is one in which all the components make a contribution to the greater good of the planet, as well as the beneficial outcomes defined by the product or service. As noted above, there is a vast and growing market of consumers who prioritize these kinds of value chains and search out products and services from companies that promote these values.

Entrepreneurs in the second half of life can build better companies by tending carefully to this business model design. The goal is to create 'good bones' for your new enterprise. This means creating a strong, resilient infrastructure supporting planning, accounting, insurance, marketing, and sales. It is easy to overlook basics when working on projects to change big global systems, but without those good bones, the weight of growth (or equally the weight of stagnation) can cripple new organizations. It is always best to take the time to build in structural strength that can put your enterprise on a path to grow and make the kinds of change you want to see in the world. It may be tempting for founders to rush past the basics to get to the storytelling phases, where they can introduce new solutions to the world. When founders and management teams are consciously committed to launching a solution that is designed to be sustainable and scalable, they are more attuned to the need to build on structures that are strong and resilient themselves.

Many great ideas are rushed to market by eager young entrepreneurs trying to beat the competition and build their reputation. Other ideas are sometimes 'pulled to market' by eager consumers looking to fix problems that a company promised to address. Older entrepreneurs who are focused on launching something intended to benefit society in the long run and make a continuing difference are more likely to understand that the model of building the plane in flight is profoundly dangerous. They know from past experience that if you truly want a sustainable outcome, you'll be wise to get the procedures and tools in place to do your 'flight check' before you take off. You may be able to survive plane-building in flight, but you are not setting a sustainable course for your new enterprise to follow and thrive.

Sustainable Organizations and Global SDGs

Organizational sustainability is an ongoing journey. Older founders derive joy from this journey, believing that each step in innovating, testing, and rolling out new solutions will ultimately create long-term value and sustainable business opportunities.

Circular economy business models keep products, equipment, and infrastructure in use for longer, increasing the value of these resources. Principles that underpin circular economy thinking include reducing waste and finding innovative ways to repair, recycle, and reuse materials by returning them to the value chain. This is an intrinsically attractive strategy and business model for ageless entrepreneurs. One could even make the case for considering new, late-life careers as a wise reuse of the talents, skills, and knowledge developed over lifetimes of work and inquiry.

Increasing sustainability within one organization creates increasing sustainability within their broader ecosystems from suppliers to buyers. This virtuous circle means that even small startups that focus on sustainable solutions can be positively leveraged as part of broader, interconnected business networks. As these networks grow in numbers, and spring up in different industry sectors, their participants have access to shared experience, new innovations, strategic skills, and increased capacity so that each network grows more valuable for everyone involved.

There are many local and regional sustainability goals. I especially like the global Sustainable Development Goals (SDGs) program led by the United Nations. These standards represent the needs of the people of the entire world and the planet we share.

The list of Sustainable Development Goals developed by the UN include:

- No poverty
- Zero hunger
- Good health and well-being
- Quality education
- Gender equality
- Clean water and sanitation
- Affordable and clean energy
- Decent work and economic growth
- Industry, innovation, and infrastructure
- Reducing inequality
- Sustainable cities and communities
- Responsible consumption and production
- Climate action
- Life below water
- Life on land
- Peace, justice, and strong institutions
- Partnerships for the goals.

Sustainable Development Goals can apply to all manner of entity types, as well as to all sizes of organizations. The SDG's have become a component of the sustainability call to action for many large global corporations. According to 'The Decade to Deliver: A Call to Business Action. The UN Global Compact–Accenture Strategy CEO Study on Sustainability 2019,' 71% of the CEOs surveyed for the report believe that business can play a critical role in contributing to the SDGs with increased commitment and action. CEOs referred to an "unprecedented shift in public expectations" that was impacting their businesses to advance sustainability to build competitiveness in their markets and trust among consumers.

Sustainability goals are ideal for entrepreneurs over fifty who are working to solve problems in communities they love or markets they care for. It is possible to imagine scenarios where older founders operating very small companies may have an outsized sustainability impact as part of a collaborative ecosystem that shares ideas and innovations. New enterprises will be able to utilize different SDGs, depending on the company focus. Identifying and deploying as many of these guidelines as possible—even if aspirational—will help new organizations thrive and prosper.

Sustainability also works as an excellent marketing platform for small scale startups. Your best potential customers will want to know what you're doing about sustainability in your own organization. Those potential customers are already on the sustainability ladder and want to improve their own organization by helping you improve yours. Serving this market is a fast track to attracting new customers, especially those with similar mindsets

I have used this approach in my own career as an entrepreneur and as the manager of nonprofit organizations. The SDGs provide a framework for all types of organizations. My own experience includes using SDGs in the planning process when launching both for-profit and nonprofit organizations. By helping put these standards in place from the beginning, later decisions about goals, strategies, and tactics could utilize a widely shared sustainability framework. The Food21 story that follows is an example of one of the projects I have been privileged to serve and learn from over the past several years, as a member of the founding team.

The Sustainability Mission of Food21

Food21 is a nonprofit started in the Pittsburgh area in 2018 with a mission to expand the breadth and depth of regional and agriculture economies through market-driven solutions and strategies. I joined Food21 as an organizer and co-founder. My role focused on early-stage business development, focusing on the six pillars of sustainability that I helped create to support the Food21 mission:

1. Expanding jobs and economic opportunity in the food economy

2. Sustainability through the applications of clean and cost-effective use of energy

3. Broad and inclusive participation in the food economy

4. Environmentally responsible in the production and processing of food

5. Advocate health and well-being through nutritional food

6. Financial sustainability via normal market exchanges

The first pillar adopted by Food21 was expanding jobs and economic opportunity. For the purposes of our new organization, we felt this goal would have the most positive immediate sustainability benefits for the communities and markets we focus on.

Expanding jobs and economic opportunities directly affects a vital Sustainable Development Goal, specifically goals related to reducing poverty. Expanding jobs and economic opportunity is one positive way to create decent work and economic growth, by supporting industry innovation and infrastructure. We felt this goal helped support sustainability for cities and communities, while highlighting responsible consumption and (especially) production. Our support for twenty-first century job training in our target industry would lead to a significant rise in quality education for our target markets.

The second goal adopted by Food21 was sustainability through clean and cost-effective use of energy. Our new nonprofit decided to work on problems focusing on the nexus of clean energy, food, and water. As clean energy alternatives emerge, we work to position Food21 and the stakeholders we serve as a front-line support system to help integrate new, cleaner technologies. While recognizing that the newest energy technologies may not be the final stop in the progression of tech, applying energy innovations to food sustainability can produce rapid results. In our early stages we are supporting indoor vertical farming projects in inner city locations, as well as a digester system to support farming and the energy systems the sector relies on.

In this case, affordable and clean energy goals inspire advances in good health and well-being, as well as new education programs geared toward integrating local citizens and the new clean energy systems. We felt that clean, cost-effective energy applications could also make immediate contributions to increasing sustainability for cities and communities and, of course, contribute in positive ways to the mitigation of climate change.

The third goal was one we felt would have a significant effect on sustainability; broad and inclusive participation in the food economy. As the food system became centralized and industrialized over the previous decades, it left in its wake many closed food businesses in underserved communities and long, fragile supply chains that did little to support people and communities that had utilized those foods. By developing the SDG goals of industry, innovation, and infrastructure, we were able to align our Food21 work with the needs of the entire food economy, starting from the ground up creating new food networks and food production capacities built around broad and inclusive participation.

The fourth goal adopted by Food21 was environmentally responsible food production. By creating options to bypass traditional food growing, production, and transportation we felt we were increasing sustainability for host communities. Increasing responsible food production capacity—from growing through processing, storage, and transportation—was a clear goal for increasing community sustainability, and one which could help mitigate the negative climate change effects of food production.

The fifth goal of Food21 was health and well-being through nutritional food. Sustainability in healthy food systems has never been a higher priority. By creating new systems to generate more local and regionally grown nutritious foods, our organization was putting into play Sustainable Development Goals such as reducing hunger and creating options for good health and well-being. Importantly, Food21 reached out to a wide variety of institutions from many walks of life including academia, industry, philanthropic groups, law and justice organizations, and energy companies to partner with to advance these important goals.

The final goal Food21 set for itself was financial sustainability via normal market exchanges. Food21 itself was formed as a nonprofit organization, but its mission is to solve issues of financial stability, especially among underserved communities and food entrepreneurs. We committed our organization to market-based exchanges. For something to be sustainable it needs to be repeatable. Normal market exchanges are a proven pathway toward equity and sustainable in transactions of all kinds. Food commerce is an especially ripe field for this approach. Innovation in the food sector based on normal market exchanges has the power and the potential to reshape broken food systems, particularly in parts of these markets where charity and philanthropy have become stretched to their limits by economic forces nationally.

In service to its sustainability charter, Food21 initiated several public/private initiatives to put those mandates into action. Three examples of the Food21 projects summarized below give a sense of the scope and impact of this program.

1. Food21 has created a regional group of food businesses and supporters called the Pittsburgh Food and Beverage (FaB) Network. This FaB network actively recruits and supports food entrepreneurs from all backgrounds to make sure we promote inclusive participation in the sector. The FaB network also promotes peer-to-peer sharing of business information and opportunities to speak to financial sustainability needs in the community. We share best practices to promote sustainable use of energy and the environmentally responsible production and processing of food.

2. Food21 has launched the Joint Center for Value Chain Development. The Center works to connect components of regional food systems to stimulate growth and economic viability of all the participants. It's first project is Farm to Tap. The project has created a fully functioning local value chain to connect growers of locally harvested

hops and malt with regional microbrewers. In less than eighteen months, a new network is in place, enabling microbrewers to use local hops and malt in the beers they are producing and selling in 2021, for the benefit of growers, breweries, and satisfied consumers.

3. To establish an ongoing culinary and food business accelerator for minority food-based businesses, Food21 has partnered with Catapult of Greater Pittsburgh. This partnership includes business and culinary training using experts in the field. This effort is building on a solid track record of similar accelerator efforts that Catapult has conducted in the retail arena. Food21 senior advisors and its Pittsburgh Food and Beverage (FaB) network of food business owners and collaborators will serve as support for the accelerator participants.

Well before I transitioned into regional food systems development, I was drawn to launch SmartSkim, a business solution invented to address an urgent and widespread problem of pollution in the world's metal manufacturing processes. Over time, the company I co-founded was responsible for significantly reducing environmental and resource problems in hundreds of manufacturing firms, in sectors ranging from heavy industry to spacecraft manufacturing. While I was not quite fifty years old when I became a co-founder, I managed this company well into my fifties. The SmartSkim story is one more example of the natural synergy between older founders and sustainability goals.

Sustainability as a Business Model at SmartSkim

Long before the United Nations Sustainable Development Goals were adopted, many early adopters were working out the pathways to implement these goals. While much of it focused on food and agriculture as it does today, I wanted to help apply these principles to heavy industry. I had long been an admirer of the futurist philosopher R. Buckminster Fuller. A short quote from Fuller's book, *I Seem to Be a Verb* inspired my business development strategies at that time. "Pollution is nothing but the resources we are not harvesting. We allow them to be dispersed because we've been ignorant of their value" (Fuller 1970).

Back in the days before the term 'recycling' was showing up in many people's vocabularies, there was rampant pollution clogging up the water and air of industrialized countries worldwide. The most common method of dealing with this pollution was to send it downstream or out a smokestack to make it someone else's problem.

Industrial manufacturing plants, then as now, relied on water based (aqueous) fluids to clean parts during the manufacturing process. Within those same processes, oil was often utilized to lubricate and cool the parts being manufactured. Inevitably the two would become mixed together degrading the quality of the manufactured parts and contaminating the aqueous fluids to the point where they did not function. These oily water fluids also would be carried into further manufacturing processes where they would be heated to high temperatures to harden the metals. At this point, the oil fluids burned onto the parts, releasing significant amounts of atmospheric carbon (as a complex, hard to treat mix of soot and CO_2) out their smokestacks.

At the time (1990s and early 2000s) pollution was the stuff of scholarly conferences and social movements, not the basis for business models. However, if the kinds of pollution we were working on could be separated back into all their component parts, and if those components could be filtered sufficiently to allow them to be reused, there were valuable resources to be harvested. My co-founders and I recognized there was value in the component constituents of many manufacturing processes, in particular the water and various oils. Filtering and reusing these components instead of dumping them into a firm's waste stream would generate savings and create a meaningful impact that could be demonstrated for manufacturing executives who oversaw these systems. That impact touched on many of the ideas that would later be collected under the UN's Sustainable Development Goals.

SmartSkim was the epitome of this aspiration. In 1997, at the age of forty-five, I co-founded Universal Separators Inc. to build systems that could recapture valuable resources from polluted fluids and keep their byproducts from becoming climate contaminants, both inside and outside the manufacturing facilities. The company was organized around a business model that focused on reducing pollution through reusing and repurposing the materials that were causing manufacturing problems and widespread pollution. Our founding vision was to transform a manufacturing process that was taking a terrible toll on every stakeholder. There was major environmental damage to the atmosphere around the plants, and to the groundwater where the heavily polluted fluids were released. This impacted the employees working in the plants, as well as the community residents living nearby.

In the 1990s, the SmartSkim process was solving a significant problem across multiple industries, but especially in the industry I was focusing on at the time, namely metal parts that went through a hot wash process during manufacturing. At this time, both large and small manufacturing companies relying on this process had a major, expensive, and messy problem. That included big brands like Harley Davidson, John Deere and Caterpillar, and auto companies.

Before we introduced SmartSkim, these companies were using a whole spate of various wastewater cleanup solutions with very limited effectiveness. The typical approach was to hang a little wheel or a rotating mop in these vast pools of oily wastewater. All those devices could do was to pull just a little bit of oil off of the surface of the washing tank. Sometimes a second step in the attempt to remove the oil would run it through devices built like the old wringer washers. Those devices were never able to keep up with the process. Almost all of the oil became residue in the fluid, which inevitably got dirtier and more contaminated with every wash. The skimming solutions were primitive and pollution was horrendous. The old ways were just ripe for disruption.

During the hot wash processing of parts, oil from the production processes would seep into the vats of critical industrial fluids meant for cleanliness and cooling and they'd become saturated with oil. In many cases, because of the industrial processes that we were focused on, the oils would come out of large industrial furnaces at extremely high temperatures, reaching thousands of degrees. During repeated cycles of washing and cooling, more and more oil would be picked up and would travel along with the parts because the source fluids weren't clean. Sometimes the excess oil would aggregate on the parts, causing them to harden out of spec.

In addition to the problem of degrading the quality of the product itself, there was also an ancillary problem in that all that extra oil would eventually be burned off leaving a carbon residue. You could see the pollution problem just by looking at the smokestacks of these places. Dense black smoke would be pouring out of the factory smokestacks because of a poor maintenance problem.

I believed that a more effective cleaning process that removed significantly more of the oil without slowing down the manufacturing process would pay for itself almost immediately in material savings. Even if the environmental benefits didn't come into the calculation for the direct buyers of SmartSkim, there was also a huge reduction in emissions, use of water, and fluid waste disposal.

My partner and I invented a two-part skimming system. As these oily fluids skimmed from the surface of these tanks flowed through these systems, the oil would get captured inside them. The clean fluids would recirculate back to the source tank, and we were able to accumulate them. That allowed the SmartSkim system to recapture a large percentage of very expensive, highly engineered oil for this specific manufacturing process—oil that had been previously discarded in the wastewater. Our system could recapture that oil in a form that was pure enough that the company could actually sell it for another use.

SmartSkim was designed to be continuously pulling oils off vast surfaces, and making those oils into a potential new product for the manufacturer. Previously allowed wasted resources (the mixture of oil and water) that were a major component of extractive societies were not only prevented from becoming environmental pollution, they were restored to a form where they could be reused as effective elements of a more regenerative society.

To paraphrase Buckminster Fuller, the inspiration for SmartSkim was recognizing that the pollution caused by discarded oil could be redefined as resources in the wrong places. We created the innovation and infrastructure to keep major industries from closing by harvesting resources from places they didn't belong and returning those resources for additional reuse.

It was a very early instance of building a new business on circular economy design and implementation models. The SmartSkim process separated and saved tens of millions of gallons of oil that had previously been discarded into the environment as pollution. Our customers were able to capture, separate, and reclaim high value oils that could be repurposed and reused. Companies that were formerly threatened with fines and even closure from regulators, were able to stay open and grow, creating new cleaner employment options for people in their communities and added economic development for their regions.

Workers in and around these plants benefited through better health and well-being from cleaner environments, both air and water. Contaminated oily fluids were kept out of the environment, as SmartSkim enabled smarter, more responsible production alternatives. Life below the water and on the land benefited. Climate action was not a term in wide circulation at that point, but our small team was able to make a major impact on climate contamination from the capture and recycling of carbon-based contaminants.

Even though we were a very small company, in the ten years that I served as its president, SmartSkim became a real force in our industry for this very focused skimming solution in the hot wash manufacturing sector. We invented our own tools to implement the solution, and obtained patents to protect the intellectual property built into our designs. Eventually, we had customers in Johannesburg and Beijing and all over Europe, as well as in North and South America. In 2007, Universal Separators was acquired by a larger corporation that has continued to implement the SmartSkim solution.

The core of this story is that there were (and are) business models that can be developed to address many pressing problems in society that people think of as endemic. In fact, it seems to me that problems that are the least glamorous, usually the dirtiest and hard to fix, offer the greatest chances to make sustainable solutions that have a lasting impact on the kind of outcomes called for, from what emerged as the UN's Sustainable Development Goals.

In the arc of the sustainability story, our company played a small but telling role. We were a group of only four people, organized around a business model that focused on sustainability. We wanted to solve a problem that was damaging to people and all life. By inventing a process that efficiently removed oils and other substances from the water used in manufacturing, the SmartSkim solution reduced water and air pollution. At the same time, we created a compelling value proposition for customers based on lowering the cost and improving the outcomes of their manufacturing process.

For our efforts, Universal Separators and SmartSkim were recognized as a 'Fast 50' organization by *Fast Company* magazine in 2003. I believe our company is the smallest organization ever to be awarded this honor. We were building solutions that would later be called sustainable. We knew that waste and pollution and environmental damage led society backwards and that it was economically foolish in the end. The only viable business option was to help make a better world. Fast Company said this about our work: "The Fast 50 are the elite of business, individuals with the vision and personal commitment to propel their companies and industries into the future."

In addition, our work was awarded the United States Small Business New Product of the Year by the National Society of Professional Engineers (NSPE), the highest engineering certification in the world. At the time, NSPE said this about our contributions: "This prestigious award honors American companies and their contributions to society. Winning products were chosen for their exceptional engineering research, design, and overall impact on our national economy."

I am proud to have been an early adopter of business goals and management practices that focused on sustainability. I am especially proud of the tools and techniques we invented to fix real problems. We were able to describe sustainability through measurable actions and outcomes.

Conclusion

Entrepreneurs over fifty represent a vast, largely untapped global resource. People with decades of experience bring knowledge, networks, and know-how to the table. In the U.S. there are about 100 million people between forty-five and sixty-five. Pre-pandemic surveys indicated about 25% wanted to launch their own small enterprise. That's twenty-five million potential startups in the queue. With twenty-five million new entrepreneurs ready to contribute creative solutions where needed, with thirty years of experience each, that's 750 million years of human experience ready to launch sustainable organizations for their own success and that of the planet.

References

Accenture (2021) Signals of Change: Business Futures 2021. Insights on Responsible Leadership https://www.accenture.com/us-en/insights /consulting/responsible-leadership. Accessed on October 16, 2021.

Crowley, J (2021) The role of HR and environmental sustainability. *PeopleHR* https://www.peoplehr.com/blog/2021/01/13/the-role-of-hr-and-environmental-sustainability. Accessed on October 16,2021.

Fuller, R B, Agel, J, Fiore, Q (1970) *I Seem to be a Verb*. Bantam: New York.

Hoffman, A (2018) The Next Phase of Business Sustainability. *Stanford Social Innovation Review*, SSIR 10.48558 https://ssir.org/articles/entry/ the_next_phase_of_business_sustainability. Accessed on October 16, 2021.

Taleb, N (2012) *Antifragile: Things That Gain From Disorder*. Penguin: New York.

Whelan, T and, Fink, C (2016) The Comprehensive Business Case for Sustainability. *HBR* online. https://hbr.org/2016/10/the-comprehensive-business-case-for-sustainability. Accessed on October 16, 2021.

About the Author

Rick Terrien is passionate about empowering entrepreneurs in the second half of life. He is a lifelong entrepreneur and co-founder of the nonprofit Center for Ageless Entrepreneurs. Terrien builds sustainability into all his companies. His first business was still running forty years after launch. His subsequent business is now well over twenty years old. He focuses on empowering older entrepreneurs around the globe who want to use their knowledge, know-how, and networks to make the world a better place through entrepreneurship. Terrien has started and run multiple for-profit and nonprofit businesses across diverse industries, with most of his achievements coming after he turned forty-five, including:

- Nine U.S. and foreign patents commercialized worldwide; focused on environmental and manufacturing sustainability
- Smallest company ever to be awarded *Fast Company* magazine's 'Fast 50' (now called 'The World's 50 Most Innovative Companies')
- Awarded the U.S. Small Business New Product of the Year, by the National Society of Professional Engineers
- AARP Purpose Prize Fellow ("Making a difference is ageless")
- Co-founder: Food21—Developing sustainable regional food networks (www.Food21.org)
- Author of *Ageless Startup: Start a Business at Any Age* (www.ageless-startup.com)
- Co-founder, the Center for Ageless Entrepreneurs (www.agelessentrepreneurs.org)

Acknowledgements

First and foremost, my heartfelt thanks to all of the entrepreneurs and founders who so generously shared their startup stories, from their founding mission to the many challenges they encountered on their paths to growth and sustainability. I learned so much from the experiences, reflections, and especially the vision of the founders who are featured in Starting Up Smarter chapters: Bill Behrens and Phil Coupe of ReVision Energy, Paul Tasner and Elena Olivari of PulpWorks, Wendy Gutterson of Physician Management Resources, Doug Peck and Josh Obeiter of Seniors Helping Seniors, Bryan Eagle of Glanris, and Jeffery Harris of Plant Power Fast Food.

Thanks also to all the over-fifty entrepreneurs and colleagues who I met in the course of researching this book. A salute to the leaders, members, and supporters of Encore, the Encore Boston Network, the Founders Over 55 Collective, and the Center for Ageless Entrepreneurs who touch so many lives, and inspire countless entrepreneurs and change makers of all ages to transform the world. The founding stories and company missions of Michael Sellers, Penny Noyce, David Weinstein, Beth McCarthy and so many more, all contributed mightily to the themes of Starting Up Smarter and to my determination to complete this book.

Boston College, and my colleagues in the Carroll School of Management, have provided much appreciated support from the early idea stages of research to the final editing and proof corrections. Special thanks to Rob Fichman, Jerry Kane, Sam Ransbotham, George Wyner, and to the world's best undergraduate Research Assistants, Jasmine Tang, Emily Nearing, and Ryan Fitzgerald, as well as to Cal Halvorsen in the School of Social Work, Jackie James at the Sloan Center on Aging and Work, Bob Mauro at the Global Leadership Institute, Katherine Smith at the Center for Corporate Citizenship, and Brad Harrington and Jennifer Fraone at the Center for Work and Family. To Tiziana Dearing and Bridget Scott Akinc; such wonderful colleagues and co-authors on prior projects, with thanks for being an invaluable circle of support over the past two years. You bring joy and inspiration in equal measure.

Many thanks to my generous friends and friendly connectors such as Laurie Barker, Drew Bonfiglio, Mike Mansfield, Scott McDermott, Jerry Wolosenko, Ruth Scheer, Katy Tynan, and Tom Anderson who listened, brainstormed, provided valuable critiques and feedback on early drafts, shared their own expertise and connected me to entrepreneurs and experts in the fields of social enterprise, mission-focused companies, regenerative sustainability, employee experience, older founders, and encore careers. The chapter on patents and invention was improved by comments from Richard Oedel, Tim Jurgensen, Thomas Pascarella, and Howard Mahler.

Abundant appreciation to the incredibly busy executives and entrepreneurs who contributed their insights and expertise in writing the chapters in Part II: Kent Johnson, CEO of Highlights; Doug Dickson, President of the Encore Boston Network, Scott Guthery, Founder and President of Docent Press, and Rick Terrien, Co-founder of the Food21 Network and the Center for Ageless Entrepreneurs. It has been an honor to work with each of you.

My commitment to building a better future is constantly renewed and strengthened by Scott, and this book is dedicated him as well as to Rebecca, Colin, Johanna, Jared, Charlotte Clementine, and August Ford who will carry their own visions into the century ahead.